"Karin Johannesson has giv̲̅   ̅:ion of
such crucial concepts as g̲̅   ̅w keys
in old locks. Simply and na̲̅   ̅iverses
with her readers about the s̲̅   ̅erspec-
tive on life as a pilgrimage.   a lot to
learn from each other with   through
this book!"
—Gunnar Weman, archbishop emeritus, Church of Sweden

"It is a great gift to the whole church that *Thérèse and Martin* is now available in English translation. In this brilliant work of receptive ecumenism, Karin Johannesson demonstrates with theological acuity and pastoral sensitivity how the Carmelite doctors of the church, Teresa of Jesus, John of the Cross, and Thérèse of Lisieux can help the Reformation to continue to flourish in the contemporary world and beyond. Johannesson's lucid and compelling book will captivate Christians across the denominational spectrum."
—Michelle Jones, The Australian Institute of Theological Education

"In this immensely readable book, with examples from the life-and-death experiences of famous mountaineers, the author draws upon the wisdom of Martin Luther and the Carmelite saints (especially Thérèse, Teresa, and John of the Cross) to guide us 'on the steep slopes of the mountains of life.' While recognizing their differences, Bishop Karin Johannesson brings out their surprising complementarity, helping today's believers address the challenge of 'secularism from within' and live a more vibrant Christian faith."
—Steven Payne, OCD, professor of historical and systematic
  theology, Catholic University of America

"The superficial character of modern secular life is a problem that occupies Christians of various traditions. The Swedish Lutheran Bishop Karin Johannesson asks for help from the Carmelite tradition. Her book is a spiritual quest and an intellectual treatise, embracing Thérèse of Lisieux and Martin Luther as lights that lead to a deepened Christian vision."
—Risto Saarinen, professor of theology, University of Helsinki

"A pioneer in spiritual theology in Sweden, Karin Johannesson invites the reader on a spiritual mountaineering adventure with the Carmelite teachers and Martin Luther as the guides. Identifying the widespread experience of 'secularization from within' as a particular form of despair, or a demon for contemporary Christians to face, she draws from the wisdom of the desert mothers, the monastics, and the reformers of the church to imagine a way forward towards a healthy and holistic religiosity."

—KIRSI STJERNA, professor of Lutheran history and theology,
Pacific Lutheran Theological Seminary

"This book shows us that Thérèse of Lisieux and Martin Luther have something very important in common: their longing for God's grace. Bishop Karin Johannesson looks not only at one Carmelite and her contribution to a more profound dialogue between Catholics and Lutherans. She also turns to Saint Teresa of Ávila and Saint John of the Cross. . . . This book is a typical fruit of the ecumenical situation in Sweden—but it has a message for Christians everywhere."

—ANDERS CARDINAL ARBORELIUS, OCD, bishop of Stockholm

Thérèse and Martin: Carmel and the Reformation in a New Light

CHURCH OF SWEDEN
Research Series

§

The Church of Sweden Research Series promotes research investigating the intersections of church, academy, and society. Its focus is on theology that is in lively conversation with the pressing issues of the world today, both from an academic and from an ecclesial perspective. What is the role of the churches in ever changing ecological, political, cultural, social and religious contexts? How is Christian teaching and practice affected by these changing currents? And how is the Lutheran tradition evolving amid such challenges? Through monographs and anthologies, the series makes available Swedish and Scandinavian scholarship in the English-speaking world, but also mirrors the worldwide connections of the Church of Sweden as part of its own identity.

General editor of CSRS (since 2020): Michael Nausner

VOLUMES PUBLISHED

1. Göran Gunner, editor, *Vulnerability, Churches and HIV* (2009)
2. Kajsa Ahlstrand and Göran Gunner, editors, *Non-Muslims in Muslim Majority Societies with Focus on the Middle East and Pakistan* (2009)
3. Jonas Ideström, editor, *For the Sake of the World. Swedish Ecclesiology in Dialogue with William T. Cavanaugh* (2010)
4. Göran Gunner and Kjell-Åke Nordquist, *An Unlikely Dilemma. Constructing a Dialogue Between Human Rights and Peace-Building* (2011)
5. Anne-Louise Eriksson, Göran Gunner, and Niclas Blåder, editors, *Exploring a Heritage. Evangelical Lutheran Churches in the North* (2012)
6. Kjell-Åke Nordquist, editor, *Gods and Arms. On Religion and Armed Conflict* (2012)
7. Harald Hegstad, *The Real Church. An Ecclesiology of the Visible* (2013)
8. Carl-Henric Grenholm and Göran Gunner, editors, *Justification in a Post-Christian Society* (2014)
9. Carl-Henric Grenholm and Göran Gunner, editors, *Lutheran Identity and Political Theology* (2014)
10. Sune Fahlgren and Jonas Ideström, editors, *Ecclesiology in the Trenches. Theory and Method Under Construction* (2015)
11. Niclas Blåder, *Lutheran Tradition as Heritage and Tool* (2015)
12. Ulla Schmidt and Harald Askeland, editors, *Church Reform and Leadership of Change* (2016)
13. Kjell-Åke Nordquist, *Reconciliation as Politics. A Concept and its Practice* (2016)

14. Niclas Blåder and Kristina Helgesson Kjellin, editors, *Mending the World? Possibilities and Obstacles for Religion, Church, and Theology* (2017)
15. Tone Stangeland Kaufman, *A New Old Spirituality? A Qualitative Study of Clergy Spirituality in the Nordic Context* (2017)
16. Carl Reinhold Bråkenhielm, *The Study of Science and Religion. Sociological, Theological, and Philosophical Perspectives* (2017)
17. Jonas Ideström and Tone Stangeland Kaufman, editors, *What Really Matters. Scandinavian Perspectives on Ecclesiology and Ethnography* (2018)
18. Dion Forster, Elisabeth Gerle, and Göran Gunner, editors, *Freedom of Religion at Stake. Competing Claims Among Faith Traditions, States, and Persons* (2019)
19. Marianne Gaarden, *The Third Room of Preaching. A New Empirical Approach* (2021)
20. André S. Musskopf, Edith González Bernal and Maurício Rincón Andrade, editors, *Theology and Sexuality, Reproductive Health, and Rights. Latin American Experiences in Participatory Action Research* (2022)
21. Karin Johannesson, *Thérèse and Martin. Carmel and the Reformation in a New Light* (2023)

Thérèse and Martin

Carmel and the Reformation in a New Light

KARIN JOHANNESSON

Translated by Gerd Swensson and Mike McCoy
Foreword by Anders Cardinal Arborelius OCD

◅PICKWICK *Publications* • Eugene, Oregon

THÉRÈSE AND MARTIN
Carmel and the Reformation in a New Light

Church of Sweden Research Series 21

Copyright © 2023 Trossamfundet Svenska Kyrkan (Church of Sweden). All rights reserved. Except for brief quotations in critical publications or reviews, no part of this book may be reproduced in any manner without prior written permission form the publisher. Write: Permissions, Wipf and Stock Publishers, 199 W. 8th Ave., Suite 3, Eugene, OR 97401

Pickwick Publications
An Imprint of Wipf and Stock Publishers
199 W. 8th Ave., Suite 3
Eugene, OR 97401

www.wipfandstock.com

PAPERBACK ISBN: 978-1-6667-4619-8
HARDCOVER ISBN: 978-1-6667-4620-4
EBOOK ISBN: 978-1-6667-4621-1

Cataloguing-in-Publication data:

Names: Johannesson, Karin, author. | Swensson, Gerd, translator. | McCoy, Mike, translator. | Arborelius, Anders, 1949–, foreword.

Title: Thérèse and Martin: Carmel and the Reformation in a new light / Karin Johannesson.

Description: Eugene, OR: Cascade Books, 2023. | Church of Sweden Research Series 21. | Includes bibliographical references.

Identifiers: ISBN 978-1-6667-4619-8 (paperback). | ISBN 978-1-6667-4620-4 (hardcover). | ISBN 978-1-6667-4621-1 (ebook).

Subjects: LCSH: Luther, Martin, 1483–1546. | Teresa, of Avila, Saint, 1515–1582. | John of the Cross, Saint, 1542–1591.| Thérèse of Lisieux, Saint, 1873–1897. | Reformation.

Classification: BV4501.3 J64 2023 (print). | BV4501.3 (ebook).

Translation from the Swedish original by Gerd Swensson and Mike McCoy.

Scripture quotations from the New Revised Standard Version of the Bible, copyrighted © 1989 by the Division of Christian Education of the National Council of Churches of Christ in the United States of America and are used by permission Scripture taken from the New King James Version. Copyright © 1982 by Thomas Nelson, Inc. Used by permission. All rights reserved.

Content

Foreword by Anders Cardinal Arborelius OCD | xi

1 The Map | 1
2 Thérèse of the Child Jesus and Grace | 29
3 Teresa of Avila and Jesus Christ | 69
4 John of the Cross and Faith | 114
5 The Compass Direction | 157

Appendix: Ten Themes for Reflection and/or Conversation | 175

Bibliography | 177

Foreword

Anders Cardinal Arborelius ocd

THÉRÈSE AND LUTHER

Several years ago, Sister Marianne, a Lutheran nun in Sweden—yes, indeed, Lutheran nuns do exist!—said that Thérèse of Lisieux is the Catholic answer to Martin Luther. At first, many of you might wonder: what on earth can this romantic Little Flower have in common with a theological giant and bulldozer such as Luther? This book, written by a Lutheran bishop who is a true fan of Thérèse, will try to show us that they have something very important in common: their longing for God's grace. On the ecumenical scene today it has become even more urgent to speak about what we as Christians have in common, rather than about our obvious and well-known differences. Receptive ecumenism is indeed necessary in order to find a new way to obtain what we all hope and long for: the coming of a new ecumenical springtime. We all know, for better or for worse, that we have dogmatic and ethical differences on so many issues. Still, we have to learn and accept that we have the most important in common: Jesus and his gospel, the Holy Trinity, baptism, and prayer. When we continue to ponder on what we share, we can become quite overwhelmed by thankfulness and wonder that we actually have much more in common than we thought. We can never thank God enough for this fact and this grace.

This book is about grace. Without grace we are nothing. "*Tout est grâce,*" said Thérèse. With all her human, female force and spiritual authority as a Doctor of the Church, Thérèse wants us to receive this message of the gospel. Everything in our existence can, in one way or another, show us God's immense love and grace. Luther's existential longing to find a gracious God is totally confirmed by Thérèse and by her personal experience. Somehow, both of them share the same fundamental insight and conviction. Together they proclaim the primacy of God's grace.

We all know from history that this issue of grace once drove Catholics and Lutherans apart. Grace *or* good deeds became more important than grace *and* good deeds. Of course, it was much more complicated than that; but still this issue had the ominous capacity to bring about one of the worst tragedies in the entire history of the Church. Gradually but slowly, this wound seems to heal, thanks to God's immense providence and the constant help of the Holy Spirit. In the year of grace 1999, Lutherans and Catholics came together in Augsburg in order to see how they could find a dogmatic solution and a way to overcome this tragic breach in their unity. Even if Catholics and Lutherans speak with different accents about their vision of grace, a common document could be produced in 1999 that stated that there was no real dogmatic difference. And so, a very important step towards unity was taken. We can hardly grasp the immense importance of this outcome and its consequences for the future of ecumenism. This book, however, can help us to grow in insight and to move forward on the path to a still deeper unity.

When we look upon Luther and Thérèse, we naturally can see both what they have in common and what differences there are. When we read this book, though, we can discern and discover their fundamental unity regarding the main message of the gospel, which proclaims that Jesus brings us the saving grace of the Father. Only in him can grace and salvation be found. Only Jesus can save us. Only he can show us the way to the merciful Father and help us to receive his grace. Thérèse and Luther might describe this in very different ways. They might have various accents in describing their theological vision and in explaining this mystery to us. Certainly, they are very different personalities: a former German monk from the sixteenth century who rejected the religious life, and a devout French Carmelite nun from the nineteenth century. Still, both of them knew that grace is all-important. At the same time, grace can be understood and explained in so many ways. We can even be caught up in very painful discussions and intense quarrels about grace. Strangely enough, grace can lead us to one of the worst and most tragic of sins, *odium theologicum*—the hatred and bitterness that arises from theological disputes. It would be interesting to compare how Dominicans and Jesuits once fought so fiercely over grace that the Pope had to prohibit them from discussing the issue of grace any further.

In her book, Bishop Karin looks not only at one Carmelite and her contribution to a more profound dialogue between Catholics and Lutherans. She also turns to the other two Carmelites who have been declared Doctors of the Church: St. Teresa of Avila and St. John of the Cross. This very fact has also a clearly theological—and ecumenical—impact. The definition of a Doctor of the Church is that he or she has a universal importance for Catholics of every age and nationality—and here we see that they can reveal something essential to Christians of all confessions and traditions. St. Teresa of Avila—or Teresa of Jesus, her official name as a Carmelite nun—is not only a saint who has followed Jesus on her way to perfection and holiness: she has also offered us a profound dogmatic insight into the mystery of the incarnation. It is similar with St. John of the Cross, who has been able to explain the universal and all-encompassing consequences of the Cross as a mystery of salvation. The dark night of the soul, masterfully described by St. John of the Cross, seems to be part of the spiritual journey of Martin Luther himself. It is quite fascinating to follow how our author tries to see similarities between Luther's vision and how these Carmelite Doctors of the Church look upon the fundamental mysteries of our faith.

For readers who are not familiar with Swedish circumstances, it is interesting to know that, in her former academic career at Uppsala University, Bishop Karin promoted spiritual theology as an important and essential branch of theology at the academic level. She can in fact be regarded as a pioneer, because spiritual theology has not always been regarded in this way in Sweden. For many scholars, spirituality was just something devotional and personal, having little impact on theology as such. But gradually, spiritual theology has become more and more important in the Swedish context—above all, as a source of inspiration for a more profound ecumenical dialogue. We can look upon this book as a typical sign of this development.

It is not only Carmelite spirituality that has been used to find new ways for the dialogue between Catholics and Lutherans. The *Spiritual exercises* of St. Ignatius of Loyola have had real success in Sweden and have helped many Lutherans to a more profound personal relationship with Jesus. But they have also been able to influence the dialogue over dogmatics. On the other hand, a Lutheran mystic, Hjalmar Ekström, has also been widely accepted as a guide to holiness by many Catholics and, at the same time, his writings are regarded as a *locus theologicus*—as a source of theological insight—and not merely as devotional literature.

Many readers might wonder why a book like this has been published in Sweden of all countries. Sweden is a very secular, post-Lutheran country with a tiny Catholic community who make up only one per cent of the population—and most of them are immigrants. It is really the same question that many asked when the joint Lutheran and Catholic commemoration of the Reformation was organized in Lund, Sweden in 2016. One reason is that the Lutheran Church of Sweden, like that of Finland, kept more of the Catholic heritage alive after the Reformation than other Lutheran communities worldwide. Another reason could be that the ecumenical scene in Sweden is quite special. The obvious dogmatic and ethical differences are the same as anywhere else—and yet spiritual ecumenism has seen tremendous development. Christians of various confessions get the same spiritual inspiration from authors from different churches. We need only mention persons such as the Lutheran Bishop Martin Lönnebo, the Carmelite Friar Wilfrid Stinissen, and the Pentecostal preacher Peter Halldorf. Spiritual theology has had a significant ecumenical impact on many Swedish Christians. But this is not so strange, really, when we think about the very secular atmosphere of Sweden; if you want to be a Christian, you have to stick together, you have to learn from each other, you have to love Jesus and follow Jesus together. This book is a typical fruit of the ecumenical situation in Sweden—but it has a message for Christians everywhere.

+Anders Cardinal Arborelius OCD

1

The Map

In December 1894, the then twenty-two-year-old Carmelite nun Thérèse of the Child Jesus, in Lisieux in northern France, was given the task of writing down her childhood memories. She was not quite sure where to begin, so she said a prayer and opened the Gospel of St. Mark in order to find some guidance. Her eyes fell on a verse that attracted her: "[Jesus] went up the mountain and called to him those whom he wanted, and they came to him" (Mark 3:13). The verse helped her to begin her work. She wrote that this verse summarized the mystery of her entire life.[1] That mystery was something she wanted to share with other people.

In the summer of 2018, I and my then nine-year-old niece Signe entered the tourist office in Lisieux. We wanted to visit the childhood home of Thérèse of the Child Jesus, the convent where she is buried, and the magnificent basilica up on the hill. We also wanted to know where we could buy a hamburger. We needed guidance, so we asked for a map.

We were given a map that proved to be excellent. It contained just enough information to help us to get to our destination. A couple of women we met outside the Carmelite Convent gave us some useful advice. There is a blue line on the pavements in Lisieux that shows the route between the places we wanted to visit. We followed the line up the steep hill and noted with great pleasure that it also led us to an ice cream vendor.

I explained to Signe that the relics of both Thérèse of the Child Jesus and her parents would shortly visit the Nordic countries. That information did not seem to make any great impression on her. However, the

---

1. Thérèse of Lisieux, *Story of a Soul*, 13.

burial chamber of Thérèse did. Signe wanted to stay there a long time. In fact, I tired of it before she did. When we came out of the Convent Church, Signe suddenly disappeared from beside me. I turned around and discovered to my horror that she had climbed a statue of Thérèse. She gave the statue a good hug and, just to make sure, a few kisses on the cheek as well. "I love Thérèse!" she cried to me in Swedish while I was apologizing in English to a French-speaking woman who was deep in prayer before the statue. Her devotions had been interrupted by a girl from central Sweden who was just as direct in her devotional expressions as Thérèse of the Child Jesus was. The woman laughed, and I drew a breath of relief.

At the train station we met a priest from Lebanon. When he heard that we belonged to the Evangelical-Lutheran Church of Sweden, he shrugged his shoulders and said that this church was "the same thing" as the Roman Catholic Church to which he belonged. I thought to myself that things are not quite that simple; but I did not say anything. As the train was arriving, the priest took a packet of biscuits from his bag and gave it to Signe. Just like Thérèse of the Child Jesus, he wanted to share what he had brought in his luggage.

We can all share something of what we have been given. The thoughts and reflections that Thérèse of the Child Jesus and other Carmelites have given us over the years are worth handing on. That is the purpose of this book. It is not exclusively about Thérèse, but its conception had to do with the visit of her relics to the Nordic countries.

This book is like the map that we received at the tourist office in Lisieux. The map did not contain all the available information, but only those details that were necessary for us to understand where we should walk. In a similar way, this book does not exhaust the subject. It only highlights a few entrances and minor roads, and points out the direction in which we can move in order to come to the right place. Sometimes it is reminiscent of the blue line on the pavements in Lisieux. Those lines not only led us to convents and churches: they also led us to an ice cream vendor, where we could have a refreshing and life-giving break on our way up the hill. When we followed that line, we came across some very ordinary people to talk to. Some of them held deeply ecumenical views of a kind that are worth encouraging.

RECEPTIVE ECUMENISM AND CONTINUED REFORMATION

A "hot" trend in contemporary ecumenical research is the method called "receptive ecumenism," which is particularly linked to the British academic, Professor Paul D. Murray. Murray is looking for a new starting point for ecumenism. Rather than engaging in doctrinal conversation of a negotiating type—where the purpose can easily become to arrive at the lowest common denominator on which everyone can agree—the ability of one's own tradition to deal with current challenges through dialog with other traditions should be highlighted as the motivation that will lead to an honest and committed search.[2]

I would like to contribute a specific example of receptive ecumenism that is open to learning from others by exploring how the spirituality of the Carmelite Order can help us in the Evangelical-Lutheran tradition to deal with a challenge that, in my view, is of decisive significance today—namely, the superficiality that worries many people besides me, and that we sometimes describe in rather vague terms as "secularization from within." During the Reformation anniversary year of 2017, we in the Church of Sweden took an interest in the need for a new Reformation. We talked about how we might hand on the Reformation. That conversation is something I would like to deepen further by illuminating how we might write the next chapter in our Reformation history with help from the Carmelite tradition.

I think that, as we bring the Reformation into the future, we do not have to be inspired exclusively by Martin Luther's (1483–1546) actions and writings. Other voices should also be permitted to speak. For myself, I would like to pay attention to three Carmelites: Thérèse of the Child Jesus (1873–1897), Teresa of Jesus/Avila (1515–1582), and John of the Cross (1542–1591). Besides being members of the same monastic order, they are also united by the fact that the pope made them all Doctors of the Church during the twentieth century. This means that the pope has highlighted them in a particular way as authorities who have something to say to all Christians throughout and around the world.

In other contexts, I have tried to define what we mean when we speak about "the secularization of the Church from within." Against the background of the work on the philosophy of language that I undertook for my PhD dissertation, like Owe Wikström and Peder Thalén I have

---

2. Murray, "Receptive Ecumenism and Catholic Learning."

characterized this secularization from within as a collective forgetfulness or loss of language. Increasingly, we lose the ability to interpret our lives and our experience by those linguistic resources and stories that the Christian tradition provides. This development leads to a spiral of silence, an escalating inability that can be described as secularization from within. This process means that people who have not yet mastered the conceptual world of the Christian tradition find it even more difficult to make it their own, since those who are able to use that tradition are not so keen on doing so for fear of being misunderstood or making fools of themselves. This is an unfortunate development, because it makes it increasingly hard for us to take advantage of the guidance that Christians of previous generations can give us. Their vocabulary and ways of expressing themselves become foreign to us.[3]

Here I intend to present secularization from within in a rather different way. Against the background of my studies of various possible expositions of Luther's understanding of the sanctification of the human person, I do not want to present secularization from within as a loss of language, but rather to understand it as a kind of despair.[4] My approach is partly inspired by Martin Lönnebo.[5] Reflecting on the devil's attacks to which the Desert Fathers and Mothers were subjected, he asks which demons we primarily need to fight against in our age and in our lives. He highlights a contemporary demon that, in his view, is the absolute worst: the demon of despair, which leads you to question whether the spiritual struggle has any meaning at all.[6]

I intend to assume that this demon or temptation affects us who are members of the Church of Sweden in a very particular way because we belong to the Evangelical-Lutheran tradition. We learn ourselves, and we teach others, that people can have a satisfactory relationship with God quite apart from their own efforts. This satisfactory relationship is God's gift through justification by faith, which takes place through grace alone and only through trust in Jesus Christ and in the promises that God fulfills through him. It is God alone who is at work in the justification of human persons. This good and satisfactory relationship with God is thus

---

3. I develop my philosophical arguments in Johannesson, *Gud för oss* and Johannesson, *God Pro Nobis*. I discuss secularization from within from a philosophical perspective in Johannesson, "Den billiga nåden som dyrköpt erfarenhet."

4. These interpretations of Luther can be found in Johannesson, *Helgelsens filosofi*.

5. A theologian and emeritus bishop in the Church of Sweden.

6. Lönnebo, *Vävan*, 87–88.

independent of people's lifestyle and actions. With regard to life following justification (which should properly be described as "life in justification" or as "holiness"), it is stressed that a person remains both a sinner and righteous at the same time, provided that God by grace grants them this justifying faith. Against that background, sin is regularly presented as a reality that cannot decrease or disappear during the earthly life of a person.

This doctrine can lead to a particular form of despair that, in this context, I will characterize as secularization from within. If it is faith alone—and not any action on our part—that is presented as significant in relation to God, the thought that God does not care about what we do might take root within us. Luther certainly stressed that believers' trust in Christ makes them spontaneously perform good deeds for their neighbors, and that these actions are significant; but many of us have experiences that are quite contrary to that doctrine. Good deeds do not spontaneously well up within us, even though we feel that we hold the faith. An explanation for our unwillingness and our inability to live as God would have us live is that, although we are certainly righteous, at the same time we are also sinners, and so we have no desire to do what is good. Our sinfulness is not something that we can deal with ourselves in any way, and particularly not by anything that we do.

From that sort of reasoning, the conclusion readily follows that we should preferably live without any ambitions that are reminiscent of the attempts by earlier generations of Christians to seek to overcome themselves and those worldly ways of thinking that, in their view, risked leading them away from God. It therefore happens that the life of following Christ in the Evangelical-Lutheran tradition is often linked to a lack of any attempt to act and to live according to the example of Christ and his instructions, since such efforts might be a form of self-justification that is based on good deeds and that has turned away from God. I will consider this complex of thoughts as an expression of secularization from within, because I believe that it often results in a lack of joy and confidence and of the power to present the Christian faith as a lived-out religion today, both in the Church of Sweden as a community and for individual people.

I do not want to claim that the confusing, paralyzing despair caused by secularization from within is the only attitude that prevails in the Church of Sweden. Not everyone who lives in that context is so problematically passive in their relationship with God as my description might indicate. Today many of us are marked instead by an excessive confidence in our own ability to approach God. We invest happily in our spiritual exercises. Like purposeful mountaineers who dream of reaching the highest peaks on Earth, we engage in meditation, retreats, or pilgrimages with more-or-less articulated aspirations that we will finally reach the answer to the question about the meaning of life, and thus become those harmonious people whom we think we ought to be. As the pace quickens in society, and as public conversations become increasingly trite, many of us long to be done with superficial ideals and meaningless wrangling. Consequently, there are many requests for environments and activities that we connect with spirituality. The Church of Sweden is also an agent in the marketplace and that raises questions. Just as in the sixteenth century, we need to reflect today on what characterize fruitful forms of devotion and advice on spiritual exercises as against objectionable expressions of justification by works.

The Carmelite tradition is a valuable dialog partner in that reflection. The Carmelite tradition often describes the characteristics of a promising spiritual development by using stories and metaphors from the context of mountaineering. These metaphors are useful because we often connect high peaks with amazing experiences of nature and fabulous views. Another reason is that the really big questions of life are often brought to a head when people move around in high alpine landscapes. At 8,000 meters above sea level, nobody can delay answering the question about what they are prepared to live or die for. Here you must act before the lack of oxygen becomes a fact. Thus, the autobiographies of famous mountaineers are full of existential questions, decisions of vital importance for life or death, encounters with deadly driving forces, and spiritual experiences. Most of us will never try to ascend the highest mountains in the world; but that does not stop us from learning something from those who have actually done so.

There is an ambivalence or uncertainty in every ascent of an 8,000-meter peak that I want to highlight, because I believe that this illustrates universal human experiences that mark people's lives—and not only in the twenty-first century. Such ambivalence was also central to the Reformation processes of the sixteenth century.

To climb in the so-called "death zone" is so risky that the question of your own driving force cannot be avoided. When I have read the autobiographies of professional climbers, I have often wondered whether it is equally risky to engage in mountaineering of the kind that the Carmelites describe. Might you perish when ascending Mount Carmel? If so, would that death be a gain or a loss? That question was central to the sixteenth-century Reformation, since Luther criticized devotions that were promoted as a way of climbing closer to God. The question about our driving forces is also a universally human one. We all wonder, from time to time, on which dreams and ambitions we should spend our time and energy. What deserves our whole-hearted commitment?

It is obvious that there might be underlying destructive motives within us that sometimes lead us to undertake adventures that we should really have avoided. It is also obvious that there is a life-enhancing longing for what is more and greater than ourselves, and for a vision of a better world or for a more perfect life, that can require us to venture bravely toward the heights. Sometimes it is not at all easy to distinguish between destructive ambitions and life-enhancing opportunities. This is something I have learnt from both living and departed climbers. With their help, I want to try to formulate a couple of life issues that are particularly relevant in our time—one in which psychiatric ill-health extends ever more widely and many of us risk experiencing burnout. Which dreams of the lofty heights really do make life worth living? And which attempts to reach the summits will kill us? How can the cloudy mountain peaks be mastered without bringing about our own demise?

THREE WORLD-FAMOUS (DEAD) MOUNTAINEERS

Rob Hall was already a world-famous mountaineer in his own lifetime. Since his death he has become an even greater celebrity. When Jan Arnold made contact with Rob on satellite telephone and walkie-talkie on the evening of May 11, 1996, she knew better than most that this would probably be their last conversation on earth. Arnold is a physician who specializes in high-altitude illnesses. She had met Hall during a study period in Nepal, and on their first date Rob suggested that they undertake a climb together. In May 1993 they were standing side by side on the summit of Mount Everest. Now they were expecting their first child. That was why Jan was at home in Christchurch, New Zealand while Rob lay dying 8,700 meters above sea level.

During the 1990s, companies that offered their services to people who wanted to reach the peaks of the highest mountains in the world began to see the light of day. Their business idea was built on the simple observation that not all of those who want to reach high altitudes are able to organize their own expedition. In fact, many people lack the experience and resources that success requires. Therefore, there is a demand for organized trips that include climbing permits, logistics solutions, experienced guides, and porters. Rob Hall's Adventure Consultants were leaders in this field, while the American climber Scott Fischer's Mountain Madness was a challenger that sought to get a foothold in this market.

Everything went wrong on Mount Everest in May 1996. The most attention-grabbing catastrophe in the history of that mountain happened. Many books, films, TV programs, and YouTube-clips portray and analyze the dramatic course of events.[7]

Jan Arnold's conversation with Rob Hall has made history. He was stranded on the South Peak, having fought for hours to try to help one of his clients to get down again. A storm blew up on Everest. The winds reached hurricane force, and the chill effect dropped the temperature to below -70 degrees centigrade.

"You sound much better than I had expected," Jan Arnold told the dying Rob Hall during the conversation, to which everyone who had radio contact in the vicinity of Mount Everest in May 1996 could listen. "How are your feet?" They spoke for a while about what name they would give their child, and about how things would be when Rob returned home. "Don't feel that you are alone," Jan said to Rob, who by that time was no longer accompanied by any other climber. "I send all my positive energy to you!" "I love you," Rob answered. "Please don't worry too much." Those were the last words that anyone heard him speak.

Why do people want to ascend Mount Everest? What is it that makes successful doctors, postmen with two jobs, well-paid lawyers, homesick parents of young children, and exhausted journalists spend large sums of money and enormous amounts of exercise time in order to get the opportunity to climb up and down a mountaintop with their lives still intact? The mountaineer who is surrounded by more myths than any other is the British teacher and son of a priest, George Mallory, who was asked during a lecture tour in the USA why he wanted to climb the highest mountain in the world. "Because it is there," was his legendary and laconic answer. Ever since, that comment has been analyzed with the same minute care as biblical scholars interpret the cryptic sayings of Jesus. Did

---

7. There are many books that describe these events. Jon Krakauer's best seller *Into Thin Air* has been translated into Swedish; Krakauer, *Tunn luft*. Lagercrantz and Kropp, *Göran Kropp*, tells Kropp's story. The Danish climber Lene Gammelgaard gives her version in Gammelgaard, *Climbing High*. The film *Everest* depicts the unfolding of those events.

Mallory express a well-thought-out philosophy of life, or did he simply cut short a tiresome journalist whom he thought should shut up?

A contributing factor to the myths surrounding Mallory is the fact that it is still unclear whether it was actually he and his climbing companion Andrew Irvine—rather than Edmund Hillary and Tenzing Norgay—who were the first people to set foot on the summit of Mount Everest.[8] If they were, this took place in 1924—almost thirty years before the climb that most regard as the first ascent of Everest. Mallory was a physically fit man with a will of steel. The last time he was seen alive, he was some two or three hundred meters below the summit of Mount Everest, dressed in a tweed suit and leather boots. His dead body was found in 1999 by an expedition that searched systematically for the answer to the question of how Mallory and Irvine lost their lives.[9] The pictures of Mallory's deathly pale back and broken legs were published in newspapers across the world, and aroused new interest in the man, the myth, and the legend. Many people—not just inveterate mountaineers—were hoping that Mallory really did reach his goal, because that would be such a sensational story. His dead body, his clothes, and his equipment were all well-preserved; but the altimeter that Mallory carried did not disclose how high he had got. It had been broken when he fell to his death.

One thing that was not found was the photo of his wife Ruth that Mallory intended to place on the summit when he reached it. Letters and notes that he carried were found intact in his pockets, but the photo has disappeared. Had it blown away when he looked at it during his last few hours alive? Or had he been able to place it on the summit as he had planned? The question is still up in the air, and it has been taken up by a Canadian research team that is interested in the weather. Their investigations show that a heavy snowstorm enveloped the summit of Mount Everest at the same time as George Mallory and Andrew Irvine fought to their last breath to reach it. It ought to have been impossible to ascend the highest mountain in the world in June 1924, but Mallory's dearest wish was to be able to put Mount Everest behind him at last and to return home to Ruth and their children. Who knows—maybe that driving force drove him to the edge of what was humanly possible?

---

8. The literature that describes George Mallory, his personality and his achievements, is extensive. An example well worth reading is Breashears and Salkeld, *Last Climb*.

9. You can read about that expedition in Hemmleb et al., *Ghosts of Everest*.

In many cases it is impossible to know what dying climbers were thinking during their final hours alive, so there is room for speculation. With regard to Alison Hargreaves, such speculations have been intense. Hargreaves was killed when a storm hit the top of K2 in August 1995. The winds reached hurricane force, with speeds of more than 160 kilometers an hour. It is believed that Alison was blown off the mountain. When the storm was over, one of her boots, a bloody anorak, and a climbing harness were found further down the mountain.

K2 is the world's second highest mountain and is considerably more dangerous to climb than Mount Everest. It is thus called "the mountain of the mountaineers." Technically, it is hard to maneuver, and its weather is very unpredictable. This is no place for amateurs. Very few have managed to reach the top. About a third of those who try are killed. Alison did reach the top before she died, but she never had the chance to answer the journalists' questions about her driving forces.

Alison had ascended Mount Everest a few months earlier without the help of Sherpas or oxygen. She was the first woman to make an independent ascent of the highest mountain in the world. Her goal was to reach the peaks of the world's three highest mountains in the same year. That was why she was on K2. She had managed remarkable climbing feats before, including—as the first person ever—having climbed all the classic north-facing walls of the Alps in one season. During her life she was presented in the media as a heroic example, but after her death she became the focus of contentious debate. Alison Hargreaves was the mother of two young children. Her son Tom was six years old when she went off to K2. Her daughter Kate was only four. How can a mother leave her two young children to undertake something as life-threatening as ascending the three highest mountains in the world? Was there something odd about Alison Hargreaves and about her sensitivities as a mother?

Two men—David Rose and Ed Douglas—were touched by the debate that followed Alison's death; so, they wanted to provide a more nuanced and multi-faceted portrait of one of the most noticed female climbers. In their biography, *Regions of the heart*, they ask why fathers who die in accidents on mountains are presented as heroes, while mothers who suffer the same fate are likened instead to demons.[10] By using Alison's diaries and stories from people who were close to her, they seek to trace her deepest driving forces. The picture emerges of a

---

10. What is narrated here about Alison Hargreaves's life and achievements is based primarily on Rose and Douglas, *Regions of the Heart*.

mountain-loving climbing-mad child who stood out because she was a girl, and so was not expected to be interested in making her way up steep cliffs. Alison's relationship with the considerably older Jim, who became her husband and the father of her children, is discussed thoroughly. He gave her the opportunities to climb. Was that why she fell for him? Was that why she stayed with him despite assaults, abuse, and financial worries? The climbing was a zone of freedom for the increasingly pressurized Alison—but was it also an increasingly demanding and suffocating career that her husband forced her to undertake, since her achievements could generate media attention that was good for his business?

Rose and Douglas believe that Alison decided to ascend the world's three highest mountains in one season in order to be able to leave Jim and support her children by herself. Since she had no education, she was not able to take a conventional job. She was able, however, to climb mountains far better than most other mountaineers. The spectacular achievement that she planned would give her a much-needed financial basis to enable her to start a new life. So, it was motherly love that drove her to the top of K2. She did not make any mistakes during the descent. It was the indomitable forces of nature that took her away from the mountain and from her children. The conclusion is that Alison Hargreaves died for a higher purpose, not just because she loved climbing.

Does this mean that her death must be ascribed to a higher purpose? Philosophers of religion have struggled with that kind of question throughout the ages. An American philosopher of religion has been particularly compelled to work on God's relationship with mountaineering accidents.

TWO WORLD-FAMOUS (LIVING) MOUNTAINEERS, AND A PHILOSOPHER OF RELIGION IN MOURNING

Alison Hargreaves could not stop the hurricane. Could anyone else have done that? Could God have done that? If God exists and is almighty, all-knowing, and completely good, why do some people die in mountaineering accidents? The philosopher of religion Nicholas Wolterstorff has struggled unusually intensively with this question. In 1983 his son Eric died in a climbing accident in the Alps.[11] He was about to ascend Ellmauer Halt, the highest peak in the mountain range of Kaisergebirge, when he fell. Nicholas remembers the telephone call from Europe and

---

11. The following is based on Wolterstorff, *Lament for a Son*.

how he answered at home in the USA. He was soon on his way to Kufstein to collect his son's body.

At Kufstein, Nicholas was not allowed to see his son's body because it was so badly damaged, but he was given the boots and the rucksack. When he looked at the well-kept footwear, the questions welled up. What was it that made Eric love climbing mountains? Could he not have engaged in something less dangerous? Why did we let him do it?

In time, Nicholas was able to find the words for some of the answers. Eric loved the physical challenge, and he sought the spiritual experiences that climbing gave him. Just like so many other mountaineers, he was striving to experience the fine-tuned collaboration between body and soul on which a successful climb depends. Eric met God on the mountains. He certainly met God in other places as well—in church, with family, among his friends—but God spoke to the deepest layers of Eric's soul, especially when he climbed the mountains. On the snowy expanses and among the cliffs, Eric's relationship with God became even more intimate. He could not live without that closeness to God that he could only experience if he were allowed to climb.

Nicholas, Eric's mourning father, was given a book about sorrow, written by another father who had also lost his son in a climbing accident. In the book, the other father expressed a belief that Nicholas could not share: that God sometimes shakes the mountain or sends a storm that makes mountaineers die by accident, because God is almighty, and so everything rests in God's hands. That means that everything that happens is governed by God. Since God is good, everything that happens is good, even though, from our human perspective, we perceive it as evil. We do not understand the ways of God, but we can receive everything that happens as a good gift from the hand of God.

Nicholas Wolterstorff knew that this is how Luther reasons in *The bondage of the will*; but he could not find any comfort in that way of thinking. He pursued other paths. For Eric's funeral he arranged an order of service founded on the funeral liturgy of the Roman Catholic Church. The congregation sang songs from the ecumenical religious community at Taizé and celebrated Mass together. The bread and the wine were shared between those who gathered around Eric's coffin. For Eric, the Mass and mountaineering were two contexts in which God met him in a very particular way. During his funeral service, both contexts spoke to each other and deepened the perspective on Eric's life.

When I tell you about Nicholas, Eric, and some of the world's most famous mountaineers, the overall purpose is to let the Evangelical-Lutheran tradition and the spirituality of Carmel converse and interact with one another. I want to contribute to a dialog that both pays attention to issues within dogmatics and relates to the life issues with which we unavoidably must struggle. Therefore, I allow not only theologians and philosophers to say something to us, but also a few living—and departed—mountaineers to add a few phrases. It is not only Doctors of the Church and reformers who have something to tell us about the risks and opportunities of mountaineering. Nor is it only monks and nuns and priests who have something to say about the importance of a continued Reformation. Mountaineers too are baptized believers, people who are searching spiritually.

Gerlinde Kaltenbrunner is one of the world's best-known and most-appreciated mountaineers. For her, mountaineering and the life of the Church are connected in a very particular way. She started her remarkable climbing career at the altar in a rural Roman Catholic church in Austria. She was a choir girl and loved to serve on Sundays. The parish priest, Father Tischler,[12] was a committed mountaineer, and he arranged summer camps and walks in the mountains for the Roman Catholic youth group. Father Tischler taught Gerlinde and her friends the basics of climbing cliffs. He taught them the importance of sticking together when you are climbing together, the importance of concentration, and how to put down your whole foot when you are walking in steep terrain. After Mass on Sundays, Father Tischler used to take the young people for a walk somewhere in the vicinity. In that way the liturgy in the church found a natural continuity in God's creation.

In 2011 Gerlinde Kaltenbrunner reached the top of K2. She thus became the second woman in the world to have ascended all fourteen mountains whose peaks exceed 8,000 meters. When she reached the highest point of K2, she knelt in thanksgiving. She describes the 45 minutes that she spent on the top, alone for a while, as a spiritual experience. She had a very strong sense of being one with existence, of being part of a larger context.

Gerlinde Kaltenbrunner's autobiography is not only a story about a person with a physique that is almost too good to imagine, but also a

---

12. Gerlinde Kaltenbrunner speaks about Father Tischler in Kaltenbrunner, *Mountains in my Heart*, 15–18. Other information about her climbs I take from the same book.

testimony to the importance of prayer and meditation. Gerlinde can be on the move for several days and nights at a stretch. She can plod forward in snow up to her waist in extreme cold. She can climb up steep cliffs with only a tiny headlamp as light. She can reach the highest points of the Earth without using oxygen. Sometimes she or another climber close to her are affected by accidents. Gerlinde describes how she handles risks and even deaths, both practically and at an existential level. As a trained nurse, she is often consulted in situations of crisis on the mountains. Following both successful and failed expeditions, many people want to talk to her. She herself used to talk to Father Tischler while he was still alive, telling him about her adventures and experiences. In the tent at the foot of the mountain, she would also meditate before starting the ascent to the top, and, if she ended up in a critical situation on the mountain, she would pray. During the sideways move on Annapurna, which was one of the riskiest and scariest things she had undertaken on an 8,000-meter peak, she prayed constantly for an hour and a half while mechanically moving her step irons and ice axes, just as Father Tischler had once taught her.

The year before Gerlinde Kaltenbrunner reached the summit of K2, the Basque climber Edurne Pasaban became the first woman to climb all fourteen mountains whose peaks exceed 8,000 meters. In her autobiography, Edurne speaks of how her life and her climbing career nearly came to an end a few years earlier when she attempted suicide.[13] She reflects on this paradoxical situation. She had walked thousands of kilometres, climbed thousands of meters upwards across cliffs and ice, always concentrating so that nothing should happen, often on tenterhooks, in order to survive. Now she had swallowed a few tablets and cut her wrists. She was at home in safety, and she immediately phoned for an ambulance herself. What had happened? Why had her will to live been blown away?

The answer is that Edurne Pasaban had been affected by depression. She was taken to hospital, and there she was soon given a treatment that required a different sort of strength than the physical strength required to ascend an 8,000-meter peak. Edurne was invited to talk about herself, her life, and her relationships. She was given the chance to reflect on her own driving forces and her dreams. She was challenged to think along new lines, to see more of herself, and to allow what she wanted to hide to emerge into the light.

---

13. This account is based on Pasaban, *Tilting at Mountains*. The description of the suicide attempt and the treatment that followed can be found on pages 151–56.

As part of her recovery, Edurne Pasaban continued to climb 8,000-meter peaks. She notes that every person must have something to live for, something to fight for, something to burn passionately for; otherwise, she will not feel well. In that sense, every person must have an 8,000-meter peak in view. She must have something to help her overcome difficulties, to find meaning, and to move toward a far-off goal. Having climbed the fourteen 8,000-meter peaks, Edurne found a new challenge that she chose to call her fifteenth 8,000-meter peak: she stopped taking the medication of which she had once taken an overdose.

When Edurne Pasaban and Gerlinde Kaltenbrunner are asked what their expeditions to all these 8,000-meter peaks have given them, they answer in very similar ways. Their hardships in the mountains have made them grow as people. They are no longer the same persons. They have matured and developed. These days they think somewhat differently than before. They see themselves rather more clearly. They can feel both their strength and their limitations. They can love more honestly. They no longer have the same need to show a nice face in their encounters with other people. Their vision is clearer, their heart more undivided in paying attention. The mountains have given them greater humility, and they find it easier to be happy about very ordinary everyday details.

In the era of the early Church, many men and women experienced the same thing as did Gerlinde Kaltenbrunner and Edurne Pasaban—that mountains provide an environment that can be beneficial for human growth and maturity. Good qualities such as love, patience, and humility can be improved. Anyone spending time in mountainous areas is exposed to dangers and challenges that make it easy to pray. Both under the starry sky and up on the peaks it is possible to experience a sense of belonging together with everything that exists and with God the Creator of everything. Physical exposure can bear fruit in a process of development in the soul and the spirit. Therefore—but not only for that reason—a growing number of Christians who lived in Egypt in the third century CE chose to withdraw to lonely areas in the mountains. There was a commitment in their relationship with Christ that I believe is the only effective cure for the Church's secularization from within. They held a faith for which they were prepared to live and die. From their circles, the Christian monastic life emerged.

THE EMERGENCE OF THE MONASTIC LIFE IN MOUNTAINOUS AREAS

In the third century CE, Egypt was part of the Roman Empire. Early in that century, the Emperor Septimus Severus had sought to unite the empire under a single religion—that is, the worship of the unconquered sun. The result was that both Jews and Christians were subjected to violent persecution because they refused to worship this god. In the middle of the century, the Emperor Decius demanded, in a similar way, that all Roman citizens show their loyalty to the empire by participating in pagan sacrifices. Christians refused, and were subjected to a new bloody persecution. Shortly after that, the Emperor Valerian claimed that the Roman Empire had been hit by pestilence, earthquakes, and other catastrophes because of the deficient loyalty of the Christians; and thus a new persecution began. The Emperor Diocletian tried in turn to unite the empire by forcibly bringing religions into line. Toward the end of the third century, he carried out the most extensive state-supported persecution of Christians in antiquity. A decade later, the tide turned: in 313, the Emperor Constantine, together with his co-Emperor Licinius, declared Christianity to be a legal religion in the Roman Empire.

The persecution of Christians, together with the steadfastness in the faith that the martyrs showed, was an important seedbed for the emergence of Christian monasticism. At the beginning of the fourth century, there were about one million Christians in Egypt. It is easy to understand that significant numbers of them doubted the possibility of living an authentic and genuine life as a follower of Christ within the narrow framework that their society imposed. It is also easy to understand their interest in the question of how you can live the kind of life that overcomes the world. The courage to risk everything for your faith, even life itself, was a much-sought-after virtue that inspired growing numbers of hermits to go and live in the desert. An undivided heart and a clear vision were their goal.

St. Anthony the Great often represents the desert hermits of the early Church. He was born into a wealthy family. When his parents died, he inherited a major fortune, which he gave away, having heard a sermon on the words of Jesus in the Gospel of Matthew: "If you wish to be perfect, go, sell your possessions, and give the money to the poor, and you will have treasure in heaven; then come, follow me" (Matt 19:21). Anthony took Jesus at his word. He sold his house and his fields and gave the money to the poor. For the rest of his life, he lived in great simplicity. He slept directly on the ground. Sometimes he would eat only once a day, and some days not at all. Sleep was replaced by watching and prayer. Eventually he fled into the desert to live as a hermit. He spent his time there alone for twenty years before he began to receive people who sought his guidance. Disciples who came to join him in the desert were accommodated in nearby caves. Anthony taught them and gathered them for common prayer.

This community around St. Anthony is often seen as the origin of Christian monasticism, even though it is certain that other Christian monastic communities formed earlier than that. When Anthony was about to go into the desert, he not only sold his property: he also placed his underage sister in the care of some nuns. Anthony did not invent the monastic life, but he soon became the ideal type for a person living the monastic life. One of the reasons is that the influential Bishop Athanasius of Alexandria wrote a book about the life of St. Anthony shortly after Anthony's death. This biography soon became obligatory reading in the emerging monastic life.[14]

Athanasius sketches an ascetic ideal that is marked by self-control, high inner moral stature, and wholehearted commitment. Asceticism, or *ascesis,* is a concept that was originally used in the sports and military contexts. It refers to the exercises to which one needs to submit to in order to be well-prepared for the fight on the battleground or in the arena. When this word was taken over by the hermits who populated the deserts of Egypt, it was used to designate the spiritual exercises, struggles, or formation that can help people to overcome the world through a systematic struggle against temptations such as pride, greed, jealousy, and despair. Modern-day Swedes encounter this concept primarily through the much-appreciated books by Martin Lönnebo on the ecumenical rosary, called *Pearls of life* (*Frälsarkransen* in Swedish). Lönnebo notes that there are physical and mental exercises as well as spiritual exercises. In his view, the spiritual exercises are the most neglected ones today, and this worries him. The lack of spiritual exercises leaves people poorly equipped for life. Lönnebo shaped *Pearls of life* as an aid or an exercise tool for contemporary people who, like the fourth century desert hermits, want

---

14. The life of St. Anthony has been translated into Swedish; Athanasios of Alexandria, *Antonios liv*. The details in the presentation of the life of St. Anthony above are taken from the introduction to that volume by Thomas Hägg and Samuel Rubenson.

to practice for the struggle that is ultimately the only struggle that can be described as life-determining.[15]

Had it not been for Martin Lönnebo's dramatic desert walk in the footsteps of St. Anthony, the *Pearls of life* would probably never have seen the light of day.[16] In the early 1990s, Martin Lönnebo and some of his friends went astray close to the cave in which St. Anthony had lived. (There is still, to this day, a monastery in the vicinity.) When I and some of my friends visited the St. Anthony Monastery a couple of years later, the Abbot become very worried, to say the least, when we announced that we wanted to spend the night in St. Anthony's cave. That was quite simply out of the question, the Abbot stated, since he did not want to risk any further incidents. St. Anthony's cave could be visited in the daytime, but nightly hermit life had to be practiced in the hostel that was situated no further away than the Abbot could see in the dark.

The daytime visit to St. Anthony's cave taught me something about deserts that I had not quite understood before. In the world of comics, cartoon figures thirsting for water crawl around in endless expanses completely without any hills; but not all deserts are flat areas filled with sand. Deserts can have steep cliff formations with areas that are just as stony as the boulders and blocks that characterize the high-altitude alpine footpaths of the Jotunheim, Norway. That insight gave new life to the biblical world of the desert for me.

BIBLICAL MOUNTAIN ASCENTS

Mountains and mountain ascents are a recurring theme in the biblical writings. The New Testament tells us that Jesus was driven into the desert by the Spirit in order to be tested by the devil (Matt 4:1–11, Mark 1:12–13, Luke 4:1–13). The Gospels do not name the desert to which Jesus withdrew, but tradition tells us that it was the mountainous desert of Judah east of Jerusalem, close to the river Jordan, and anything but a flat desert. Just before his walk into the desert, Jesus had been baptized by the desert prophet John the Baptist. John lived in the desert of Judah, where he sustained himself on grasshoppers and wild honey. He wore clothes of camel hair, and people made pilgrimages into the desert to listen to his preaching. He encouraged conversion and justice. Whoever has two shirts should share with the one who has nothing. Everyone should

---

15. Lönnebo, *Själen*, 7–8.
16. Halldorf, "Öppning," 4.

receive what they need to survive, and nobody should resort to threats or violence to make a fortune. So many people took his words seriously that he became a danger to the worldly powers who lived by quite different ideals. John was imprisoned and beheaded in a grotesque fashion.

The Bible describes how the devil took Jesus up to a very high mountain in the desert to show him all the kingdoms of the world and their glory (Matt 4:8–19). The devil tempted Jesus with promises of remarkable success. In a similar way, modern-day climbers can be lured by the promise of a sensational triumph when they are affected by 'summit fever'. "All these I will give you, if you will fall down and worship me," the devil said to Jesus. "Away with you, Satan!" Jesus answered, with reference to what is written in the Law (the Torah): "Worship the Lord your God and serve only him" (Exod 20:1–5, Deut 5:6–9).

There is nothing in the Gospels to indicate that Jesus made his way into the desert at any other time after he had overcome the temptations to which the devil had subjected him. However, the evangelist St. Matthew recalls with great enthusiasm a number of significant mountain ascents. Jesus went up a mountain to find space to teach the crowds, and his preaching is summarized in what we call the Sermon on the Mount (Matt 5–7). He also took Peter, James, and John with him up a high mountain (Matt 17:1–8, Mark 9:2–8, Luke 9:28–36). When they were alone at the top it turned out that they were in fact not as alone as they had thought. The frightened disciples saw how Jesus was transfigured. His clothes became as dazzling white as the light, and he stood there and talked with the most prominent desert figures of the Old Testament, Moses and Elijah. We are also told that, when Jesus needed to be by himself and pray, he went up a mountain (Matt 14:23). When he arranged to meet his disciples after his resurrection, it was of course to a mountain that he commanded them to go (Matt 28:16).

Mount Horeb in the Sinai desert played a decisive role for the Old Testament prophets, Moses and Elijah. Here they met God in a very special way. Horeb—usually known as Mount Sinai today—is in Egypt. When I visited it in the mid-1990s, you could hire a camel to ride on if you did not feel like walking all the way up the 2,880-meter peak. Up there, it was possible to buy sweets and drinks from a little kiosk.

The Book of Exodus tells us that it was at the foot of Mount Horeb that Moses met God in the burning thorn bush (Exod 3:1ff.). Moses had run away from Pharaoh, the Egyptian king, because he had killed an Egyptian who had killed a Hebrew man—that is, one of Moses's countrymen. The Hebrew people were oppressed and taken advantage of by the worldly powers of Egypt. Through the thorn bush, God encouraged Moses to return to Egypt to liberate the people from their captivity. It was in the desert that God informed Moses about what he should do.

Moses returned to Egypt to lead the people on a forty-year-long desert walk. From time to time there was dreadful murmuring in the ranks. People thought that God was absent. When they pitched camp at Mount Sinai, dramatic events took place (Exod 19:16ff.). The Bible recalls how God appeared on the top of the mountain in clouds, thunder, and flames. The people stood at a distance while Moses went up into the darkness to meet God. God and Moses talked together at the top. Then Moses went up and down the mountain several times as messenger between God and the people. On Mount Sinai, he received the Ten Commandments. While he was up the mountain to receive the first set of stone tablets with the commandments, the people gave in to temptation. They made themselves an idol out of their own riches. They tried to make a cast for their own happiness in the shape of a golden calf, which they worshiped. When Moses came down from the mountain and saw what they had done, he was so angry that he broke the stone tablets that God had given him. The Bible says that then the Lord comforted Moses, and put him in a cleft on Mount Sinai. When the Lord passed by, he covered Moses's eyes with his hand. Nobody can see the face of God and live. When the Lord had passed by, Moses was allowed to see him only from the back, and he was given a new set of stone tablets with the commandments.

God also spoke to the prophet Elijah in a cave on Mount Horeb. Elijah was on the run from Queen Jezebel (1 Kgs 19:11ff.). He had taken part in what can best be described as a sacrifice duel between himself and 850 prophets who worshiped the god Baal and the goddess Asherah. The duel took place on Mount Carmel, and Elijah emerged victorious from the fight. The outcome had made Queen Jezebel furious, and her wrath drove Elijah out into the desert. There he sat down under a broom bush and longed for death. "It is enough," he said to God. "Take my life." When he fell asleep, an angel came and touched him. "Get up and eat," the angel said—and then the angel came back with further instructions. For forty days and forty nights, Elijah walked through the desert to Mount Horeb. There he met God.

"What are you doing here, Elijah?" God asked, and Elijah gave an answer that indicated that he too was struggling with the despair of secularization from within.[17] "I have done my utmost for the Lord of Hosts," Elijah answered, "but it does not seem to be of any use. There are no believers anymore. Everything seems to go wrong, and I can do nothing to stop this development. Now it is enough. I give up. I cannot cope any longer." "Go out and stand on the mountain," God responded. "I will pass that way." There was a strong wind that rent mountains and broke the rocks to pieces. But God was not in the storm. Then came an earthquake, and then a fire, but God was not in the earthquake, nor in the fire. After the fire there came a still small voice. Then Elijah went out of the cave and stood at the entrance. "Go, return," God said to Elijah. "I will make sure that there will be people who will not bend their knee to idols." With that promise, Elijah went down from the mountain.

MOUNTAIN GUIDES FROM THE PAST AND THE PRESENT

St. Catherine's Monastery is situated at the foot of Mount Sinai. According to legend, it was founded in the fourth century by Helena, the mother of the Emperor Constantine. St. Catherine's Monastery is considered to be the oldest Christian monastery that is still in use. A large number of impressive manuscripts are kept here, and one of the most influential devotional books was collated here by a desert hermit called St. John Climacus.

We do not know very much about this John. The most trustworthy sources say that he came to Sinai at the age of 16. Here he first lived under the guidance of a spiritual father called Abba Martyrius.[18] After three years of testing, Abba Martyrius admitted John as a monk in the chapel at the top of Sinai by shaving off his hair. Soon afterwards John started to live as a desert hermit and maintained that way of life for forty years. Then he was elected Abbot of St. Catherine's Monastery against his will. However, it was as abbot of the most prominent monastery in the Christian world that John wrote *The ladder of divine ascent*. He did this at the urging of the abbot in a neighboring monastery who had realized that John could give other hermits the good guidance that they so sorely needed.[19]

---

17. In what follows I paraphrase 1 Kgs 19:9ff.

18. "Abba" means "father." For spiritual mothers, the term "Amma" ("mother") is used.

19. The introduction by Kallistos Ware in John Climacus, *Ladder of Divine Ascent*, 3–6.

In *The ladder of divine ascent,* John describes how a person can gradually make a break with the world's way of thinking and habits, practice virtue, and—if all goes well—reach a contemplative vision of God. John summarizes his insights in 30 chapters, presented as steps on a ladder that reaches up to heaven. In the Eastern Church tradition, John's book is a classic that has become just as significant as Thomas à Kempis's work *On the Imitation of Christ* has become in the Western Church tradition.[20] John's work is not available in a Swedish translation; but that does not mean that it has passed us Swedes by completely. Several exercises can be found in Martin Lönnebo's major book, *Väven (The weave),* which is obviously inspired by John's teaching. It is evident that Lönnebo has been sitting in his rowing boat outside Gräsö and meditating on *The ladder of divine ascent.*[21]

John often comes back to the importance of how we use and react to words. For John, holding back before you make a judgment about other people, or comment on their efforts, or express some opinion about their views or person, is something of a key or cardinal virtue for anyone who wants to make progress on the pathway to God. The same applies to the ability to accept criticism in the right way and to be able to relate to other people's words, judgments, and conclusions when they comment on your own efforts. It is quite obvious that John did not live in our contemporary tweeting and opinionated culture; but even though he had no company and no mobile phone, he still had to struggle with challenges and temptations with which we also need to be able to deal in order not to become totally insufferable in our own context.

The structure of John's work is related to themes that can be discerned, even though his writing is sketchy and impressionistic. *The Sayings of the Desert Fathers,* another classic that summarizes the teachings of the early Christian hermits, follows a different approach. Here we find stories about spiritual guides and their words of wisdom, given in alphabetical order by name. The first is Abba Anthony and the last is Abba Or. Altogether, 86 Desert Fathers speak to us in the Swedish edition, entitled *Ökenfädernas tänkespråk (The Sayings of the Desert Fathers).* Besides the Desert Fathers, three Desert Mothers also turn up between the covers; Amma Theodora, Amma Sara, and Amma Syncletica stand out, and are thus often given extra attention by modern-day readers. Luckily, they

---

20. The introduction by Kallistos Ware in John Climacus, *Ladder of Divine Ascent,* 1, 12–13.

21. Lönnebo, *Väven,* 86–88.

have sensible things to say. Amma Sara stresses that, if we want all people to be happy with us, we must become like penitents at each and everyone's door. It is far better for us to ask for a pure heart toward everyone.[22] Amma Syncletica takes us to the sports arena, and notes that, just as a successful athlete needs to develop in accordance with the pace at which they encounter better opposition, so we too need to become better and better at dealing with the tricks of the devil. She also notes that we need to be able to distinguish between good spiritual exercises and demonic forms of asceticism that do not foster humility in us but lead to pride.[23] Amma Theodora thought along similar lines when she stressed that it is not *ascesis*, watching, or prayers of any kind that can save us: only humility can do that.[24]

The Benedictine nun Laura Swan has made significant research efforts to deepen our knowledge of the Desert Mothers and their life conditions and teachings. In her book, *The forgotten Desert Mothers: Sayings, lives, and stories of early Christian women*, she refers by way of introduction to Palladius of Galata who, in a piece of writing from the fifth century, estimated that there were around twice as many Desert Mothers as Desert Fathers.[25] Swan notes that, in many cases, it is the stories about the men and their words of wisdom that have been preserved for future generations. The hermits strove to cover up any traces of themselves and their efforts. The women were often more successful in doing that, Swan thinks.[26] However, Swan's research has made it possible for her to present no fewer than 78 desert-influenced women who, in various ways, served as examples and leaders in the early Church.

Swan herself belongs to a monastic order that has its origins on the mountain of Monte Cassino in Italy. Here Benedict of Nursia and his followers built a monastery in the sixth century. Benedict wrote a rule for their common life that became the model for monastic life in the West. Benedict himself had lived as a hermit from a young age, for some time in a cave situated about fifty kilometers from Rome, the city where he had

---

22. *Ökenfädernas tänkespråk*, 150, § 5. For an English translation; Swan, *Forgotten Desert Mothers*, 39.

23. *Ökenfädernas tänkespråk*, 153–54, §§14, 15, 18. For an English translation; Swan, *Forgotten Desert Mothers*, 54–55, 57.

24. *Ökenfädernas tänkespråk*, 72, § 6. For an English translation; Swan, *Forgotten Desert Mothers*, 67.

25. Swan, *Forgotten Desert Mothers*, 3.

26. Swan, *Forgotten Desert Mothers*, 16.

grown up. When he moved to the loneliness of the cave, he was only 14 years old.

On Mount Carmel, where Elijah's sacrifice duel took place, another monastic order, the Carmelite Order, was founded. The Carmelite Order came to Europe in the thirteenth century and would play a significant role in the processes of reformation that began in the sixteenth century. The Carmelite Order was then reformed by a Spanish woman from Avila. In the religious life her name was Teresa of Jesus. She fought the same ecclesiastical decline as Luther did, but she used other means and had other opportunities. She and her followers can enrich our reflections on the significance of the Reformation, both now and then.

MOUNT CARMEL IN FOCUS

Unlike the Benedictine Order and many other monastic communities, the Carmelite Order is not named after any founder. It emerged in the form of a community of hermits on Mount Carmel toward the end of the twelvth century. Brothers who found their spiritual ideal embodied in the prophet Elijah—he who had done his utmost for God—lived here. They built a small church dedicated to the Virgin Mary because they wanted to live under her patronage. In the early thirteenth century, the hermit Brothers on Mount Carmel turned to the Patriarch Albertus of Jerusalem because they realized that they needed to organize their community in some way. Until then they had not had much contact with one another, and their lifestyle had been transmitted to newcomers by oral tradition. The Patriarch wrote a rule for the community in which the stress was on solitude, silence, and unceasing prayer. The hermits, who had been spread out, united under the leadership of a prior, and the existence of the Carmelite Order was officially confirmed by the pope in the year 1226.[27]

Toward the end of the thirteenth century, the Brothers were forced to move gradually to Europe because fighting between Christians and Muslims made it impossible for them to continue their monastic life on Mount Carmel. In 1291 the monastery on Mount Carmel was invaded by the Saracens and the remaining hermits were murdered. By that time, Carmelite monasteries had been founded in France, England, Italy, and Germany. The order kept its contemplative character when it moved to Europe, but now the monasteries and convents were usually founded

---

27. Steinmann, *Karmelitorden*, 9–10; *De första munkarnas bok*.

in cities rather than in remote mountainous areas. The task of assisting people by offering spiritual guidance thus became more pronounced.[28]

The Carmelite Order came to Sweden relatively late. In the fifteenth century there were four known Carmelite monasteries within what are today the boundaries of Sweden, at Örebro, Landskrona, Varberg, and Sölvesborg. The Reformation in the sixteenth century turned Sweden into an Evangelical-Lutheran nation. However, that revolutionary chain of events has many roots that go deep into Carmelite soil. A number of influential Swedish reformers were deeply marked by the tradition of Carmel, since they had had Poul Helgesen as their teacher.[29] Helgesen came from Varberg, and was one of the most outstanding Nordic theologians at that time. He entered the Carmelite Order early in his life, and later became Director of the Carmelite Study House in Copenhagen. One of his disciples was Frans Vormordsen, who for a while was a Carmelite Brother in the monastery at Elsinore. During the Reformation he became the first superintendent of the Diocese of Lund.[30] Today we would have called him a bishop, but in the sixteenth century Protestants avoided that title, since it was associated with the papacy. The best-known Swedish reformer, Olaus Petri, may have received his basic education with the Carmelites at Örebro.[31]

I would like to claim that the gap between the Evangelical-Lutheran faith and the Carmelite tradition did not appear particularly wide to the Swedish reformers of the sixteenth century. At that time, it was not always easy to determine who represented the new Evangelical-Lutheran teaching and who kept faith in the original Carmelite ideals. The fate of Poul Helgesen, among others, testifies to that. He was accused of being a supporter of Luther's doctrines, but eventually he was killed because that was not what he was.

Today things are different. To contemporary Evangelical-Lutheran Christians, monastic life in the Carmelite Order usually seems to be the direct opposite of justification by grace through faith-filled trust in Jesus Christ, which Luther preached. The Carmelite nuns who live in strict enclosure within the walls of a convent, and who do not leave it except in extreme need, seem to be locked into a form of life that Luther identified

---

28. Steinmann, *Karmelitorden*, 10–12.
29. Nyman, *Förlorarnas historia*, 208–12 discusses Poul Helgesen's life and thought.
30. Steinmann, *Karmelitorden*, 13, 16.
31. Nyman, *Förlorarnas historia*, 45.

as one of the very clearest expressions of justification by works, and which he abhorred. Just like over-ambitious mountaineers, they have been affected by summit fever, and they commit everything to striving to please God in the hope that they will be rewarded accordingly. However, they neglect the everyday care of fellow human beings outside the monastic walls that Luther appreciated so much. This is how we might sum up a standard Evangelical-Lutheran objection to the hermit-focused monastic life, if it were particularly directed at Carmelite nuns.

The strict enclosure of Carmelite nuns was introduced by Teresa of Jesus in the sixteenth century. Teresa entered the Convent of the Carmelite Sisters at Avila in 1535. At that time Martin Luther had published his ninety-five theses against indulgences in Germany; he had been excommunicated by Pope Leo X; and he had been outlawed by Emperor Charles V. After twenty years in the monastic life, Luther had left the Augustinian Order to marry the former nun, Katharina von Bora, and start a family. There were such lively discussions around the table in their home and sometimes one of the dinner guests wrote down what was said in order to preserve it for the future. By the 1530s, Luther was a well-known figure who had become a catalyst for the ecclesiastical process of change whose effects were felt as far away as Spain.

In the Carmelite Convent at Avila, Teresa of Jesus gradually began to worry about the same decay of the Church that Luther thundered against. Teresa shared the convent with some two hundred nuns. Some of them were rich, others were poor. The financial gaps were noticeable in the life of the convent. Rich nuns were permitted their own rooms with soft cushions and feather beds. They also had servants to attend them, while the poor nuns had to make do with considerably simpler conditions. They also had to carry out tougher work, and would never be appointed to leading positions within the monastic community. The regular life of prayer was neglected. The wealthy nuns were able to come and go as they pleased. They attended friends' parties outside the convent walls, where they could talk and socialise in the same way as everyone else.[32]

Teresa's experience of decaying community life is reminiscent of Luther's shocking discoveries during his pilgrimage to Rome, which he undertook in 1510–1511. Some scholars believe that Luther's pilgrimage marks the actual starting point of the Reformation. Had Luther not traveled to Rome, he would not have discovered the extent of the

---

32. Bilinkoff, *Avila of Saint Teresa*, 112–16.

ecclesiastical decay. His visit awakened Luther's desire for a Christian life that was characterized by other ideals than this moral decay that he found in the ecclesiastical capital.

Teresa of Jesus also longed for an authentic life of following Christ. Just like the prophet Elijah, she wanted to do her utmost for God; but she thought that her life in the convent did not allow space for that. She therefore sought new opportunities to live a life that was more clearly marked by the solitude, silence, simplicity, and renunciation that characterized the lives of the first monks on Mount Carmel. In time her longing led to permission for her to found new convents with a lifestyle that was in greater accord with the original ideals of the order. Thus Teresa became the reformer of the Carmelite Order. Just like Luther, Teresa wanted to return the whole Church to its central core, to an original ideal and content that had become superficial as a result of the deterioration of the Church, by sorting out deficiencies in the life of worship and devotion.

Teresa's influence as a reformer reached far beyond the Carmelite Order. Because of her visions, she is regarded today as one of the world's most prominent mystics. Philosophers of religion take a keen interest in her remarkable experiences. Through her writings, she guides people from various Christian traditions who long for a deeper and often wordless life of prayer. The British theologian Alister E. McGrath stresses Teresa's importance in his book *Historical theology*, in which Teresa is the only woman whom McGrath describes as a "key theologian." In that respect she is in the good company of 28 men, including St. Athanasius of Alexandria and Martin Luther.[33]

In the past, Teresa's work and the reformatory processes in which she was involved were usually described as part of the so-called Counter-Reformation. However, McGrath is careful not to use that loaded concept, which is based on the assumption that Teresa and other "counter-reformers" were primarily reacting against Luther and that they were governed by his reformatory agenda. Today we know better. Not all the reformatory events of the sixteenth century revolved around Luther and the ninety-five theses that he reportedly pinned to the church porch at Wittenberg. There were other independent agents who sought to deal with the same ecclesiastical deterioration that Luther criticized. Teresa of Jesus was one of them.

---

33. McGrath, *Historical Theology*.

In the year 1970, the pope appointed Teresa of Jesus as a Doctor of the Church—the first woman to receive that distinction. Having considered carefully whether women could be presented as good teachers for the whole Church without being in conflict with the Bible, the pope concluded that it is possible to give both men and women that status and function.

This book agrees with the view that the Carmelite Doctor's of the Church are good teachers for the whole Church. My aim is to explore how Teresa of Jesus and two of her followers, John of the Cross and Thérèse of the Child Jesus, can help us in the Evangelical-Lutheran tradition to continue the Reformation. My reflections on what we can learn from these three Carmelites focus on two key concepts—namely, grace and faith—and on one primary person, Jesus Christ. The reason is that these two concepts and that one person are completely determinative of Luther's understanding of justification by faith. Having grace, faith, and Jesus in focus, I want to highlight our opportunities to counter the secularization from within with the help of the Carmelites—but without abandoning the doctrine of justification, which Luther believed we must preserve in order to remain the Church. Originally the name "Carmel" comes from a word that means "God's garden of fruit trees." My hypothesis is that the spirituality of Carmel could bear fruit in the Church of Sweden's Evangelical-Lutheran tradition as well.

2

Thérèse of the Child Jesus and Grace

The mountaineer Edurne Pasaban grew up in the Basque town of Tolosa. In her autobiography she says that she found it difficult to feel comfortable among her contemporaries. They were not interested in the same things as she was, and she did not feel that she could share her innermost thoughts with them. As a teenager, she ended up, by chance, on a course that the local climbing club had arranged. On that course and in the climbing club she found friends for life. In their company she could be herself. The club arranged outings to the Pyrenees at weekends. In that mountain range, Edurne Pasaban encountered challenges that gave rise to her longing to climb to higher altitudes.

Just like Pasaban, pilgrims like to find their way to the Pyrenees. Many of them choose to begin their walk to Santiago de Compostela at Saint-Jean-Pied-de-Port. It is not easy to find your way to "St. James-at-the-Foot-of-the-Pass," the travel agencies explain on their websites, but it is doubtless worth the effort. The Pyrenean mountain areas around Saint-Jean-Pied-de-Port offer some of the most beautiful daily legs of the pilgrimage.

Every year, more than 100,000 people receive their pilgrimage diploma at Santiago de Compostela. This diploma certifies that the holder has walked the last 100 kilometers of the Camino—the path to the traditional site of the grave of the apostle James at Santiago—and that this has taken place for a religious or spiritual purpose. Some of those who have walked along the way of St. James speak of their experiences and of the insights that this walk has given them in media interviews and blogposts. The current popularity of pilgrimages led an international group of researchers to carry out a major investigation by questionnaire in order to sketch the contours of this popular movement in walking boots that has also made its mark in Sweden's woods and mountains.

When 1,000 pilgrims were asked why they had walked to the grave of the apostle James, 51.8 per cent agreed with the statement that, for them, a very significant goal was "to find themselves."[1] This motivation appeared to be the most important in the investigation. In second place came "to find a break from everyday life" (40.2 per cent), and in third place, "to enjoy the quiet stillness" (39.2 per cent). Among other motivations that were stressed as central were "to experience the spiritual atmosphere" (34.6 per cent), "to experience nature" (34.4 per cent), and "to enjoy the beautiful landscape" (32.9 per cent). About a quarter of those asked (23.4 per cent) ticked "religious reasons" as very important for their walk, while only 6.6 per cent stressed "to arrive at the pilgrimage goal" as a determinative driving force. What took place along the way was described as more significant than the final destination of the walk. In line with this view, 22.2 per cent said that the opportunity to spend time with the family during the pilgrimage was a very important cause for their walk. "To experience adventure" (20.9 per cent), "to be part of the pilgrimage community" (19.1 per cent), and "to get some exercise" (17.3 per cent) were other popular reasons that underline the importance of what happens during the days of walking. The same applies to the answer "to work out a life crisis" (14.2 per cent).

Against the background of these statistics, researchers have identified five ideal-type pilgrims who are on the move along the Camino: the spiritually searching pilgrim, the religious pilgrim, the sporty pilgrim, the adventurous and experience-seeking pilgrim, and the culture- and landscape-focused pilgrim. It is worth noting that the researchers describe all these ideal types as "pilgrims." A significant feature of modern pilgrimage research is the reluctance to draw a sharp distinction between "real pilgrims" who are driven by religious motivations and "ordinary tourists" who visit pilgrimage destinations for other reasons.[2] This reluctance is because people's motivations are complex. Even among those who state that they undertake the walk in order to get some exercise, a spiritual search may also be an important driving force. Even for pilgrims who stress that they walk in penitence before God (16.6 per cent in the

1. In the following I refer to Jensen, *Pilegrim*, 77–81. The survey by questionnaire was carried out in 2010.

2. Cf. Jensen, *Pilegrim*, 74.

investigation), an adventurous break from humdrum everyday life could also be part of the motivation.

Historically focused pilgrimage researchers stress that these complex motivations are nothing new. In centuries past, people went on pilgrimage for many different reasons. During the thirteenth century, pilgrimages in Europe enjoyed a considerable upturn when both the lust for adventure and financial incentives were significant background factors, besides reasons that can be described as religious.

There are not only different reasons why people choose to make a pilgrimage: different turning points in life also tend to encourage people to do so. Sometime the desire to "find oneself" or the need to "have a break from humdrum everyday life" becomes unusually relevant. In order to describe when in life people tend to carry out a longer pilgrimage, researchers have identified five types of life transition that often constitute the underlying reasons for such a walk.[3]

First, people tend to undertake mid-life pilgrimages. In mid-life, many of us reflect on the choices we have made in life. We realize at a deeper level that our lives here on Earth will come to an end one day, and at that time much will remain undone. Some people then undertake a longer pilgrimage—preferably on their own, with their diary as a significant companion. They want to gain a fresh perspective on things. Maybe they also need to find a new direction in life.

Second, some people make a pilgrimage when something sad has happened. It may be a divorce that they have gone through, or the death of someone close to them. During such pilgrimages, good encounters with other pilgrims can be just as liberating as the fellowship in the climbing club was for Edurne Pasaban. By talking about what you have experienced yourself, and learning about the experiences of other people, you can have the chance to discover opportunities that you had not seen before.

Third, some pilgrims go for what we might call a "catch-your-breath" walk. Such walkers want to have time to adopt an alternative lifestyle in which mobile phones and professional titles are put aside and permitted to remain absent.

Fourth, there are pilgrims who are on the move and are looking for new insight, a fresh start. They are about to leave some important stage of life behind, and they work on that transition during their walk.

---

3. The following account is based on Jensen, *Pilegrim*, 83–86.

The recently retired, or parents whose children have recently left home, belong to that category.

Fifth, there are pilgrims who are on their way into a new and significant stage of life, and who can therefore be characterized as new-start walkers. Recently ordained clergy, or those who have just completed their degrees as business administrators and put on their boots to walk to Santiago de Compostela, may belong to that category.

The tendency to undertake a pilgrimage at significant transitions in life is not a new phenomenon. Earlier generations of travelers also went on pilgrimage at significant turning points in their lives. A Christian pilgrim who undertook something that might be described as a life-crisis walk at a young age is a saint whom we in Sweden have made our own in a very special way. Every year, innumerable children walk in honor of St. Lucy, a young woman from Syracuse in Sicily. She herself honored the grave of St. Agatha by visiting it. That visit reminds us that the Christian pilgrimage movement emerged during periods of persecution, when the specific goal was thought to be of decisive importance. You did not go on pilgrimage to just anywhere, or in just any kind of way. You made your way to the relics.

RELICS AND PILGRIMAGES

During the final stage of the Diocletian persecution, around the turn of the fourth century, the young Lucy suffered martyrdom. The legend tells us how her fiancé was so disappointed when she gave away her dowry to the poor that he told the authorities that she was a Christian. Lucy was tortured and sentenced to serve in a brothel, but, when she was about to be taken there, it turned out to be literally impossible to move her. So, she was killed by a man who stuck a spear through her throat.[4] It is reported that, before she died, she tore out her eyes and sent them to her fiancé.

As a young girl, Lucy had made a pilgrimage together with her sick mother to the grave of St. Agatha, who had suffered martyrdom during the persecution of Christians that the Emperor Decius had initiated in the middle of the third century. Agatha was reportedly imprisoned at Catania and brought before the Judge Quintian, who instantly fell so much in love with her that he wanted to marry her. Agatha refused the proposal by answering that she was already engaged to a man, Jesus Christ. That only made Quintian subject her to horrendous torture. She

---

4. Martling, *En sky av vittnen*, 408.

was whipped bloody, and her breasts were cut off. Eventually she died from this dreadful assault.[5]

The account of Lucy's pilgrimage to Agatha's grave is a story of the Christian pilgrimage movement during the first few centuries of the history of the Church. The bloody persecution of Christians led them to meet together at the graves of the martyrs in order to remember, honor, and revere those who had sacrificed their lives for professing their faith in Christ. In the fourth century, the practice of meeting at the graves of the martyrs to pray together had become an integral part of liturgical life in Rome. Christians who did not live in Rome started to make pilgrimages to the city to take part in the services.[6] The churches that were later built over the graves of the martyrs testify to the importance of these places in the early Church. The Emperor Constantine, for example, who ended the persecution of Christians, had a church built on the spot where the apostle Paul was reportedly buried. Today San Paolo Fuori le Mura is one of Rome's major tourist attractions.

Once Christianity had not only been permitted but also been declared the official religion of the Roman Empire, other locations besides Rome also began to attract pilgrims. Increasing numbers found their way to Palestine, the Holy Land, to visit the places we read about in the biblical writings. One of these pilgrims was Helena, the mother of Constantine. Not only did she found the Monastery of St. Catherine at the foot of Mount Sinai, but she also brought home a new kind of relic: items with which Jesus had supposedly been in contact.

Another pilgrim who visited the Holy Land was Egeria. She traveled from "the farthest coast of the Western Sea," which has led scholars to believe that she came from either north-western Spain or south-western France. Thus she must have started her travels somewhere in the vicinity of Edurne Pasaban's home. While she was traveling, she sent letters home to her "dear ladies and sisters" to tell them about her experiences. Egeria's letters from her travels make up the only written work by a woman from the fourth century that has been preserved. In the letters, Egeria tells her readers about her ascent of Mount Sinai, among other things.[7] Egeria was one of many wealthy women who became key persons in the emerging Christian pilgrimage movement. Then, as now, it was not everyone

---

5. Martling, *En sky av vittnen*, 60–61.

6. Jensen, *Pilegrim*, 96.

7. Tournier, "Egeria," 108–9, 118–22. The description of Egeria's ascents of Mount Sinai and Mount Horeb are found in Egeria, *Resebrev från det heliga landet*, 33–37.

who had the time and the means to undertake a pilgrimage or to organize an expedition to the mountain tops. Egeria belonged to a privileged group. Like her, the pilgrims of the past were not only interested in the places that they visited: they also sought guidance from devout people who lived near those places. The Desert Fathers and Mothers received visits. However, some hermits regarded this as a growing problem. The Church Father Gregory of Nyssa, who spent a few years in the Holy Land, complains in his letters about the pilgrims and tourists—primarily women—who disturbed the quiet calm of the holy places.[8]

In the early Christian Church, monastic life and the pilgrimage movement emerged in association with each other. People who wanted to pray and who wanted to live close to the biblical sites came together in communities that, among other things, took on the task of serving the pilgrims who visited the holy places in various ways. Desert Mothers and Fathers assisted travelers who journeyed to biblical sites with advice on how to live. Others provided food, shelter, and the opportunity to celebrate services of worship. When the numbers of pilgrims increased, pilgrim hostels opened, often overseen by monastic people who were sometimes themselves former pilgrims who considered it their vocation to help other pilgrims on their travels.

The emergence of the Carmelite Order has some connection to the Church's attempts to facilitate pilgrimages to the Holy Land. In the seventh century, the Islamic Caliphate extended its power to include Jerusalem. That city is a holy place for Muslims, since the Qur'an tells how the Prophet Mohammed made a night journey to the Temple Mount, where he met God and was taken up to heaven. Christian pilgrims could still visit Jerusalem during the time of Muslim rule. In practice, however, it became far more dangerous. Partly for this reason, sites of pilgrimage in Europe became increasingly significant during the Middle Ages. The new pilgrimage locations were linked to relics, which in some cases were items that had been brought home from Palestine. In other cases, the relics were the remains of holy people who had died nearby. In the midtenth century, the first pilgrim walked toward Santiago de Compostela, where the relics of the apostle James are still believed to remain.

The increasing interest in the pilgrimage movement in the eleventh century had dire consequences for the population of Jerusalem. In the year 1095, Pope Urban II encouraged the first crusade. The pope wanted

---

8. Tournier, "Egeria," 109, 112–13, 117.

to make it possible for Christian pilgrims to visit biblical sites safely. Thus Jerusalem was conquered by the Crusaders in the year 1099. They laid siege to the city and, in less than a year, more than half of the Jewish and Muslim population of Jerusalem had died. A Christian kingdom was established in the city, but its rule did not last for very long: it was overthrown by the Sultan Saladin and his troops in 1187.

Not all the Crusaders returned to Europe after the fall of Jerusalem. Some of them withdrew to be hermits on Mount Carmel. Among them was Berthold from Calabria, who had originally come from south-western France. Now he and the other hermits used more peaceful means in their battle for the Christian faith and for the protection of pilgrims. Like the Desert Fathers and Mothers, they spent time in prayer and engaged in battle against the demons. From their circles, the Carmelite Order emerged.

MARTIN LUTHER AND THE LIFE OF PILGRIMAGE

In our own time, interest in pilgrimages has grown; and this raises the question of how the Church of Sweden, which stands in the Evangelical-Lutheran tradition, can arrange pilgrimages while maintaining its true identity. In an article in the Swedish Tourist Association's annual publication, Åsa and Mats Ottosson provide a possible answer: maybe it is about adaptation to the market. Under the heading "Gudomlig guidning. Låt tankarna vandra" ("Divine guidance. Let your thoughts wander"), they write:

> Someone has worked out that, between the years 1150 and 1450, some 20 to 50 per cent of the adult population of Europe went on pilgrimage. At that time, it was a popular movement. You would walk in penitence or to collect plus-points before God. The German priest and professor of theology Martin Luther, who started the Protestant Reformation in 1517, was opposed to this. He thought that it was not possible to merit salvation either by good deeds toward other people or by walking hither and thither to visit one or another holy place. It was only God himself who could grant salvation through faith. As a consequence, Gustav Vasa forbade pilgrimages altogether.
>
> Pilgrimages in Sweden began again in earnest in the 1990s. Somewhat unexpectedly, the Church of Sweden has taken the initiative. The attitude is open and free; many organizers simply turn to those who look for some spiritual fellowship—yes, even to all who in some way seek some deeper meaning in life, who

want to spend time in nature, to use their body, and to experience something together with other people. That does of course widen the areas of contact for the churches behind this initiative, many of which greatly need to attract more people. And it seems to work.[9]

A question that must be asked about the growing interest in pilgrimage in our time is this: What are the characteristics of pilgrimage activities that work well? That question can only be answered if we consider the purpose of the journey. Luther reflected on that question during his pilgrimage to Rome in 1510–1511. He travelled across the Alps; but there are no lyrical accounts of the beautiful scenery in Luther's collected works. Luther walked in the company of another monk, and he was shocked when he realized that a life of luxury was lived at the cost of the faithful, both in the monasteries that they visited along their way and in the dwellings of the ecclesiastical authorities in Rome. He felt dejected about the double moral standards and the *Geschäft* ("business") of which he found proof during his pilgrimage. That led him to criticize the medieval pilgrimage movement by building on the objections that had been voiced ever since the fourth century.

The Church Father Gregory of Nyssa complained not only about curious pilgrims and tourists, particularly women, who disturbed the peace at biblical sites. He also stressed the risks of undertaking a pilgrimage.[10] Gregory thought that a holy life was open to all people, regardless of where they were. Many people believe, wrongly, that the Holy Spirit is bound to certain places—but that is not the case. The Spirit can come to us wherever we are. According to Gregory, a holy life is marked primarily by chastity. During a pilgrimage, chastity is severely tested, since women and men travel together. Women, in particular, found themselves in a vulnerable position, since they had to travel together with men who would show them the way and help them up into the saddle and down again. In order not to subject themselves and others to unnecessary temptations, they would do well to stay at home, Gregory argued.

During the Protestant Reformation of the sixteenth century, Gregory's fourth-century remarks against pilgrimages were again brought to the fore. Roger Jensen has investigated Luther's criticism of the pilgrimage

---

9. Ottosson and Ottosson, *Gudomlig guidning*, 122. Gustav Vasa was king of Sweden 1523—1560. The Reformation took place during his reign.

10. Gregory's criticism is summarized in Aurelius, *På helig mark–pilgrimen i historia och nutid*, 35–39.

movement of the Middle Ages, and summarizes Luther's objections in six main points.[11]

First, Luther underlines that pilgrimages are made on the mistaken perception that you must leave home in order to meet God. Luther stresses that God meets us just as much in our nearest parish church as in any other church that people might want to visit because it is a pilgrim destination. We do not have to go on pilgrimage to be closer to God.

Second, Luther thinks that pilgrimages are often linked to immorality. In his writings he often stresses the particular greed to which groups of pilgrims succumb. Souvenirs and pilgrimage certificates are offered for sale at cathedrals, even though they have no value whatsoever from the perspective of eternity.

Along these lines, Luther stresses, third, that the goal of the pilgrimage can easily become an idol that is worshiped instead of God. Like our modern climbers, people of the Middle Ages spent large sums of money on pilgrimages. Thus they pinned their hopes on a place rather than on God.

Fourth, Luther thinks that we neglect our neighbors when we go on pilgrimage. The time and money that we spend on our pilgrimage would be better spent on taking care of our day-to-day commitments and of the people we live with. Pilgrimages are too often perceived as a good deed for God. In some cases, such journeys are an egoistical action that is motivated by our hope that God is going to like us a bit more and be a little more generous toward us because we have undertaken a pilgrimage. Luther rejects that kind of exchange, and stresses that, in the eyes of God, good deeds are loving actions that we undertake for our fellow human beings.

Fifth, Luther stresses that pilgrimages are a religious practice that lack any support in the Bible. He emphasizes that the Church, with the pope at the helm, abuses its power by decreeing pilgrimages in spite of the lack of biblical support. Religious practices that lack a biblical foundation should not be imposed upon anyone.

In line with that objection, Luther emphasizes, sixth, that pilgrimages are an expression of the unbiblical justification by works that in his view we need to fight against in order to preserve the faith. The practice of going on pilgrimages keeps people captive to a reign of terror in which nobody can be certain that they have done enough for God.

11. The following report is based on Jensen, *Pilgrim*, 139–47.

In the Middle Ages, the practice of going on pilgrimage was linked to the same penitential system as the trade in indulgences. People were encouraged to buy indulgences and to go on pilgrimage in order to be liberated from so-called temporal penalties in this age or in purgatory. Seen in their historical context, Luther's ninety-five theses against the trade in indulgences thus become a critical confrontation with other devotional practices as well. His theses paved the way for a more extensive criticism that embraced pilgrimages, relics, reverence for saints, and the monastic life.

INDULGENCES AND PILGRIMAGES

Many people know that Martin Luther published his ninety-five theses against the trade in indulgences in October 1517. The event is often seen as the start of the Protestant Reformation. In those theses, Luther confirms that the true treasure of the Church is the most holy Gospel of the glory and grace of God.[12] Luther's purpose when he published his theses was to initiate a deeper theological reflection on the idea that there is a collective treasure of the Church that consists of the merits of the saints, and that the pope or his representatives, the bishops, can share out among the faithful through indulgences. Luther thinks that this idea has been wrongly interpreted by far too many preachers, and therefore people do not receive the pastoral care that they need.

In order to understand Luther's criticism of the trade in indulgences, we need to start, as he did, with his conviction that God does not leave sin unpunished because God is good. If the highest power were to leave sin unpunished, Luther argued, it would mean that it gave full scope to evil. And then that power would no longer be the highest good. If God acted in that way, God would no longer be perfectly good.

However, the penalty for sin must not necessarily be borne or served by the person who has committed the offense. When Jesus dies on the cross, God lets our misdeeds fall on him. God acquits us by letting our death sentence fall on Jesus.

When we confess our sins in private confession or in a service of worship and receive the forgiveness of sins, God liberates us from what is called the eternal punishment—that is, an existence without communion with God, an existence in hell. Since God in Jesus Christ takes on the eternal punishment, we can escape that. We are acquitted, given grace,

---

12. Luther, *Ninety-Five Theses*, 31:31 (Thesis no. 62).

because Jesus has served the sentence. His merits are accounted to us as our good. We receive this acquittal by confessing our sins. The forgiveness of sins shuts the gates of hell and opens the kingdom of heaven for us.

However, the forgiveness of sins does not liberate us from what is known as the temporal punishment for sin. Even though the sin is forgiven, its consequences are not obliterated. What is done is done and cannot be undone. It remains, and it chafes. This leads to an imbalance between good and evil that needs to be dealt with before a person can live forever in complete heavenly communion with God, who is good. The balance is restored through what are called the temporal penalties. You could say that God and humanity even out the imbalance between good and evil by our being sentenced to, and serving, the temporal penalties—the recompense that cures or heals the disharmonious relationship. The penalties are temporal, since they are limited to a period. Penalties that should be served in the place of purification after the earthly death of a person—called purgatory—belong to this category, since they have an end. Even here on Earth, people can go through a period of purification, thanks to various forms of penitence. Penitence is a temporal penalty, which means that a person takes on or is ordered to do something for God and the good. The deficit of goodness is adjusted, and that means that the need for purification in purgatory is reduced, Luther argued.

During the Middle Ages, pilgrimage was a common form of penitence. People walked to Santiago de Compostela and other places of pilgrimage after they had made their confession and received absolution. The pilgrimage was seen as an expression of regret; it was a temporal punishment for the sin, motivated by the Church's promise of indulgence. "Indulgence" means that the Church remits some penitence, including in the form of temporal penalties in purgatory, with reference to the view that other people, the saints, have engaged in so much penitence that a surplus has been generated. They have, so to speak, even carried out other people's penitence and their good deeds. When a person receives an indulgence, it means that the merits of the saints are ascribed to them, and this shortens their temporal penalty in a way that is reminiscent of how Christ's merits are accounted to us and release us from eternal punishment. There is thus a perception of ecclesiastical joint property in the trade in indulgences. The starting point is that sin and its consequences are a common concern that we combat together. In a corresponding way, the good that we do is a common treasure of which the Church is the steward. If a person does more good deeds than could reasonably be expected of them, a surplus of goodness is generated. The Church redistributes that goodness through indulgences, so that parts of the surplus are credited to sinners who suffer from a deficit of goodness.

The trade in indulgences that Luther reacts against meant that people could buy indulgences by donating money to good causes, including the building of the Church of St. Peter in Rome. In the ninety-five theses, Luther attacks several aspects of this trade in indulgences. He believes, for example, that the pope is so rich that he could pay for the building of the Church of St. Peter himself. Donations of money for this particular purpose should therefore not be a priority. In particular, he criticizes what he sees as poor pastoral care. Indulgence preachers, such as Johann Tetzel, frighten poor people and comfort the rich on the wrong grounds. The letters of indulgence risk making wealthy people unrepentant. They think that they do not need to go to confession or to carry out any acts of penitence, since they have bought letters of indulgence. Rather than purchasing such a letter, they ought to confess their sins, improve themselves, and undertake some penance, Luther thinks. Poor people could be tempted to spend their meagre savings on letters of indulgence for the purpose of reducing their dead relatives' temporal penalty in purgatory. The Church, which has the power to grant indulgence even to those who are not able to donate any money, ought to encourage them instead to use their money in some better way.

In the ninety-five theses, Luther does not reject the actual idea of indulgence, nor the view that there is a place of purification after death, purgatory, where people serve temporal penalties before they enter the kingdom of heaven. However, he does do that later in his life. In the light of his reformatory discovery, the medieval system of penance, as well as many other forms of devotion that were encouraged within that framework, appear to be human attempts to merit the grace of God by doing such things that, because of poor pastoral care, we understand to be good deeds. And we imagine that God is obliged to reward such good deeds in the name of justice. For Luther, the medieval system of penitence is a prime example of justification by works. He thinks that it has been built on non-biblical misconceptions, since, according to the biblical writings, humanity is only justified by grace and by trusting faith in Jesus Christ. Luther realizes that this is what the biblical writings teach when he makes his reformatory discovery.

MARTIN LUTHER'S REFORMATORY DISCOVERY

The publication of the ninety-five theses is linked to a specific date, but the precise date of Martin Luther's reformatory discovery remains unknown. Some scholars think that it was as early as 1513; others believe that it was as late as 1520; and many maintain that Luther made his reformatory discovery in 1518. Even though a specific event was decisive for the development of Luther's thought, his reformatory discovery was, by and large, a process. Luther himself explains that, as a monk, he sought to be an exemplary monastic Brother and Christian. He often went to make a long confession. He prayed, did penance, and tried to improve himself; but he was frequently aware of his shortcomings. He was not able to live as he should; and that made him very scared, because he knew that God, who is good, cannot leave sin unpunished. Luther vividly described his torments and severe temptations. Things went so far that he began not only to loathe himself, but God too, because he was so very scared of God. In an attempt to make Luther think about something other than his own successes or failures, his pastoral carer and supervisor, Johann von Staupitz, gave him the task of reading the Scriptures more deeply. Luther was sent to Wittenberg, where in due course he became a professor at the young university in that city.

One day, when he was working on St. Paul's Letter to the Romans, Luther read a verse that spoke to him in a new way. In Romans 1:17 it says that, in the Gospel, the righteousness of God is revealed through faith for faith, which means that the righteous person will live by faith. A little further on, Romans says that God justifies the person who believes in Jesus. Luther was struck by the insight that it is God—not the human person—who achieves this good and satisfactory relationship with God called righteousness. A person may receive righteousness as a gift through faith. The righteousness that exists in Jesus, God grants entirely graciously to people. Not even the reception of the gift of faith is something that a person can achieve by their own efforts. Since it is God who gives them faith, it is God who enables their justification.

What is characteristic of justification by works—and of all the forms in which it can be expressed—is the idea that people can do something to appease God, or at least to gain a good or better standing before God. That is not possible, Luther claims. The thought that it might be possible gives rise to temptations and a lack of peace. People are turned in on themselves by constantly brooding on how God views them. In contrast, the insight that God makes people righteous by grace alone, by faith alone, and only through Jesus Christ, gives rise to freedom and joy. When people do not need to worry about their own blessedness, they can instead commit themselves to the good of their fellow human beings. When people are not forced, or do not feel forced, to carry out what are considered to be good deeds, but which in actual fact keep them captive in imagining that they can contribute to their own salvation, they can confidently engage in the really good deeds that are marked out by the fact that they contribute to the well-being of other people.

Luther's reformatory discovery made him note, among other things, that if people live in the trust and confidence that God grants them, they will not be setting off for Santiago de Compostela, Rome, Jerusalem, or any other pilgrimage destination. It is the tempted person who lacks peace who wrongly believes that they need a pilgrimage. Luther writes:

> Thus a Christian man who lives in this confidence toward God knows all things, can do all things, ventures everything that needs to be done, and does everything gladly and willingly, not that he may gather merits and good works, but because it as a pleasure for him to please God in doing these things. He simply serves God with no thought of reward, content that his service pleases God. On the other hand, he who is not at one with God, or is in a state of doubt, worries and starts looking about for ways and means to do enough and to influence God with his many good works. He runs off to St. James, to Rome, to Jerusalem, hither and tither; he prays St. Bridget's prayer, this prayer and that prayer; he fasts on this day and that day; he makes confession here and makes confession there; he questions this man and that man, and yet finds no peace. He does all this with great effort and with a doubting and unwilling heart . . . And even then they are not good works and are in vain. Many people have gone quite crazy with them and their anxiety has brought them into all kinds of misery.[13]

For the purpose of avoiding the horrors of justification by works, Luther stresses that there is a need for good pastors. He notes that there are keen and childish Christians who we must put up with. They might need to be "enticed with external, definitive, concomitant adornment, with reading, praying, fasting, singing, churches, decorations, organs, and all those things commanded and observed in monasteries and churches,

---

13. Luther, *Treatise on Good Works*, 44:27–28.

until such time as they too learn to know the teachings of faith."[14] However, such devotional practices—which include pilgrimages, the monastic life, the worship of saints, and visits by relics—we ought to wean people off from in due time through good teaching.

RELICS ON PILGRIMAGE

Luther chose to publish his ninety-five theses on the Feast of All Saints in 1517. During that feast, the general public were able to view the record collection of relics that the Elector Frederic the Wise had in his possession. In 2017, when the 500th anniversary of this occasion was celebrated, the pope and the archbishop of the Church of Sweden met in Lund Cathedral to pray together. At earlier anniversaries of the Reformation, such a display of ecumenism would have been inconceivable.

In the year 2018, we who live in the Nordic countries had another opportunity to rejoice over reformatory insights when the relics of St. Thérèse of the Child Jesus visited our countries. Sometimes saints' relics travel around the world and are shown to the public, just as they were in Wittenberg that same weekend that Luther published his ninety-five theses. If the five hundredth anniversary of that event could lead to an embrace between the pope and the Church of Sweden's archbishop before a large media presence, it is quite possible that the 2018 tour of the relics through Sweden might also have spread the same friendly goodwill a little further down the ecclesiastical ranks. They were not just any relics that traveled through our countries; they were those of one of the most cherished saints of the Roman Catholic Church. Thérèse of the Child Jesus was a grassroots Christian who loved the small things and the little people in a very particular way. Just like many Swedes, she was a landscape pilgrim in the sense that she met God in nature. In her own garden she could be affected by the same reverence for creation that an alpinist might experience on the summit of K2.

When Thérèse's relics visited the USA a few years ago, 1.1 million people gathered in the churches, convents, and cathedrals where the relics were exposed. People queued for hours to catch a glimpse of the reliquary or to touch, maybe even kiss, the plexiglass around it. Coach tours arranged to the places where the relics where shown were soon fully booked. Elizabeth Ficocelli notes that some of the visitors came because they were curious. Others came because they sought help in some way.

---

14. Luther, *Treatise on good works*; *Luther's Works*, vol. 44, 35.

Most people came because the pilgrimage of the relics through the USA gave them a unique opportunity to show respect to a much-loved friend.[15]

When Thérèse's relics made their pilgrimage through the Nordic countries, the attention was not as great as that described by Ficocelli, but some people were renewed in their faith, found their way back to their deepest commitment, grew in love, and found greater peace in their hearts.[16] Luther would regard these consequences as good ones; but his experience of the exposition of relics leads to a view that is radically different from Ficocelli's. Luther highlights the risks of a wrong focus on relics. He stresses that misconceptions and abuses may obscure our understanding of the faith that brings justification.

During the visit to the Nordic countries, Thérèse's relics travelled together with those of her parents. Zélie and Louis Martin were canonized in 2015—the first married couple to be canonized together. In the Evangelical-Lutheran tradition, marriage is presented as a God-given form of life, unlike the monastic life. In their relationship with their partner, and together with their family, a person is given unique opportunities to meet God and to grow in faith. To bring up children to be good neighbors is a central task of married life.

Zélie and Louis Martin's marriage, and the stories about the children they brought up, are fascinating. The couple had nine children; four of whom died young. Thérèse was the last child to be born into that family. When Thérèse was four years old, Zélie died of breast cancer. Louis Martin lived the rest of his life as a single father. The oldest daughter, Marie, was 17 in the year that her mother died; and so she acted as "mother" to the fourth daughter, Céline, who was eight years old. The second daughter, Pauline, was 16, and she acted as a surrogate mother to the then four-year-old Thérèse. In the middle of the siblings was Léonie, who was 14 in the year that Zélie died. Many hope and believe that Léonie will be the next member of the Martin family to be canonized.[17]

Thérèse was an unusually sensitive child. All her biographers agree on that.[18] They describe her sensitivity in a way that leads my thoughts

---

15. Ficocelli, *Shower of Heavenly Roses*, 16–17.

16. Cf. Ficocelli, *Shower of Heavenly Roses*, 17.

17. As noted later, the process that could lead to her canonization was begun in 2015.

18. Thérèse tells the story of her life in Thérèse of Lisieux, *Story of a Soul*. A good introduction in Swedish is Stinissen, *Den enkla vägen till helighet*, in which he describes the life and teaching of Thérèse of the Child Jesus.

to the vulnerability that the mountaineer Edurne Pasaban voiced in her biography. Thérèse suffered badly from having to leave the safety of the family home in order to go to school. She was easily saddened by hurtful comments by people who did not understand. It was not always easy for her to make friends or to get along with other children. Just like Edurne Pasaban, she was emotionally very dependent on her family. Her father and her sisters were extremely close to her. To some extent, this can be explained by the loss of her mother at such a young age.

When Thérèse was nine years old, she suffered another difficult separation. Pauline, her older sister and surrogate mother, entered the Carmelite Convent at Lisieux. Now Thérèse could no longer crawl into Pauline's arms and tell her about her worries. She had lost Pauline, and she reacted very strongly to that loss. For two months she was seriously ill. The family members and the doctors were in two minds. Afterwards Thérèse wrote: "I can't describe this strange sickness, but I am now convinced it was the work of the devil. For a long time after my cure, however, I believed I had become ill on purpose."[19]

Her recovery was just as strange as her illness. On the Day of Pentecost in 1883, her pain became intense and, in her need, Thérèse turned to a statue of the Virgin Mary that stood by her bed. She asked the Virgin Mary to show her compassion at last. Thérèse says:

> All of a sudden the Blessed Virgin appeared *beautiful* to me, so *beautiful* that never had I seen anything so attractive; her face was suffused with an ineffable benevolence and tenderness, but what penetrated to the very depths of my soul was the "*ravishing smile of the Blessed Virgin.*" At that instant, all my pain disappeared, and two large tears glistened on my eyelashes, and flowed down my cheeks silently, but they were tears of unmixed joy. Ah! I thought, the Blessed Virgin smiled at me, how happy I am.[20]

Thérèse often recalled how the statue of Mary had smiled at her. The Virgin Mary had shown her special grace and care. In her, Thérèse found a new and heavenly mother to whom she could always turn with her joys and sorrows. She continued to be a very sensitive child, but after her recovery her sensitivity found a new expression. Now she became affected by the same kind of temptations and scruples as Luther had

---

19. Thérèse of Lisieux, *Story of a Soul,* 62.
20. Thérèse of Lisieux, *Story of a Soul,* 65–66.

been. She had an over-sensitive conscience, and she was terrified by the thought that she might have committed some serious sin.[21] She searched her heart with anxious carefulness, and she ended up in floods of tears for the slightest reason.

CHRISTMAS GRACE

At Christmas in 1886, something happened that Thérèse of the Child Jesus describes as a miracle. When the family came home after the Midnight Mass, their father Louis sighed when he saw the then fourteen-year-old Thérèse's shoes—which served as Christmas stockings—standing by the open fireplace. He was tired and felt that Thérèse was now old enough for the family to stop the traditional exchange of Christmas presents. "Thank goodness this is the last year!" he exclaimed, thinking that Thérèse had not heard him. But she had. His comment pierced her heart, and Céline, who could see the tears welling up in Thérèse's eyes, advised her to delay pulling out the surprises from those magic shoes; but Thérèse was no longer the same. In her autobiography she says that Jesus had transformed her heart. She writes:

> Forcing back my tears, I descended the stairs rapidly; controlling the poundings of my heart, I took my slippers and placed them in front of Papa, and withdrew all the objects joyfully. I had the happy appearance of a Queen. Having regained his own cheerfulness, Papa was laughing; Céline believed it was all a *dream*! Fortunately, it was a sweet reality; Thérèse had discovered once again the strength of soul which she had lost at the age of four and a half, and she was to preserve it forever! On that *night of light* began the third period of my life, the most beautiful and the most filled with graces from heaven. The work I had been unable to do in ten years was done by Jesus in one instant... He made me a fisher of *souls*. I experienced a great desire to work for the conversion of sinners, a desire I hadn't felt so intensely before. I felt *charity* enter my soul, and the need to forget myself and to please others; since then I've been happy![22]

A few months before Thérèse experienced what has been called "the Christmas grace," her oldest sister, Marie, had entered the Carmelite Convent at Lisieux. Thérèse had felt a desire to do the same for a long time, but there were some ecclesiastical regulations that put a spoke in the

---

21. Foley, *Context of Holiness*, 97 ff.
22. Thérèse of Lisieux, *Story of a Soul*, 98–99.

wheel. You had then, and you still need, to be old enough to be allowed to become a Carmelite nun; and the teenaged Thérèse was not considered old enough yet. During a pilgrimage to Rome, Thérèse made a personal appeal to the pope himself to be granted permission to become a Carmelite nun, even though she was only 15. The pope answered kindly that this was a matter for the bishop to decide. After some toing and froing, Thérèse did at last gain permission to enter the Convent of the Carmelite Sisters at Lisieux, aged 15. She felt straight away that she was now where she truly belonged.[23] By the time that she made her solemn vows, she had reached the age of 17.

A few years later, following the death of Louis Martin, Céline also entered the Carmelite Sisters' Convent at Lisieux. Thus, Thérèse could live her religious life surrounded by three of her biological sisters, to whom she was very close, even though the monastic family was her real family in many respects. During her final period here on Earth, her biological sisters—Pauline in particular, who in the religious life was called Sister/Mother Agnes of Jesus—were very significant, not only for Thérèse, but also for us. With the encouragement of Mother Agnes of Jesus, Thérèse began to write down her life story with a focus on the mental and spiritual development that God had allowed her to go through. When Thérèse lay dying, her religious Sisters—particularly Mother Agnes of Jesus—wrote down everything she said and did. Those notes have been published as *St. Thérèse of Lisieux. Her last conversations*. Thanks to the Sisters' encouragements and notes, we can participate in Thérèse's world of experience.

On Good Friday in 1896, Thérèse coughed up blood for the first time. That was a sure sign that she had contracted tuberculosis. A year and a half later, the then twenty-four-year-old Carmelite nun died from that illness. Her final year was filled with drawn-out sufferings. Like a mountaineer at 8,000 meters above sea level, breathing became increasingly difficult for Thérèse. She had so much pain in her body that the Sisters did not know how they would manage to turn her over without subjecting her to unbearable pain. Everyone waited for her death, but it did not seem to come. Eventually, toward the end of September, Thérèse of the Child Jesus could no longer draw any breath. She died, surrounded by her religious Sisters, including Marie, Pauline, and Céline.

Léonie, the one sister who had *not* become a Carmelite nun, fascinates many people besides me. In the case of the Martin family, it seems

---

23. Letter to M. Martin (Thérèse's father), July 31, 1888. Thérèse of Lisieux, *Letters of St. Thérèse of Lisieux*, 1:451–52 (LT 58).

that she made a very original and independent choice not to enter the Carmelite Sisters' Convent at Lisieux. For the greater part of her life, Léonie lived in other convents. At the age of 23, she entered the Convent of the Poor Clares at Alençon, but she did not stay there for very long. Six weeks later she was back home with her family. The following year she made another attempt to find her way into the religious life. She entered the Convent of the Visitation Sisters at Caen. After six months she again moved back home to her family; but six years later she re-entered the same convent. Now she stayed for two years and was clothed in the habit, but she didn't make any vows. She moved back home yet again. Four years later, after the death of Thérèse of the Child Jesus, Léonie returned to the convent at Caen. She made her profession, and then lived as a nun in that convent until her death. She had had a very lively correspondence with her sister Thérèse, whose autobiographical writings she had read. Thérèse had helped Léonie to discover how human weakness can become a strength when it is used by God. As a nun, Léonie was called Françoise-Thérèse, and in 2015 the process that could lead to her canonization was begun.

Both Zélie and Louis Martin had nursed dreams of entering the religious life for themselves, but they had been denied that opportunity. Louis could not become a monk because he did not know Latin, and Zélie could not become a nun because it was considered that she did not have that vocation. Louis became a clockmaker instead, and Zélie ran a little lace-making company. They brought up their children together in a spirit of faith, hope, and love. In time, their youngest daughter, Thérèse of the Child Jesus, became one of the most beloved saints of the Roman Catholic Church. Wilfrid Stinissen notes that the reason might be that "Thérèse is a wonderful example of how a person who is mentally wounded is not predestined to a life of failure."[24] We are all mentally wounded, and most of us lack the strength required to ascend Mount Everest. Thérèse had another kind of strength, one that impressed the doctor who treated her during her last illness. If a journalist had been given the opportunity to ask her how she had gained that strength, her answer would have been that everything is grace.

---

24. Stinissen, *Den enkla vägen till helighet*, 17.

ALL IS GRACE

In the 1520s, a violent theological debate broke out between one of the most influential theologians at that time, Erasmus of Rotterdam, and Martin Luther. Erasmus had been accused of being a follower of Luther's teaching, since he had expressed a similar criticism of the Church. Just like Luther, Erasmus was also upset about the trade in indulgences and the decay of the Church that, among other things, found expression in *Geschäft* along the pilgrimage routes. Erasmus defended himself in various ways against the accusations of being a Lutheran. He published a work entitled *On the Freedom of the Will* to highlight a very important difference between his own theological starting points and those of Luther. Erasmus and Luther held different views on the possibility of human beings collaborating with the grace of God.

Erasmus argued for the view that the good relationship of human persons with God, the communion with God that saves people from death, is certainly a gift that God gives quite independently of any human achievements. However, a person must do something important in that context—namely, receive that gift. A person does that by saying "Yes" to God, just as the Virgin Mary said "Yes" to God when she replied that she was willing to become the Mother of Jesus. God did not abuse the Virgin Mary. God waited for her "Yes," and only then did God give her the gift.

Erasmus's position is summarized in a hymn that we often sing in the Church of Sweden: "The love of God is like the beach and the grass, is wind and vast expanse and an infinite home. We were given freedom to live there, to go and come, to say 'Yes' to God and to say 'No'" (Swedish Hymnal 289:1). Erasmus thought it quite decisive that we have this freedom to say "Yes" or "No" to God. If we were lacking that freedom, we would be unjustly condemned or maliciously treated if God punished us because of our sins. Thus God would be evil. Such a concept of God is not found in the Bible.

Luther was furious about the attack by Erasmus. His written reply, *The bondage of the will*, is an extensive argument for the view that people lack the opportunity to say "Yes" or "No" to God—or rather, unless God intervenes and converts the person so that they can say "Yes" to God, they can only say "No" to God. However, if God does intervene and enters into a life-giving relationship with a person, God can govern that person in such a way that they cannot say anything but "Yes" to God, just as a rider can direct a horse using the reins. Luther stresses that a person cannot do anything at all for themselves to either create or sustain that good and life-giving relationship with God. The idea that a person could do something by themselves—for example, say "Yes" to God—negates the entire thought that a person is justified by grace alone. Thus, this is an expression of justification by works.

Erasmus sought to make Luther think along different lines by offering an example. Imagine a father who has a nice-looking apple.[25] His little child would very much like that apple, and the father wants to give it to the child, but the child cannot take the apple himself, since he cannot walk or crawl that far. Therefore, the father will take the hands of the child, raise him up, and support him so that he can walk up to the apple. Having arrived at the apple, the child cannot take it because his hands are too small. So the father will take the apple, open the hands of the child, and put the apple into them. Erasmus thinks that God is like that father and that people are like that child. God certainly makes every effort to help the child to receive the apple, but the child also needs to do something in that situation.

Both Erasmus and Luther understand the question of a person's opportunity to turn to grace in order to receive it, or to turn away from grace by rejecting God's gift, as entirely decisive. That is why they became such irreconcilable enemies. Luther underlines that persons can do nothing of themselves in order to influence their relationship with God. He stresses that the ability to receive grace, the gift of God, is also itself a gift from God. For some inscrutable reason, God gives some people the opportunity to receive grace. They are saved by God's decree—by God's "Yes" to them—for eternal life. Why God says "No" to some people—if God really does do that—is something we should not speculate about. We should rather adore, revere, and fear God who is so great and powerful that God can do something like that.

Some 350 years later, a young French Carmelite nun meditated on our total dependence on God. In the monastic life she was called Elizabeth of the Trinity (1880–1906) and, like Luther, she found peace in what theologians describe as the doctrine of predestination. God has decided in advance that some people should go to heaven and that others cannot do that.

Thérèse of the Child Jesus lived as a nun in a different French Carmelite Convent at the same time. The grace of God was also the center of

---

25. Erasmus, *On the Freedom of the Will*, 91.

her life, but she would never have thought of developing any doctrine of predestination. Nor would she ever have read Erasmus's and Luther's writings to the end—even if she had started them. She would have thought it a waste of time, and that she would rather spend her time loving God and her fellow human beings.[26]

For Thérèse, the possibility for a person to say "Yes" to God was not an abstract concern, but something that makes life worth living. With curiosity and passion, she sought every opportunity to say "Yes" to God. She wanted to say "Yes" to God in as many languages as possible, and that soon brought her to realize her own incapacity. Her attempts to live a holy life resulted in her insight that "everything is a grace."[27] Thérèse understood that she would never manage to fulfill her intentions if she strove to do so on her own. Fortunately, God revealed to her "the Little Way" that became her reformatory discovery. To her prioress, Mother Marie de Gonzague, Thérèse explained:

> You know, Mother, I have always wanted to be a saint. Alas! I have always noticed that when I compared myself to the saints, there is between them and me the same difference that exists between a mountain whose summit is lost in the clouds and the obscure grain of sand trampled underfoot by passers-by. Instead of becoming discouraged, I said to myself: God cannot inspire unrealizable desires. I can, then, in spite of my littleness, aspire to holiness. It is impossible for me to grow up, and so I must bear with myself such as I am with all my imperfections. But I want to seek out a means of going to heaven by a little way, a way that is very straight, very short, and totally new.[28]

The purpose of the Way that Thérèse discovered was that a person should not become greater or achieve more. Rather, she should become smaller, allow herself to be ever more emptied of everything in order to be able to receive even more of God's grace. When Thérèse was a child, Pauline had explained to her how the grace of God fills the life of every person. She had taken their father's cup and Thérèse's little thimble and filled them both with water.[29] Both vessels overflowed, but since the cup was larger than the thimble, there was more room for water in the cup.

---

26. Cf. Thérèse of Lisieux, *Her Last Conversations*, 261 (Céline, July).
27. Thérèse of Lisieux, *Her Last Conversations*, 57 (June 5, point 4).
28. Thérèse of Lisieux, *Story of a Soul*, 207.
29. Thérèse of Lisieux, *Story of a Soul*, 45.

Thérèse understood the point. The greater the empty space that a person has within, the more God can fill that person with grace.

A characteristic of the Little Way is the absence of any discussion about who should do what, or to whom honor should be ascribed if anything good has been done. In an ordinary family, people sometimes fall out over who should take out the rubbish, for example. Or family members make an agreement that whoever has done the cooking does not have to do the washing-up. On the walk in the Little Way together with Jesus, it is not necessary to exhaust oneself with such disputes or agreements. Jesus and the person help each other with everything, and there is no need to clarify exactly who needs to do what.

When Thérèse describes the Little Way, she frequently returns to the image of an elevator—one of the technological inventions of the late nineteenth century. It seems that, to begin with, this was an image that Pauline (Mother Agnes of Jesus) also used.[30] Thérèse seizes on that. She writes: "We are living now in the age of inventions, and we no longer have to take the trouble of climbing stairs, for, in the homes of the rich, an elevator has replaced these very successfully." She continues: "I wanted to find an elevator which would raise me to Jesus, for I am too small to climb the rough stairway of perfection. I searched, then, in the Scriptures for some sign of this elevator, the object of my desires, and I read these words coming from the mouth of Eternal Wisdom: '*Whoever is a LITTLE ONE, let him come to me*' (Prov. 9:4)." Thérèse sensed that she was about to discover something important, so she continued her search, and "this is what I discovered," she wrote: "*As one whom a mother caresses, so will I comfort you; you shall be carried at the breasts, and upon the knees they shall caress you*' (Is. 66:12–13). Ah! never did words more tender and more melodious come to give joy to my soul. The elevator which must raise me to heaven is Your arms, O Jesus! And for this I had no need to grow up, but rather I had to remain *little* and become this more and more."[31]

When Thérèse made a pilgrimage to Rome, she passed the high peaks of the Alps. "Ah! Mother, how much good these beauties of nature, poured out *in such profusion*, did my soul." She wrote afterwards: "I hadn't eyes enough to take in everything. Standing by the window I almost lost my breath; I would have liked to be on both sides of the

---

30. Cf. Thérèse of Lisieux, *Her Last Conversations*, 48–49. (From May 21 to 25, point 11).

31. Thérèse of Lisieux, *Story of a Soul*, 207–8.

car. When turning to the other side, I beheld landscapes of enchanting beauty, totally different from those under my immediate gaze."[32] Later in life she likened the Little Way to the mysterious ascent of a mountain, which is mostly reminiscent of an underground trip in an elevator that lifts the person to the top of the mountain even though she cannot see any signs that she is on her way there.

In a letter to Sister Agnes of Jesus (her sister Pauline), Thérèse describes that strange mountain ascent. She uses metaphorical language that leads our thoughts to the Desert Mothers and to the bridal mysticism that Teresa of Avila developed. Thérèse calls herself "the little hermit," and describes a remarkable travel plan. Before she sets out on her life pilgrimage together with Jesus, it seems to her as if Jesus—whom she, like Teresa of Avila, describes as her betrothed—asks her to which countries she wants to travel and which direction she wants to take. Thérèse, the little fiancée, answers that she has only one desire: she wants to get to the top of the Mountain of Love. There are several ways she can choose to get there, but she is not a sufficiently good mountaineer to climb any of those routes by herself. So, she says to Jesus, whom she calls her divine guide, "You know where I want to go, You know *for whom* I want to climb the mountain, for whom I want to reach the goal. You know the one whom I love and the one whom I want to please solely; it is for Him alone that I am undertaking this journey. Lead me, then, by the paths which He loves to travel. I shall be at the height of my joy provided that He is pleased." Thérèse continues her parable by telling how Jesus then takes her hand and leads her through an underground passage. "I don't see that we are advancing towards the summit of the mountain since our journey is being made underground," Thérèse writes, "but it seems to me we are approaching it without knowing how."[33] She does not have to climb up steep mountain walls. She travels together with Jesus inside the mountain, in the elevator of grace.

THE "LITTLE WAY" OF PILGRIMAGE

As a child, Thérèse had once said that she wanted to go away far into the desert and live alone. Later in life she discovered that the Carmelite

---

32. Thérèse of Lisieux, *Story of a Soul*, 125.

33. Letter to Sister Agnes of Jesus (Pauline), August 30–31, 1890. Thérèse of Lisieux, *Letters of St. Thérèse of Lisieux*, 1:651–52 (LT 110).

Convent in Lisieux was the "desert" to which she could withdraw.[34] Here God hid her from the world, and here, like the Desert Mothers and Fathers, she had the opportunity to practice virtues such as using words sparingly, being patient with other people's shortcomings, and learning the art of giving and receiving criticism in the right way.

Thérèse often likened herself to a grain of sand—tiny in comparison with the sky-high peaks of the Alps or the expansive desert. Paradoxically, entire desert areas or major mountain ranges can be contained within a tiny grain of sand. There is no need to travel to Egypt or to ascend Mount Everest in order to experience a life-changing adventure. Thérèse, and many others with her, emphasize that it is sufficient to go into oneself. Metaphorically speaking, all people have to walk in deserts or ascend mountains during their pilgrimage through life.

Both Thérèse and Martin Luther were affected by temptations that forced them to face their own shortcomings. In the same way, now and again we too are scared by our own smallness. For that reason we try to appear happy, safe, peaceful, strong, honest, and caring, even though we cannot always be those things. We want to cover up our weakness, both from other people and from ourselves. Even if we have sung "God's love is like the beach and the grass" (Swedish Hymnal 289:1) innumerable times, we still want to cover up our weakness and smallness before God as well. We are afraid of the reaction that might follow when God sees who we really are, deep down. Sometimes it is said that our human fear of God has become the most untreated of all pastoral problems today. We know that, ideally, we need not fear God, and so we do not have the courage to confess that we actually are fearful.

Thérèse believes that we must have the courage to remain in our own weakness. It should not be hidden away in the darkest corner of a cellar, nor be rolled up in messy talk about God's love that might sit on the surface. Instead, our weakness should be put in the hands of God. God's grace can work major miracles with our smallness once we stop inflating it into gigantic and scary proportions.

Abbé Bellière was a young priest for whom Thérèse was given special pastoral responsibility. He suffered from temptations that were similar to the anxious fear before God's greatness and our own smallness with which Luther and Thérèse also struggled. Toward the end of her life, Thérèse wrote two farewell letters to Abbé Bellière. Some key sentences in

---

34. De Meester, *Med tomma händer*, 15.

those letters describe the trusting surrender to God that Thérèse specifically associates with the Little Way. Rather than mulling over their own mistakes and shortcomings again and again, a person should show the same trusting confidence in God that a child puts in good parents. Small children often break things. Their parents might be angry with them sometimes—and the children might need to ask for forgiveness and to make things right again as best they can—but good parents do not stop loving their children, even when they smash their very best chinaware vase. God is perfect, unlike even the best parent. Therefore, Thérèse never tires of reminding everyone that we can have even greater trust and confidence in God than we could ever imagine.[35]

Thérèse encourages Abbé Bellière to crawl into the arms of Jesus with the same confidence that small children show when they crawl into the arms of adults whom they trust. "I beg you, do not *drag* yourself any longer to *His feet*," Thérèse writes; "follow that 'first impulse that draws you into His arms.' That is where your place is."[36] The Little Way is that the soul is "called to raise itself to God by the ELEVATOR of love and not to climb the rough *stairway* of fear."[37] The courage that is needed for that journey is the courage to come before God with "empty hands."[38]

Most climbers who die on K2 perish during their descent. The reason is that people find it much easier to climb upwards. We are nurtured in various ways into the perception that our task in life—the meaning of life—is to strive toward those attractive heights where successful people can enjoy their achievements and the rewards that they have gained. We invest in our careers, we admire celebrities, we hope to win millions of dollars, and we publish photos on Facebook that aim to give the impression of a happy and successful life.

Just like many professional mountaineers, Thérèse stresses that it is the descent that is the most significant part of the journey if we want to survive. So often we miss the point of life because we invest too much in attempts to reach heights that in reality exist only in our collective imaginations. We become affected by various kinds of summit fever. The

---

35. Cf. Letter to Léonie, July 12, 1896. Thérèse of Lisieux, *Letters of St. Thérèse of Lisieux*, 2:965–66 (LT 191).

36. Letter to Abbé Bellière, July 26, 1897. Thérèse of Lisieux, *Letters of St. Thérèse of Lisieux*, 2:1164 (LT 261).

37. Letter to Abbé Bellière, July 18, 1897, *Letters of St. Thérèse of Lisieux*, 2:1152 (LT 258).

38. Thérèse of Lisieux, *Story of a Soul*, 276–77 (Act of oblation, June 9, 1895).

symptoms may be a damaging admiration for the strong, for those who come first, who can manage the most, are liked by most people, or take the most decisions. In a letter to her sister Céline, Thérèse prescribes a medicine that can be taken as a cure against the misunderstanding that it is vitally important to be the first man or woman to reach the summit. While mountaineers run up mountains, Thérèse suggests that we should run in the opposite direction. She presents freedom from jealousy as the compass we should use to find the right direction. She writes:

> The only thing that is not *envied* is the last place; there is, then, only this *last place* which is not vanity and affliction of spirit . . . we surprise ourselves at times by desiring what sparkles. So let us line up humbly among the imperfect, let us esteem ourselves as *little souls* whom God must sustain at each moment. When He sees we are very much convinced of our own nothingness, He extends His hand to us. If we still wish to attempt doing something *great* even under the pretext of zeal, Good Jesus leaves us all alone. "But when I said: 'My foot has stumbled,' your mercy, Lord, strengthened me . . . [Ps XCIII]." YEs, it suffices to humble oneself, to bear with one's imperfections. That is real sanctity! Let us take each other by the hand, dear little sister, and let us run to the last place . . . no one will come to dispute with us over it . . . [39]

Reading Thérèse's writings, you can see clear traces of a deliberate practice in mountain descent. The content and the character of these exercises vary to some extent during Thérèse's life, depending on how much of the Little Way she has discovered. To begin with, she primarily perceives the sought-after smallness as humility, which means that you should not strive to be great, successful, and gifted, nor devout, small, and humble in the eyes of other people. Humility also means having the courage to be small in one's own eyes. You do not become either desolate or incapable of taking action when you discover the traces of your own weakness or sin. Later in life, when Thérèse has understood more of the Little Way, she stresses more clearly that our weaknesses are constructive opportunities for God. Her attention is no longer focused on people and their attempts to deal with their shortcomings. Rather, God is at the

---

39. Letter to Sister Geneviève (Céline), June 7, 1897. Thérèse of Lisieux, *Letters of St. Thérèse of Lisieux*, 2:1121–22 (LT 243).

center: God can use our weakness to do great things with us, just as God did great things with the Virgin Mary.[40]

Since our weaknesses are God's opportunities, Thérèse does not become sad when she realizes that she is "weakness itself." On the contrary, she boasts of her weakness, and she is prepared to discover new shortcomings in herself every day.[41] She does not become despondent, nor does she lose her ability to act when she realizes that she is still stamping around in the same place as before. The mountain descent does not make the weaknesses disappear gradually. That would be a mountain *ascent*. Rather, it is the attitude to your own smallness and incapacity that changes during that journey. Thérèse says to Mother Agnes of Jesus:

> I have my weaknesses also, but I rejoice in them. I don't always succeed either in rising above the nothings of this earth; for example, I will be tormented by a foolish thing I said or did. Then I enter into myself, and I say: Alas, I'm still at the same place as I was formerly! But I tell myself this with great gentleness and without any sadness! It's so good to feel that one is weak and little![42]

"Small" and "tiny" are the favorite words of Thérèse of the Child Jesus, and they were frequently used in her conversations with the Sisters while she lay dying. They made loving and humorous comments about her little hair, her little life, her little face, and her little brain. Sometimes they called her "the Little One." When Thérèse was asked what they should call her when they asked for intercessions in heaven after her death, she answered, "You can call me Little Thérèse."[43]

If Little Thérèse had written a book of good advice for the journey along the Little Way down the mountain, it would not have been particularly thick, but its content would have been significant. To take the elevator up into the arms of Jesus is not a passive attitude for Thérèse of the Child Jesus. It is, rather, an active rest of the kind in which climbers engage on their days off at the base camp. Since small movements reduce the risk of high-altitude sickness, they take short walks around the camp of small tents, talk to their neighbors, and do their laundry.

---

40. Cf. De Meester, *Med tomma händer*, 20, 37–42.
41. Thérèse of Lisieux, *Story of a Soul*, 158, 224.
42. Thérèse of Lisieux, *Her Last Conversations*, 73–74 (July 5, point 1).
43. Geneviève of the Holy Face, *My Sister Saint Thérèse*, 54.

THÉRÈSE'S SMALL PIECES OF ADVICE FOR EXERCISES

Wilfrid Stinissen notes that there is an unfortunate tendency to tone down or even to neglect completely the importance of *ascesis* in the life and teaching of Thérèse of the Child Jesus.[44] If we do not pay attention to the meaningfulness of spiritual exercises, there is a major risk that we will transform Thérèse's message into the kind of preaching that contributes to the secularization from within. If everything is grace, and it is only a matter of taking the elevator up to God, it will probably not matter what we do, since God loves us anyway and lifts us up into his arms.

Thérèse never asked those questions—evidence that she thought along different lines. She did not conclude that *nothing* that we do makes any difference because everything is grace. Rather, she thought that *everything* that we do makes a difference because everything is grace. That everything is grace means that every little thing that we do, every little word that we say, and every little thought we think is something divine.

Just like Amma Theodora, Thérèse could have said that it is not our *ascesis* but our humility that makes it possible for God to save us. Just like Amma Syncletica, Thérèse understood that the spiritual exercises require discernment, since there are both good and demonic forms of *ascesis*. Just like Amma Sara, Thérèse is particularly interested in the importance of discernment in how we relate to other people's judgments and about how we ourselves express justified criticism without behaving badly. Our walk along the Little Way should not turn us into penitents at everyone's door. We should rather pray for a pure heart toward everyone.

An important aspect of Thérèse's *ascesis* is her practice of not paying too much attention to what other people say about her. She does not try to defend herself or to explain unnecessarily when she has been misunderstood or judged unfairly. She makes no effort to excuse herself, which she finds very difficult.[45] Toward the end of her life, while she was seriously affected by her illness, she was sometimes canonized in advance by people who were impressed by her steadfastness and good temper. Then she had to prove her ability not to care in the wrong way about words of praise either.

In her last conversation, Thérèse mentions an occasion that made her realize that the judgments of other people can vary a great deal, and that it is wise not to give too much weight to them. Thérèse writes:

---

44. Stinissen, "Om Thérèses andliga utveckling," 47–50.
45. Thérèse of Lisieux, *Story of a Soul*, 159.

One day, after I received the Habit, Sister St. Vincent de Paul saw me . . . and she exclaimed: "Oh! how well she looks! Is this big girl strong! Is she plump!" I left, quite humbled by the compliment, when Sister Magdalene stopped me in front of the kitchen and said: "But what is becoming of you, poor little Sister Thérèse of the Child Jesus! You are fading away before our eyes! If you continue at this pace, with an appearance that makes one tremble, you won't observe the Rule very long!" I couldn't get over hearing, one after the other, two such contrary appraisals. Ever since that moment, I have never attached any importance to the opinion of creatures, and this impression has so developed in me that, at this present time, reproaches and compliments glide over me without leaving the slightest imprint.[46]

Another important feature of Thérèse's *ascesis* aims to teach her to live with the weaknesses and shortcomings of other people without being too irritated by them. In the Carmelite Convent at Lisieux in Thérèse's day there were some twenty nuns. There was one Sister whom Thérèse instinctively did not like very much. Thérèse says that "her ways, her words, her character, everything seems *very disagreeable.*"[47] Thérèse decides to be extra friendly and caring toward that Sister. She helps her with various tasks, always smiles at her, and prays to God for her every time they meet. For Thérèse, this is an exercise in coming before God with empty hands. In a letter to Céline, she writes,

> [W]hen I *am feeling* nothing, when I am INCAPABLE *of praying,* of practicing virtue, then is the moment for seeking opportunities, *nothings,* which please Jesus more than mastery of the world or even martyrdom suffered with generosity. For example, a smile, a friendly word, when I would want to say nothing, or put on a look of annoyance, etc. etc.[48]

For a while, Thérèse was responsible for teaching the novices in the convent. Just before she died, she gave one of the novices, Sister Marie of the Eucharist, the good advice to read a chapter of *The imitation of Christ* entitled "On forbearance with the faults of others." This classic by Thomas à Kempis was one of Thérèse's favorite writings, and the chapter on how

---

46. Thérèse of Lisieux, *Her Last Conversations,* 111–12 (July 25, point 15).
47. Thérèse of Lisieux, *Story of a Soul,* 222.
48. Letter to Céline, July 18, 1893. Thérèse of Lisieux, *Letters of St. Thérèse of Lisieux,* 2:801 (LT 143).

to put up with other people's shortcomings was something she thought had done her a great deal of good.[49]

As Novice Mistress, Thérèse had the opportunity to practice giving justified criticism without being affected afterwards by fruitless or distorted scruples. Discernment is required with regard to both spiritual exercises and human imperfection. We are not always meant to put up with or to adapt to the behavior or customs of other people. Sometimes we must reject them—and say so. Thérèse noted: "We should never allow kindness to degenerate into weakness. When we have scolded someone with just reason, we must leave the matter there, without allowing ourselves to be touched to the point of tormenting ourselves for having caused pain..."[50] When she had unintentionally caused anyone any hurt, she asked God to repair it, and then she did not worry any more about the matter.[51]

Thérèse's autobiography includes several examples of ascetic practices that hardly appear to be life-enhancing. Thérèse speaks to one of her Sisters about a priest who abstained from alleviating a terrible illness. "As for me, I prefer to practice mortifications in other ways, and not in such irritating things," Thérèse comments. "I can't control myself in that way."[52] As they speak about various penitential instruments, Thérèse underlines that one must be moderate in using such measures, since they can be used as part of unsound self-harming behavior.[53] She tells Mother Agnes of Jesus that she used to wear an iron cross next to her body, but that it made her sick. This made her realize that it was not God's will that she or anyone else should engage in such severe mortification of the flesh.[54] She also speaks of the abstinences she has practiced at meals. In the past, she used to think of unpleasant things while she was eating, "[b]ut afterwards, I found it very simple to offer to God whatever appealed to my taste."[55] Consequently, she practices offering the good things to God through abstinence at meals by not drawing anyone's attention to the fact that she has not been served the gravy or the salad. Toward the

---

49. Thérèse of Lisieux, *Her Last Conversations*, 252 (July 11).
50. Thérèse of Lisieux, *Her Last Conversations*, 38 (April 18, point 4).
51. Thérèse of Lisieux, *Her Last Conversations*, 93 (July 13, point 9).
52. Thérèse of Lisieux, *Her Last Conversations*, 127 (August 1, point 6).
53. Thérèse of Lisieux, *Her Last Conversations*, 130 (August 3, point 5).
54. Thérèse of Lisieux, *Her Last Conversations*, 115 (July 27, point 16).
55. Thérèse of Lisieux, *Her Last Conversations*, 178 (August 31, point 12).

end of her life, she speaks of all the bad omelettes she has eaten in the refectory of the convent without complaining. "You must pay particular attention after my death not to give bad fare to the poor Sisters."[56]

You might question whether all the ascetic practices to which Thérèse subjected herself really fulfilled their purpose. If she liked squeezing peaches, did she really have to abstain from them? If she wiped her brow an extra time so that other people might see that she was sweating, was any harm done? Thérèse herself sometimes reflected on such issues. A technique that she seems to have brought with her from home was always to manage with "the least possible."[57]

If we applied that technique more often, the world would no doubt be in a better state. It is only too easy for us to succumb to the damaging temptation of over-consumption. Sometimes we are aware that we eat too many sweets or drink too much alcohol. Sometimes we are not aware that we ought to change our lifestyle. Sound *ascesis* can help us to discover and break with damaging habits that endanger our own well-being as well as that of other people and of the entire creation. Our misguided attempts to try to live as we ought to may also fulfill their purpose. "[O]ne feels that to do good is as impossible without God's help as to make the sun shine at night."[58] Those who have never tried it will never make this reformatory discovery.[59]

HEAVENLY HUMAN KINDNESS

Martin Luther never identified the date of his reformatory discovery, but he sent a short account of what he had come to realize to the pope. That work was published in 1520, and is one of the most beloved of Luther's books. *The freedom of a Christian* is in many respects not only a Lutheran but also a Theresian document. Luther's starting point is that human persons are justified by faith; and faith means that a person is united with Christ as intimately as a bride and bridegroom are united with one another.[60] Thus Luther makes connections with bridal mysticism. This unity means that the bride and the groom have everything in common. The

---

56. Thérèse of Lisieux, *Her Last Conversations,* 108 (July 24, point 2).

57. Thérèse of Lisieux, *Her Last Conversations,* 120 (July 30, point 12). Cf. also 242 (August 27).

58. Thérèse of Lisieux, *Story of a Soul,* 238.

59. Cf. Stinissen, *Den enkla vägen till helighet,* 70.

60. Luther, *Freedom of a Christian,* 31:351.

sins, guilt, and weaknesses of humanity become the possession of Christ through this unity. In the same way, Christ's righteousness, his relationship with God, and his love become the possession of people. When we in the Evangelical-Lutheran tradition speak of "this blessed exchange," it is the mystical union between the believer and Christ that we are thinking of. Sometimes this blessed exchange is primarily likened to a court hearing, which means that God acquits people from the penalty for sin by ascribing to them the righteousness of Christ. However, Luther does not only present the believer's relationship with Christ as a legal matter: he also describes it as a loving union, which means that Christ moves into the believer and lives in them.

Luther underlines that, thanks to this intimate unity with Christ, people can love their fellow human beings with the love of God. When a person no longer needs to worry about how God views them because they know that they have been justified by faith, they can confidently get involved in better things than anxious self-reflection. Time and energies are set free, so that a person, just like a tree that has a fresh root, can bear fruit in the form of good deeds. Through faith, a person becomes a Christ for their neighbor, a heavenly fellow human who can love other people and the whole of creation with the love of Christ.[61]

For Luther, it is important that we should not connect justification with any form of *ascesis*, because the result of that would be justification by works. Rather, ascetical practices are something that belong in the life of an already justified person. The purpose of such exercises is that the lifestyle of the person becomes more attuned to God's loving will. Putting it simply, we could say that good *ascesis* will help people to love their fellow human beings and the whole of creation with the love of Christ. *Ascesis* clears away the weeds, helping the root of the healthy tree to become better settled in the soil. Luther explains the importance of *ascesis* when he writes:

> Although, as I have said, a man is abundantly and sufficiently justified by faith inwardly, in his spirit, and so has all that he needs, expect insofar as this faith and these riches must grow from day to day even to the future life; yet he remains in this mortal life on earth. In this life he must control his own body and have dealings with men. Here the works begin; here a man cannot enjoy leisure; here he must indeed take care to discipline his body by fastings, watchings, labors, and other reasonable

61. Luther, *Freedom of a Christian*, 31:361–62, 367–68, 371.

discipline and to subject it to the Spirit so that it will obey and conform to the inner man and faith and not revolt against faith and hinder the inner man, as it is the nature of the body to do if it is not held in check.[62]

Thérèse of the Child Jesus understands such a moderate and life-enhancing *ascesis* in the same way as Martin Luther. It helps people to discover their dependence on God and it opens the possibilities for God to perform acts of love here on Earth through us. Thérèse emphasizes that Jesus does not demand anything impossible from us. He knows our weaknesses and imperfections, and he knows that we can never love other people in our own strength as he wants us to love them. That is why he becomes love within us and loves our neighbors through us. "[W]hen I am charitable, it is Jesus alone who is acting in me," Thérèse writes.[63] She becomes a Christ for her fellow human beings, and thus she "has to borrow God's love," so to speak, in order to love God and other people with that love.[64]

When Thérèse of the Child Jesus expounds the heavenly human kindness on Earth, her teaching is in line with that of Luther. For Thérèse, however, there is no sharp boundary between our temporal existence and eternity. She rests in the assurance that she will continue to exercise the heavenly human kindness even after she has completed her time here on Earth. "I really count on not remaining inactive in heaven," she writes. "My desire is to work still for the Church and for souls. I am asking God for this and I am certain He will answer me."[65] This heavenly loving kindness that she will practice after her earthly death includes in a self-evident way people in this temporal life—that is, on Earth or in purgatory. When Sister Geneviève of the Holy Face (Céline) says, "You will look at us from up there in heaven, right?" Thérèse answered spontaneously, "No, I shall come down!"[66] Thérèse told Mother Agnes of Jesus (Pauline) a little more about her heavenly plans. She said, "If God answers my desires, my heaven will be spent on earth until the end of the world. Yes, I want to spend my heaven in doing good on earth."[67]

62. Luther, *Freedom of a Christian*, 31:358–59.
63. Thérèse of Lisieux, *Story of a Soul*, 221.
64. Thérèse of Lisieux, *Story of a Soul*, 256.
65. Letter to P. Roulland, July 14, 1897. Thérèse of Lisieux, *Letters of St. Thérèse of Lisieux*, 2:1142 (LT 254).
66. Thérèse of Lisieux, *Her Last Conversations*, 228 (September 26, point 1).
67. Thérèse of Lisieux, *Her Last Conversations*, 102 (July 17).

Thérèse imagines that, just as she and Christ have been united on earth, so they will continue their teamwork in heaven. Death is no obstacle to their joint project of salvation. Thérèse never specifies who does what in the collaboration between God and humanity. With regard to the loving kindness that she will exercise in heaven, however, she can say who wants what. Thérèse says that "God will have to carry out my will in heaven because I have never done my own will here on earth."[68] That way of speaking seems to suggest that God can reward people in heaven by giving them greater space to act if they have been obedient on Earth. In fact, Thérèse assumes that her will in heaven will be completely in tune with the will of Jesus. On earth, their wills might sometimes differ—and then Thérèse strives to act in accordance with the will of Jesus and not in accordance with her own will—but, in heaven, she and Jesus will always want the same thing. It is therefore possible to say that he wants what she wants.

Communion with Christ is the foundation of Thérèse's hope for the future. Against the background of *The freedom of a Christian,* we can say that Thérèse is confident, since she and her bridegroom own everything together. She has no good deeds or great merits for which God might reward her. She cannot put her hope in anything that she herself has achieved; but the assets of her bridegroom are hers as well. His righteousness is hers also. His deeds are hers also. Therefore, Thérèse says,

> I am very happy to go to heaven very soon, but when I think of these words of God: "My reward is with me, to render to each one according to his works," (Rev.22,12) I tell myself that He will be very much embarrassed in my case. I haven't any works! He will not be able to reward me 'according to my works.' Well, then. He will reward me 'according to His own works.'[69]

With regard to purgatory and the merits of the saints, Thérèse of the Child Jesus has a message to which Martin Luther would have been receptive in 1517, but that he would not have appreciated a few years later. Thérèse does not worry about going to purgatory. She hopes instead that, from heaven, she will be able to intervene in purgatory to liberate souls who are there by suffering in their place.[70] Thérèse takes it for granted

---

68. Thérèse of Lisieux, *Her Last Conversations,* 92 (July 13, point 2).

69. Thérèse of Lisieux, *Her Last Conversations,* 43 (May 15, point 1).

70. Thérèse of Lisieux, *Her Last Conversations,* 56 (June 4), 81 (July 8, point 15) and 118 (July 30, point 3).

that there is a collective treasure of the kind on which the indulgence system is founded. Some people have undertaken penance or endured sufferings that have generated a surplus of goodness that can be transferred to other people in order to balance their deficits. Thérèse often expresses a wish to suffer with Christ. The background is that she imagines that, in that way, she can save souls. She wants to exercise heavenly loving kindness by bearing the sufferings of others—already here on Earth, but also in heaven. The penance that she takes on has not only the purpose of making her will more attuned to the will of God; she also thinks that her penance can be credited to other people. In the same way, she imagines that she can serve other people's temporal penalties in purgatory.[71] Thus the dying Thérèse can say to a Sister,

> Will you hand me my Crucifix so that I can kiss it after the Act of Contrition, in order to gain the plenary indulgence for the souls in purgatory; I can give them no more than that!
> Give me the holy water now; and bring close to me the relics of Blessed Anne of Jesus and Théophane Vénard; I want to kiss them.[72]

Thérèse of the Child Jesus wanted to collect merits—"Yes, but not for myself; for poor sinners, for the needs of the whole Church; finally, to cast flowers upon everybody, the just and the sinners."[73] What particularly distinguishes her indulgence system from that which Luther criticized in the sixteenth century is the absence of money and of the pope. Thérèse distributes flowers quite freely, without the pope having said anything about the matter. The treasures of the Church are redistributed from heaven, not from Rome. Basically, it is the will of Jesus that governs the redistribution; but Thérèse is no stranger to the thought that those who are in heaven—and who there want the same thing as Jesus—take part in the work of redistribution. She believes that God wants the saints to mediate grace to one another and to other people through intercessory prayer.[74]

Here on Earth, Thérèse showed such heavenly loving kindness and such perseverance in suffering that people told her she was a saint. "No,

---

71. Letter to P. Roulland, March 19, 1897. Thérèse of Lisieux, *Letters of St. Thérèse of Lisieux*, 2:1069–73 (LT 221).

72. Thérèse of Lisieux, *Her Last Conversations*, 188 (September 11, point 5).

73. Thérèse of Lisieux, *Her Last Conversations*, 152–53 (August 18, point 3).

74. Cf. Thérèse of Lisieux, *Her Last Conversations*, 99 (July 15, point 5).

I'm not a saint," she answered, "I've never performed the actions of a saint. I'm a very little soul upon whom God has bestowed graces; that's what I am. What I say is the truth; you'll see this in heaven."[75] Thérèse obviously thought that it was not only great saints, but also little souls, who would be given divine opportunities for ever to show heavenly loving kindness. Not only rare eagles, but also very ordinary little sparrows, fly under heaven.

NATURE AND GRACE

Thérèse was very fond of devotions of the kind from which Luther thought we ought to be weaned. She loved processions with the sacrament, she caressed images of the saints, and she decorated statues of Mary with flowers. When on pilgrimage to Rome, she managed to put her little finger into a tiny slot so that she could touch the nail from the cross of Christ that Helena, the mother of the Emperor Constantine, had brought back from the Holy Land.[76] Thérèse saw no need to be weaned of such "childish practices." Rather, she cultivated her inventiveness. She came up with new little symbolic acts that reminded her of grace and smallness and that people are the children of God. She offered grapes to Jesus and fanned the images of the saints with a fan that she had received from the Carmelite Convent in Saigon.[77]

In the pilgrimage movement of our own age, there are some agents whose inventiveness is reminiscent of that of Thérèse of the Child Jesus. The Pilgrim Center at Vadstena is a significant place for pilgrims to gather, and a source of inspiration here in Sweden. In *Pilgrimsvandring på svenska* (*A pilgrimage in Swedish*), Anna Davidsson Bremborg describes the work at Vadstena. She also highlights various symbolic acts and items that are used in Church of Sweden pilgrimages.[78] When the gym Friskis & Svettis ("Healthy & Sweaty") or the Swedish Tourist Association organize pilgrimages, they sometimes use the same symbolic actions and items, but then with a completely or partly different meaning. Actions and items do not interpret themselves. It is we who provide their meaning-carrying significance. It is we who perceive—or do not perceive—something as a

---

75. Thérèse of Lisieux, *Her Last Conversations*, 143 (August 9, point 4).

76. Thérèse of Lisieux, *Story of a Soul*, 139.

77. Thérèse of Lisieux, *Her Last Conversations*, 114 (July 27, point 10) and 119 (July 30, point 11).

78. Davidson Bremborg, *Pilgrimsvandring på svenska*, chapters 4 and 7.

ramble or as a pilgrimage. We can describe many different kinds of walk as pilgrimages.

As mentioned earlier, Thérèse of the Child Jesus made a pilgrimage to Rome. In ordinary circumstances she liked to make a pilgrimage walk in the family's garden. It was not only the rites of the Church and her little symbolic actions that reminded Thérèse of the grace of God and that human beings are the children of God: she saw all of nature as a proclamation. The flowers, the birds, the sun's rays, and the snowflakes—all spoke to her. Their address was not only a general proclamation of the kind that is highlighted in what we often call the teleological proof of God's existence: "See how well everything fits together. There must be creator who has made all this." The message to Thérèse was often more specific. She received guidance from Jesus through a flower, a snowfall, or some stars. Her love of nature puts Thérèse of the Child Jesus on the same wavelength as all those Swedes who catch their breath during a walk through the forest or while on pilgrimage. She can help us to discover not only how something divine in general, but also how Jesus as a person, can speak to us through nature. I see this as a significant ecumenical contribution that the little nun from Lisieux can give us. Like Gunnel Vallquist, I too believe that Thérèse has even more surprises to offer us.

When Thérèse's autobiography was published in Swedish, Vallquist wrote in one of the major daily Swedish newspapers "that this little nun, without any theological speculations and without any polemics . . . cleared up exactly the same misconception that Luther had been storming against with so much noise and hullabaloo—namely, the demand that you had to achieve something in order to merit God's love."[79] Like Luther, Thérèse of the Child Jesus was very familiar with the biblical writings, and she was particularly fond of the same letter that catalysed Luther's reformatory discovery. In her prayer book she kept a little note that linked two texts from the Letter to the Romans, "Blessed are those whom God reckons as righteous regardless of any deeds. Whoever has deeds to point to will receive his wages, not as a gracious gift but as a due. But without having any merits, they are justified by his grace as a gift, through the redemption which is in Jesus Christ."[80] Martin Luther would have been happy to join in that song of praise.

---

79. Stinissen, "Om Teresas andliga utveckling," 69.
80. De Meester, *Med tomma händer,* 87. Thérèse links together Rom 4:4–6 and Rom 3:24.

Wilfrid Stinissen notes that "Thérèse's ecumenical significance is probably much greater than we have realized so far, and in this field, we probably have many surprises to look forward to."[81] It is impossible to predict surprises, since they are, by definition, unpredictable. What can be predicted is never a surprise. We do not know what ecumenical insights we might draw from Thérèse's magic shoes or from her little walking boots. However, with regard to opportunities to counter the secularization from within with the help of Thérèse of the Child Jesus, it is easier to be prophetic. It does not require a wild guess to see that Thérèse can help us who stand in the Evangelical-Lutheran tradition to discover more of the space for action within grace and of the proclamation of Christ through nature. With regard to Christ and the question of how we can cultivate our friendship with him, another Carmelite nun, Teresa of Avila, has several important insights that she wants to share with us.

---

81. Stinissen, *Den enkla vägen till helighet*, 160.

3

Teresa of Avila and Jesus Christ

EARLY IN THE MORNING, Rob Hall called the base camp from the south summit of Mount Everest. Dr Caroline Mackenzie answered, and quickly noticed that he sounded confused. Rob said that his legs felt strange and that he was too clumsy to move. Even so, Mackenzie plucked up the courage to ask the question that everyone was wondering about. How had things gone for Doug Hansen? "Doug is dead," Rob said, and then he broke off the radio link to the base camp. Later, when the base camp made contact with him again, nobody said anything about Doug.

Doug Hansen was a forty-seven-year-old postal worker from the USA who was making his second attempt to ascend the highest mountain in the world. The year before, Rob Hall had forced him to turn back only 100 meters from the summit because it was late in the day and the top was buried under a deep cover of unstable snow. Since then, no day had passed without Doug thinking about the incident. Now Rob had persuaded him to return to Mount Everest to make a new attempt. He had been given a substantial discount on the fee. Doug did not belong to the same income class as other clients on the mountain. He was not a well-paid doctor or a lawyer rolling in money. He had worked night shifts at the post office and had taken an extra job at a building site in the daytime to be able to afford the trip. The pupils at a state school in Washington State had also helped him financially by selling T-shirts.

Doug Hansen was no elite alpinist, but, unlike many of the other clients, he did have experience of climbing without the assistance of professional guides. Some of the women he had known in his life would probably have described him as besotted with mountaineering, but he was able to combine his interest with family life. He had managed to bring up two children as a single parent. They were adults by the time Doug ascended Mount Everest.

Rob Hall always announced a time on the day of the ascent itself as the latest hour when everyone in the group had to start the descent from the mountain, regardless of where they were at that point. Both the person who still had several hours left before reaching the top and the one who only had another 100 meters left had to turn back. That deadline was meant to give climbers the best possible safety margin. The idea was that everyone should have sufficient energy and oxygen left to be able to return to the highest camp in daylight.

On May 11, 1996, Rob Hall compromised his principles. Doug Hansen reached the top of Mount Everest more than two hours after the time when it was said that everyone must turn back. During those hours, Hall had been in "the death zone," waiting for Doug, who was below him. Seeing the worn-out postal worker approaching, he went to meet him and shoved him up the last bit to the summit. Doug was able to fulfill his life's dream that he had worked so hard to realize. Soon after that, his powers and his oxygen came to an end.

While Doug was struggling to reach the summit, another of Rob Hall's clients experienced a strange incident. Lou Kasischke, a lawyer who was about the same age as Doug Hansen, was further down the mountain, and he noted with increasing surprise that many continued to ascend upwards, even though it was getting late.[1] He tried to estimate the time and to decide what he should do. He was so short of oxygen that he could not force his brain to make a decision. Suddenly his heart started to race and pound uncontrollably. He had never experienced anything like it. He became both unsteady on his legs and terror-stricken. Using all the energy he could muster, Lou Kasischke drove his ice axe firmly into the ground and fell on his knees. He prayed intensely, with closed eyes. What was happening?

When he opened his eyes, he could see more clearly. He watched the climbers moving on further ahead on the route. He heard the whining wind and felt his frozen fingers. There were two contradictory voices locked in passionate argument inside him. He knew that he would probably be able to reach the summit, but he also knew that he ought to turn back. Some climbers on their way up had passed the praying Lou without

---

1. The story is taken from Kasischke, *After the Wind*, 167–79.

disturbing him. He was given the time that he needed to make the discovery that saved his life.

It is not Mount Everest that is the greatest challenge. Overcoming the summit fever that makes a person believe that the meaning of life is to reach the highest peaks is an even greater challenge.

Lou Kasischke was still on his knees when everything suddenly fell silent around him. He took a firmer grip on the ice axe and watched the snow whirling around him, now in slow-motion. Many years later, when he chose to describe in a book what had happened on Mount Everest, he clothed his experience in words aided by the biblical story of the prophet Elijah. Elijah was caught in a storm on Mount Sinai, but God was not in the storm. After the storm came a still small voice, and God was in that voice. Lou Kasischke stood up on Mount Everest, pulled out the ice-axe, and descended the mountain. That conversion, that turn-around, saved his life.

Most of those who were on Mount Everest in May 1996 and survived told their stories relatively soon afterwards in books, films, and interviews. Lou waited twenty years before he published *After the wind*. Unlike other books on the events that led to eight people losing their lives, Lou Kasischke's book does not include any photographs of either living or dead mountaineers. It does, however, include stories about prayers and reflections on the really major questions of life. What does God want us to do here on Earth? Lou Kasischke returned home to his family. Mount Everest gave him the chance to receive life—and God—at a deeper level.

RELIGIOUS EXPERIENCES

Richard Swinburne is one of the world's most influential philosophers of religion. He has developed a way to categorize religious experiences to which many other philosophers of religion refer.[2] Swinburne believes that first of all, a person can experience that they are meeting God, or Ultimate Reality, mediated through a common, sensory, public object—for example, in a sunrise that everyone in that place can view. Second, a person can experience a meeting with God through a publicly available object that, in some way, breaks with the natural law, or makes a break with what we can reasonably expect. When Moses met God in the burning bush, he had a religious experience of that kind. Third, a person

---

2. Peterson et al., *Reason and Religious Belief,* 14–16.

can experience meeting God through a private experience that can be described in ordinary language. Lou Kasischke experienced a silence and stillness on Mount Everest that other climbers who were there did not notice, and he described that experience using ordinary language. Fourth, a person can experience meeting God through a private experience that cannot be described by ordinary words, since it is indescribable. Other people in the same place do not experience the same thing, and the person who has the experience feels that it cannot be described in any adequate way. Fifth, a person can experience a meeting with God that is not mediated by any sensory object; they can, for example, experience that God governs and leads them in a particular direction and into a greater understanding of existence as a whole. This fifth category includes mystical experiences as well as experiences that find expression in a heightened degree of awareness or a deeper consciousness. If a person feels that they become one with the whole of existence, they have a religious experience of this fifth kind.

Philosophers of religion who are interested in religious, spiritual, or mystical experiences are usually most interested in experiences that cannot be captured in language or described within the framework of natural laws. The reason is that an important question for philosophical research into mysticism has been, and to some extent still is, whether it is possible to build a good argument in favor of God's existence from people's experiences of meeting God. Experiences that are natural and that can be described with the help of ordinary language are not considered very useful in this context: they do not give rise to any particularly strong arguments that God might exist and be active, since the frameworks of interpretation to which the person who had the experience has access are what mark the experience. It could have been that person's language and interpretation that created the experience. That possibility is not considered to be as prominent in experiences that transcend language and ordinary awareness.

Most people who encounter Swinburne's characterization of religious experiences interpret them in a hierarchical way. It seems that the model is built on the assumption that it is "better" or "more exclusive" to have a religious experience of the fourth kind than of the first kind. That interpretation is justified. Since philosophers of religion are primarily interested in mystical experiences, this categorization is regularly used to separate "authentic" mystical experiences from "ordinary" religious experiences that are not considered equally useful if you want to argue in favor of God's existence. Lou Kasischke's experience on Mount Everest may have had decisive life importance for him, but for many philosophers of religion it is only one more example of how we can interpret natural events in a more supernatural way than the circumstances permit us to do.

It is possible to problematize Richard Swinburne's categorization in several different ways. In this context, I will focus on one critical objection. Swinburne seems to imply that some mystical experiences that belong to the fifth category are "the best." It is primarily men with a thorough theological education who have reported that they have had experiences of that kind. Women, who within a certain tradition are described as mystics, report more often that they have had experiences that belong to the fourth category. Richard Swinburne places Teresa of Avila's religious experiences in this category, which is in itself quite remarkable. Teresa certainly wrote that words are not enough to describe the beauty of Jesus; but she nevertheless describes her experiences in very ordinary everyday language. She does not regard her experiences as ineffable, and therefore the greatest mystic of Christendom ought to be placed in Swinburne's third category, "normal religious." For that reason, many people have wondered if there might be something wrong with Swinburne's categorization. If the most famous example of a mystic does not end up in the mystical category, one might well ask whether this framework really does capture what we mean by mysticism.

MYSTICISM THROUGH THE AGES

The philosopher of religion Grace Jantzen has written a ground-breaking book that problematizes the understanding of mysticism that Richard Swinburne and many others use as their starting point.[3] Jantzen analyzes how the power to identify who is an "authentic" mystic has been exercised for millennia; and she notes that the understanding of mysticism that Swinburne proposes is a twentieth-century phenomenon. In earlier centuries, things other than those that Swinburne proposes were considered the characteristics of a mystic.

The word "mysticism" comes from the Greek word *muein*, which means "to remain silent." What people kept silent about in the Greece of antiquity were the initiation rites that you went through when you were admitted to a religious cult. When the concept was taken over by

---

3. In the following I summarize Jantzen.

the early Christian Church, it was used primarily to describe people who were given the grace of God to discern deeper levels of meaning in biblical texts. They were, so to speak, able to reveal the divine message that was hidden in the Bible that other people were not able to discover without the help of the mystics. Theologians, Bible translators, and preachers could be mystics in this sense. They could read, and then guide people using what they had understood from the texts.

Later on in the history of the Christian Church, the concept of "mysticism" was extended to include more than interpreting the biblical writings. Anyone who was able to discern, expound, or reveal God's message through nature or through historical events could also be described as a mystic. Against that background, practices emerged that aimed to help people to see and hear God's guidance more clearly. Roadmaps for the pilgrimage of the interior life were put together. There was a focus on discerning different stages in a person's way to God and/or God's way to a person. The purpose of these mapping exercises was to help people to relate to God in a constructive way. The various stages had recommendations attached to them that stated how a person might avoid going backwards, falling into a ditch, or simply sitting by the roadside.

In the sixteenth century, during the lifetime of Martin Luther and Teresa of Avila, the concept of "mysticism" had developed even further in the Christian tradition. At that time, people imagined that a mystic was a person who, with the help of God, clearly revealed what life as a follower of Christ could mean. Thus, a mystic was not only able to discern God's message through biblical texts or through nature and history, but also, with the help of God, to live to a very great extent in accordance with God's will. We could say that Teresa indirectly confirms that understanding of mysticism when she denies the accusation of those who think that she has been possessed by the devil or has fallen victim to her own imagination when she has received a number of revelations. Teresa was no stranger to the thought that some of her experiences could be the work of the devil or of her own imagination; but she stressed that, in some remarkable way, she had become a better person. She regarded her development as a clear sign that God was at work in her life, quite independently of her own efforts or ambitions. A deeper or more honest imitation of Christ is not something that either the devil or a mere mortal could achieve.

Jantzen stresses that we use the concept of "mysticism" in a way that is different than that of previous generations. When modern-day philosophers of religion take an interest in Teresa of Avila, the reason is not that she was an exceptionally good person. The reason, rather, is that she often experienced Jesus revealing himself to her and speaking with her. She even experienced something that could best be described as a heavenly orgasm.[4] That particular event is something that a number of scholars have analyzed in minute detail. Their interest shows that today we primarily connect mysticism with intense inner experiences. A mystic will experience something very special, something beyond the commonplace. In order that this experience be considered "authentic," it should preferably be impossible to describe.

Jantzen is critical of the current understanding of mysticism for various reasons. Among other things, she believes that it considerably distorts our reading of texts written by Christian women in earlier generations. The book *Philosophy of religion. Selected writings* is an anthology that illustrates the problems that Jantzen highlights.[5] Teresa of Avila is one of very few women who contributed to this collection. The editors included a heavily abbreviated extract from her autobiography. They omitted Teresa's reflections on how the meetings with Jesus that she experienced had transformed her. They also omitted her account of her conversations with her confessors about these remarkable events. Only her description of how Jesus showed himself to her and spoke with her remains. The stress is on the supernatural and the ineffable. One paragraph of the text has been cut in such a way that the line of reasoning becomes distorted. The reasoning that is ascribed to Teresa is not the line of thought that she herself developed.

Bernhard McGinn is another scholar who, like Grace Jantzen, stresses that our current formation of concepts makes it more difficult for us to understand previous generations' world of experience. He notes that many people today speak appreciatively of spirituality. However, it is often not clear what that concept means. McGinn recalls how, without too much effort, he was able to find thirty-five different definitions. He himself contributes an overview of the history of concepts, which is reminiscent of Jantzen's exposition of the history of the concept of "mysticism."

---

4. The so-called transverberation is a vision described in Teresa of Avila, *Book of Her Life*, 252 (29:13). Transverberation is a mystical grace wherein a person's heart is pierced with a "dart of love."

5. The example is mine. The book in question is Peterson et al.

THE BIBLICAL BACKGROUND OF SPIRITUALITY

Bernhard McGinn took on the task of answering the question of how the concept of "spirituality" emerged, and what it has meant in different centuries. He began by paying attention to the Old Testament writings.[6] The Hebrew word for "spirit," *ruach*, originally meant "wind." The Old Testament underlines that God is Spirit. The Book of Genesis says that, having formed a man from the dust of the Earth, God blew life into his nostrils. Since God has created humanity in God's image, humanity is also spirit. The spirit in humanity is linked primarily to the movable, energy-filled, and emotional life within them. The spirit is the driving force in people, the will that motivates their good deeds and the heart that makes them compassionate. To be filled with the spirit is to be filled with power. Some of the Old Testament authors believe that, when a person dies, their spirit returns to God.

Sometimes the Old Testament describes how chosen people receive the Spirit of God in a very special way. They receive divine power or deeper insights when the Spirit of God "falls upon them" or "runs upon them." Now and then the concept of "spirit" is used in contrast to the concept of "flesh." In the Old Testament, the purpose on such occasions is primarily to stress the differences between strength and weakness, or between wisdom and foolishness. "Flesh" stands for incapacity and foolishness, while "spirit" signifies power and wisdom.

The New Testament authors build on and develop the Old Testament concepts. The Greek word for "spirit" is *pneuma*. Originally it meant "wind," "a breeze," or "a current of air." God's Spirit plays a major role in the Old Testament hope for the Messiah and for the recreation of the world. A new kingdom, the reign of God, would come. In that kingdom, the power and wisdom of the Spirit would be the guide. The New Testament authors stress that God's reign has come into the world, and that it comes to us through Jesus.

St. Luke the Evangelist stresses that Jesus had the power of the Spirit within himself. On the first Day of Pentecost, the disciples received the Holy Spirit. The house in which they were sitting was filled by the roar of a storm wind, and they saw tongues as of fire distributed and resting on

---

6. In the following I refer to McGinn, "Letter and the Spirit," 26–29. With regard to the biblical writings, I also refer to *Svenskt bibliskt uppslagsverk*, "ande" (*Swedish Biblical Encyclopedia*, "spirit").

each one of them. Then they started to speak in other tongues and tell of God's wonderful deeds (Acts 2:1–11).

St. Paul the apostle links the risen Jesus with the Spirit, and develops the Old Testament distinction between "spirit" and "flesh" further. He uses it to describe the differences between the sphere of life that is governed by God (in which weakness also exists and can be valued) and a sphere of life that is turned away from God and is governed by evil, the world, or the devil (in which strength can be worshiped in the wrong way). Paul stresses that people are sanctified by baptism by the Spirit. As a Christian, a person is made a partaker of the Spirit (*pneuma*) and becomes spiritual (*pneumatikos*). In the light of this, Paul writes to the Christians in Galatia, "Live by the Spirit . . . If we live by the Spirit, let us also be guided by the Spirit. Let us not become conceited, competing against one another, envying one another." Paul stresses that it is easy to see what the flesh brings—namely, enmity, strife, intolerance, anger, intrigues, dissension, heresies, power struggles, drunkenness, licentiousness, and other such things. If instead the Spirit leads us, we will bear good fruit in the form of love, joy, peace, patience, kindness, goodness, faithfulness, humility, and self-control.[7]

Sometimes Paul describes even more remarkable gifts of grace that the Holy Spirit can give to people. He stresses that the Spirit is revealed in different ways in different people. Individuals are given special gifts of grace for the joy and use of other people and the whole creation. Through the Spirit, one is given the gift of speaking wisdom; another, with the help of the same Spirit, can impart knowledge. One is given faith through the Spirit, another is given the gift of curing those who are sick through the same Spirit, and a third is given the power to work miracles. One is given the gift of prophetic speech, and another the ability to discern between different spirits. All this is the work of one and the same Spirit who distributes gifts to each one as the Spirit chooses.[8]

In his so-called farewell speech in the Gospel of St. John, Jesus describes the Holy Spirit as "the Helper and Advocate." The Advocate will always be with the disciples, teach them everything, and remind them of everything that Jesus has told them. The Advocate will testify to Jesus and guide the disciples so that they too can bear witness to Jesus. The Advocate is "the Spirit of truth" by whose help we can distinguish between sin

---

7. I have paraphrased Gal 5:13–26 and quoted Gal 5:16 and 25–26.
8. Paraphrase of 1 Cor 12:4–11.

and righteousness.[9] When the concept of "spirituality" began to be used in the early Church, it was intended to encourage people to receive the help of God.

A FORMER HERMIT AND SOME PHILOSOPHERS

In the early Church, the New Testament texts were translated into Latin so that the population of the Roman Empire would be able to understand them. At about the same time as Christianity became the state religion in the Roman Empire, the pope commissioned the former hermit Jerome to produce a single, authorized Latin translation of the whole Bible. His translation is known as the *Versio vulgata* ("the universal translation"). In the Vulgate, the adjective *spiritualis* (spiritual) is used as a translation of the Greek word *pneumatikos*. It is against the background of that translation that the noun "spirituality" (*spiritualitas*) appears for the first time. The first verified appearance is in a letter from the fifth century that has been ascribed to Jerome. In it, the writer encourages the addressee to "act in such a way that you may grow in spirituality." Bernhard McGinn believes that this exhortation should be interpreted in line with the biblical development of this concept. The meaning is that the receiver of the letter should act in such a way that he (or she) increases his (or her) grip on, or becomes increasingly gripped by, the Spirit of Jesus Christ, the source of the Christian life. The few occurrences of the concept of "spirituality" that have been confirmed from the early Middle Ages should be understood along these same lines.

From the twelfth century onward, it is possible to discern a scholastic understanding of the concept of "spirituality" that certainly underlines some aspects of the biblical world of ideas, but that at the same time lets others fade into the background. The scholastics strove to explain the tenets of the faith by recourse to reason. Following this line, they described "spirituality" as linked to the human soul as against the human body. Spirituality was considered to be that which distinguished human beings from animals. The understanding of spirituality in our own time as a deep dimension of human existence, as something that is found within every person, has some similarities with the scholastic interpretation. There are also some similarities between the scholastic exposition and Old Testament passages that present the spirit as the principle of human life. During the Middle Ages, the accepted understanding of spirituality

---

9. See particularly John 14:15ff.; 15:26-27; and 16:12-15.

(to be influenced or affected by the Spirit of Jesus Christ) lived side by side with the scholastic interpretation. According to the accepted understanding, there was no strict separation between body and soul. To be influenced by the Spirit of Jesus Christ was something that affected the body as well as the soul.

During the sixteenth and seventeenth centuries, however, a shift of meaning took place that led to the primary connection of "spirituality" with the inner life of a person, with a person's dispositions to act, or with different states of the soul. Bernhard McGinn emphasizes that, when John of the Cross used the concept of "spirituality" in the sixteenth century, he wanted to discuss various signs of the life of the Spirit in the inner life of a person. When the Enlightenment philosopher Voltaire used the concept a couple of centuries later, yet another shift of meaning had taken place.[10] Unlike John of the Cross, Voltaire spoke ironically about spirituality, which shows that by then the concept had negative connotations: one would prefer not to be accused of being interested in spirituality or in other "woolly" thoughts. In the eighteenth century, the Roman Catholic Church's condemnation of Quietism—a piety that was accused, among other things, of underestimating the importance of the traditional devotional life of the Church—had led to the association of the concept of "spirituality" with heresies of various kinds. Both Roman Catholics and Protestants therefore normally used other concepts, speaking of "piety" or "devotion" instead.

Today "spirituality" is again viewed in a positive light. Bernhard McGinn believes that this can be described as something of a miracle in the history of ideas. For unclear reasons, French Roman Catholic thinkers in the early twentieth century began to use the concept of "spirituality" in an appreciative sense. Their works were translated into English, and in the 1970s it was obvious to many people that the English word *spirituality* had positive associations. McGinn notes jokingly that nowadays it is only God who knows in which different senses the concept of "spirituality" is used. Today many people describe themselves as "spiritual" or as interested in spirituality, and they take it for granted that this is something different from being "religious." In academic contexts, it is now common to speak, for example, of "Muslim spirituality," in spite of the background

---

10. It is worth noting that John of the Cross had Spanish as his mother tongue, while Voltaire had French. The concepts that we translate with the English word "spirituality" sometimes have different connotations in different languages. McGinn does not discuss this in the text to which I refer.

of this concept in the Christian history of ideas. In Christian contexts, the concept of "spirituality" is sometimes used to denote a deep dimension of human existence ("All people are spiritual"). Sometimes the concept is used in the older sense ("Act in such a way that you can be gripped by the Spirit of Jesus Christ"). When the spirituality of a specific Christian tradition is discussed, the presentation usually includes various attitudes or activities that are perceived to facilitate the work of Christ in a person's life. Simply put, you could say that what is then highlighted is how we can act in order to make it easier for the Spirit of Jesus Christ to "grip us" or to "affect us."

Some expositions of Luther's theology imply that there can be no Lutheran spirituality, since Luther stressed that people cannot do anything themselves to come to faith or to grow in faith. It is the Spirit alone who achieves this within us (*solus Spiritus in nobis*). Luther does, however, allow for human collaboration with God.[11] Some scholars focus on that thought and seek to demarcate what might be described as a Lutheran spirituality. Their work should be seen in the light of a significant shift in twentieth-century research on Luther. That shift concerns Luther's attitude to mysticism.

MARTIN LUTHER AND MYSTICISM

In the Lutheran tradition, and in research on Luther, it was long taken for granted that Martin Luther was not a mystic. Mysticism was presented as a self-centered religious fancy that despised God's external messages through the Bible. The mystic was seeking God within themselves. Such a search was considered emotional, anti-intellectual, and unmasculine in contrast to the masculine reasoning that characterized Lutheranism, which stressed that Jesus meets persons through baptism and Holy Communion, not through any strange experiences that a person might have in their private chamber. To seek God within oneself was depicted as a dead end that leads to becoming turned in on oneself—something that Luther continually warned against.

At the end of the nineteenth century, Luther's collected works began to be published in the Weimar edition, giving even more scholars access to his writings. It also meant that the Luther texts that had not so far attracted much attention became objects of closer study. This led to the flourishing of the so-called Luther renaissance in the early twentieth

---

11. Luther, *Bondage of the Will*, 33:242–43.

century. The ecumenically influential professor and archbishop Nathan Söderblom was part of that scholarly community.

Söderblom was himself a historian of religions, and was interested in the mystical traditions of various world religions.[12] He distinguished between two different forms of mysticism: infinity mysticism and personal mysticism. The ideal in infinity mysticism is that a person should abandon their bonds to Earth in order to rise to greater heights. The mystical experiences that belong in Swinburne's fifth category are experiences of infinity mysticism. In personal mysticism, the ideal is described instead as a personal, lively relationship with an active, saving God. Söderblom underlines in several works that Luther described the Christian faith as a kind of personal mysticism. For Luther, faith is not primarily an acceptance of the teaching of the Church, but Christ's own mystical presence within the person. In his book, *Humor och melankoli och andra Lutherstudier (Humor and melancholy and other studies on Luther)*, Söderblom stressed that "Luther is the authentic perfecter of the mystic devotional tradition of the church in its deepest furrow." Söderblom described Luther's understanding of the intimate union between a person and Christ through faith as a "faith mysticism" and a "mysticism of trust."[13]

Not all Luther scholars were convinced by Söderblom's presentation of Luther as a "hero of mysticism." They certainly agreed that Luther had been influenced by the mystic Johannes Tauler, who taught that the mystical union provides the power to live one's everyday life as a follower of Christ. It was also known that Luther had commented on and arranged for the publication of *Theologia Deutsch*, an anonymous work from the fourteenth century that he valued highly. Influential scholars on Luther, however, usually describe "evangelical theology" or "Lutheran theology" as essentially separate from "mystical theology."[14] The similarities that did exist were based on concepts, not on content, and thus they lacked any importance.

In the mid-1960s, the third *International Congress on Luther Research* took place in the Finnish town of Järvenpää. The theme was "Church, mysticism, sanctification and the natural world in Luther's thought." In a

---

12. The following is based on Hoffman, *Hjärtats teologi*, 218–19.
13. Hoffman, *Hjärtats teologi*, 219.
14. Hoffman includes surveys of research that describes how various scholars and schools have presented Martin Luther's attitude to mysticism. See Hoffman, *Hjärtats teologi*, 200–203 for a summary. Cf. Hoffman, *Hjärtats teologi*, chapter 11.

lecture,[15] the historian of theology Heiko A. Oberman described how Luther, in terms of both concepts and content, made links to and developed lines of thinking that are of central significance in Christian mysticism. In the Evangelical-Lutheran tradition, the theological emphasis is on *Christus pro nobis*, Christ for us. Christ has fulfilled the law on our behalf, and his righteousness, which comes to us from outside, is accounted to us through faith. Oberman asked how Luther understands *Christus in nobis*, Christ in us. By comparing Luther's writings with the teaching of mystical authors, Oberman concluded that one would be justified to speak of Luther's understanding of the Christian life as a democratized form of mysticism. In his lecture, he also suggested that it might be valid to understand some of Luther's thoughts as expressions of a Bible-centered form of mysticism.

Sometimes Luther's reformatory discovery is perceived as a mystical experience. Luther was suddenly carried away out of himself, enraptured (*raptus*), when the Bible opened itself to him in a new way. He was given wider perspectives and reached greater freedom. Many Luther scholars who are interested in Luther's relationship with mysticism are therefore interested in the use of various Latin concepts that have to do with enrapture and ecstasy. They might point out, for example, that we often say that Luther believed that good theologians are characterized by their ability to distinguish correctly between the law and the gospel. It is more rarely stressed that Luther also says that you become a good theologian through enrapture and ecstasy.[16]

Many of us like to stress that Luther's understanding of the circumstances of the life of a Christian can be summarized in the phrase that a person is at the same time both justified and a sinner (*simul iustus et peccator*). During the conference at Järvenpää, Oberman noted that we might just as well summarize Luther's theology using two other concepts that are deeply anchored in Christian mysticism. Luther describes the Christian person as simultaneously groaning and enraptured (*simul gemitus et raptus*). *Gemitus* designates the trembling experience of falling into the hands of God, while *raptus* is a concept that reminds us that Luther's understanding of justification can never be reduced to the legal acquittal of a person before a heavenly court. Aided by the concept of *raptus*, Luther points out that a person's trusting relationship with Christ

---

15. Oberman, "Simul gemitus et raptus."
16. Hoffman, *Hjärtats teologi*, 99. Cf. Hoffman, *Hjärtats teologi*, 151.

can be experienced here on Earth. That is one of the reasons why the union with Christ by faith can affect both a person's inner life and their outward actions.[17] The blessed exchange is not a theoretical matter, but a reality based on experience. Jesus takes away the sin, guilt, and death of humanity, and we are given the forgiveness, life, and immortality of Jesus.

In the years that have passed since the conference at Järvenpää, many studies of Luther's view of mysticism have been published. Nowadays it is no longer controversial to say that Luther was affected by, and positively disposed toward, Christian mysticism. There is also a degree of unity over the characterization of Luther's mysticism or his understanding of mysticism. The Swedish historian of theology Bengt Hägglund had already pointed out during the conference at Järvenpää that Luther understands mysticism as an aspect of normal Christian life.[18] The union between the person/the bride and Christ/the bridegroom that so many Christian mystics describe takes place through faith. The Roman Catholic historian Erwin Iserloh noted in turn that Luther's view of mysticism can be described as a "Christ mysticism."[19] Through faith, Christ becomes present in every believer. That presence can be characterized as a mystical union.

Christian Braw is one of the scholars who have investigated the inheritance from mysticism in Martin Luther's works. He stresses that Luther emphasizes the importance of the outward Word more than the mystics by whom he has been influenced do. If Luther were to be asked how a person is united with God, his answer would be that it takes place through the Word and through faith. Therefore, in the case of Luther, we can speak of a mysticism of the Word of God or a mysticism of faith. Braw also points out that Luther personalizes mysticism and gives it a clearly Christocentric force. All of Luther's theology focuses on a person—the person of Jesus Christ. He is the Word of God, and when a person is united with him through faith, it means, according to Luther, that "Christ becomes me, and I become Christ." Braw underlines that the mystical union with Christ through faith characterizes all Christians, not just a few. Luther thinks that Christ really becomes present in the Christian person through faith. Christ leads the person and gives them strength to do good from the center of their personality, their heart. Christ sanctifies

---

17. Cf. Hoffman, *Hjärtats teologi*, 98–101 and Hoffman, *Hjärtats teologi*, 151–55.
18. Hägglund, *De homine*; see particularly 94.
19. Iserloh, "Luther und die Mystik," see especially 61, 67.

people. He makes them divine. He transforms a person from within and makes it possible for that person to bear good fruit. The good deeds that that transformation inspires are nothing for which mere mortals can take any credit. It is "God in you" or *Christus mysticus* who guides you, so that you can and want to do what is good.[20]

Christian Braw's description of Luther's view of mysticism is based on his work in the field of the history of ideas. Braw compares views that Luther has expressed with thoughts that occur in the mystical writings and traditions that influenced Luther. The Danish theologian Else Marie Wiberg Pedersen works in a similar way when she compares Luther's theology with the teaching of Bernhard of Clairvaux.[21] Like Bernhard, Luther uses the metaphors of bridal mysticism when he describes the union of people with Christ through faith.

Teresa of Avila is the most prominent bride-mystic of the Christian tradition. To illuminate how she can help us to deal with the secularization from within—and maybe the secularization from without as well—I want to investigate how her presentation of a person's friendship with Jesus Christ relates to Luther's understanding of how a person is justified by trusting faith in Jesus Christ. I am not the only one who finds such a comparison interesting. A few years ago, the then Bishop of the Roman Catholic Diocese of Stockholm, now Cardinal Anders Arborelius, wrote:

> During the year 2015 Teresa of Avila—or rather, Teresa of Jesus, which is her official name, both as a Carmelite nun and as a Doctor of the Church—will be celebrated, studied and analyzed all over the Catholic world. During the year 2017, the memory of the Reformation by Martin Luther will be celebrated, studied, and analyzed all over the Lutheran world. It would be extremely interesting to make some kind of comparison between Teresa and Luther. It would be very well worth undertaking an ecumenical venture with this focus, which could illuminate both differences and similarities with regard to theology and spirituality between this woman and this man, who even today are so important for so many people.[22]

We know that Martin Luther and Teresa of Avila did not read each other's writings. We also know that they lived and worked far away from

---

20. Braw, *Mystikens arv hos Martin Luther*, 22, 98, 108, 145, 148–49, 160, 170, 173–74.

21. See, for example, Wiberg Pedersen, "This Is not About Sex?"

22. Arborelius, "Förord" in *Andliga redogörelser och Själens rop till Gud*, 11.

each other in different cultural environments: he lived north of the Alps and the Pyrenees, while she was south of these mountain ranges. However, they both strove to reform the same Church. Today they are role models who inspire people from different denominations. The question is how they can help us to engage in receptive ecumenism.

PERFUMES AND DECORATIVE CUSHIONS

According to her father's notes, Teresa de Cepeda y Ahumada was born at about five o'clock in the morning of the twenty-eighth day of March 1515.[23] She entered this world as part of a Spanish aristocratic family who owned a house in Avila as well as a rural property at Gottarrendura. Teresa's father, Alonso Sánchez de Cepeda, was a widower and father of two children when he met Teresa's mother, Beatriz Dávila y Ahumada. The couple had ten children together. In her autobiography, Teresa says that there were three sisters and nine brothers. The oldest child, Maria, was nine years older than Teresa, while the youngest child, Juana, was thirteen years younger than Teresa. Teresa herself was in the middle of the siblings. Rodrigo, who was a few years older than Teresa, and Lorenzo, who was a few years younger than her, became her faithful supporters while they were growing up.

In her autobiography, Teresa recalls a happy childhood. Her father was an honorable man who showed a great care for poor people and for his servants. Since he loved books, the family had a large library, which even included writings in the local language of Castilian. That means that the children had the opportunity to learn to read. Teresa's mother was gentle and very intelligent. She taught her children to pray and to make their devotions to the Virgin Mary and the saints. Teresa and Rodrigo liked to read the lives of the saints. They were fascinated by the stories of the martyrs and reflected on what they should do to participate in the heavenly glories that they had read about. They agreed that the best way would be to go to "the Land of the Moors," an area under Muslim rule, in order to be decapitated. On their way there they would beg for alms. The two children set off, but just outside the walls of Avila a relative caught up with them and brought them back home.

---

23. With regard to the life of Teresa, my information comes from Álvarez and from Teresa's autobiography: Teresa of Avila, *Book of Her Life*. I provide page references when using direct quotations.

Following that failed attempt to become martyrs, Teresa and Rodrigo decided to become hermits instead. They built hermitages in a garden on the family's property, "piling up some little stones which afterward would quickly fall down again. And so in nothing could we find remedy for our desire."[24] Teresa did not play only with her brothers while she was growing up; sometimes she was together with other little girls, and then they sometimes played at being nuns in a convent.[25]

Teresa's mother died when Teresa was thirteen years old. Like Thérèse of the Child Jesus, she then turned to the Virgin Mary, whom she asked to become her mother. She notes that, "although I did this in simplicity it helped me. For I have found favor with this sovereign Virgin in everything I have asked of her, and in the end she has drawn me to herself."[26]

Teresa's biological mother enjoyed reading novels about knights and, following her death, Teresa began to enjoy the same kind of literature. She was consumed by the stories of beautiful virgins and honorable men, and she was continually on the look-out for a new book. Her reading had to take place in secret, however, since her father did not approve of her being influenced by that kind of literature. Afterwards Teresa said that she "didn't think it was wrong to waste many hours of the day and night in such a useless practice." She also had other memories from her teenage years. Teresa recalls, "I began to dress in finery and to desire to please and to look pretty, taking great care of my hands and hair and about perfumes and all the empty things in which one can indulge, and which were many, for I was very vain."[27]

Teresa spent a lot of time with male cousins of the same age. "[W]e always went about together," she tells us. "They liked me very much" and "I engaged in conversations with them about all the things that pleased them." She also had a relative of the same age who became her best friend in their early teens. "She was so frivolous that my mother tried very hard to keep her from coming to our home." Teresa stresses that, for her own part, she had no inclination to take any wrong turns. What she wanted was relaxation and nice company.[28]

---

24. Teresa of Avila, *Book of Her Life*, 55 (1:5).
25. Teresa of Avila, *Book of Her Life*, 56 (1:6).
26. Teresa of Avila, *Book of Her Life*, 56 (1:7).
27. Teresa of Avila, *Book of Her Life*, 56–57 (2:1, 2:2).
28. Teresa of Avila, *Book of Her Life*, 57–59 (2:2, 2:3, 2:6).

Teresa says that her father had an immeasurably great love for her. She was the apple of his eye. He made sure that she would attend the College of Santa Maria de Gracia, where young aristocratic ladies lived as boarders and were educated under the leadership of Augustinian nuns. Teresa stayed with the Augustinian nuns for a year and a half, and here her fascination with what is eternal was again aroused. The move to the convent boarding school meant that Teresa had not to be at home on her own, without a mother and subject to the risks that "bad company" could bring. Many years later Teresa says that she was unhappy in the convent for the first eight days, but that after that she felt much more at ease. She notes that "[a]ll were very pleased with me, for the Lord gave me the grace to be pleasing wherever I went, and so I was much loved. And although at that time I was strongly against my becoming a nun, it made me happy to see such good nuns, for there were many good ones in that house."[29]

Toward the end of her stay with the Augustinian nuns, Teresa began to reflect seriously on the question whether God wanted her to become a nun, even though she herself did not want that. She did not want to enter the Augustinian Order (to which, incidentally, Luther belonged) since the life of the Augustinian nuns seemed to her to be excessive. Having reflected, spoken with wise people, and asked God for guidance, Teresa eventually concluded that she wanted to enter the Convent of the Carmelite Sisters at Avila, where a friend of hers was a nun. Teresa recalls how the longings of her childhood now appeared in a new light. She writes, "I began to understand the truth I knew in childhood (the nothingness of all things, the vanity of the world, and how it would soon come to an end) ... And although my will did not completely incline to being a nun, I saw that the religious life was the best and safest state, and so little by little I decided to force myself to accept it." Many years later Teresa noted that "in this business of choosing a state, it seems to me I was moved more by servile fear than by love."[30] However, during her 47 years of life in the convent, her driving force changed.

After reading a pastoral letter by Jerome, Teresa plucked up the courage to tell her father that she wanted to become a nun. He was not happy. "So great was his love for me that in no way was I able to obtain his permission," Teresa recalls, "or achieve anything through persons I

---

29. Teresa of Avila, *Book of Her Life*, 60 (2:8).
30. Teresa of Avila, *Book of Her Life*, 63 (3:5, 3:6).

asked to intercede for me. The most we could get from him was that after his death I could do whatever I wanted."[31] It all ended when the then twenty-year-old Teresa—who was a decisive person—left her parental home and entered the Convent of the Carmelite nuns at Avila. This time she managed to escape together with her Brother Antonio, who wanted to become a monk. Antonio soon moved back home again; but Teresa remained in the Convent of the Incarnation. By the time she began her novitiate, her father had consented. He committed himself to make sure that in the convent she had a bed complete with a duvet and some decorative cushions, a bedspread, a white blanket, a thick woolen blanket, six thin linen sheets, six pillows, two mattresses, a mat, two small cushions, a bed of ropes, clothes, and nuns' habits made of fine cloth that could be used for everyday wear. He also committed himself to make sure that she had three petticoats—one scarlet, one white, and one from Palencia—and two mantles—one scarlet and one homespun. And besides that, he also promised to provide her with a calf's skin, toilet articles, shirts, shoes, and books.[32]

As a nun, Teresa de Cepeda y Ahumada was called Teresa of Jesus. She experienced several reformatory discoveries or experiences of conversion that led her to abandon her piles of cushions in order to sleep on a hard bed of straw, just like Luther did in the monastery at Erfurt. Luther, however, travelled in the opposite direction: he gave up the bed of straw in favor of a pleasurable family life with Katharina von Bora. In that sense their reformatory discoveries went in completely opposite directions.

TERESA'S REFORMATORY DISCOVERY

The scholar and Carmelite Tomás Álvares stresses that, in the 1530s, Avila was "a city deprived of young men. The magic and allure of the American adventure continued to seize hold of the best of the young men of the city."[33] Maybe that contributed to the relatively high number of women in convents at that time. When Teresa entered the Convent of the Incarnation, almost a hundred nuns lived there. That number would soon double. The historian Jodi Bilinkoff describes the considerable class

---

31. Teresa of Avila, *Book of Her Life*, 63 (3:7).
32. The list is reported in Álvarez, *Teresa av Avila*, 37.
33. Álvarez, *Teresa av Avila*, 30.

differences that existed in the convent.[34] Teresa and other Sisters who came from high-ranking families had little flats with their own kitchens. A number of relatives of Teresa, including her youngest sister Juana, periodically lived with her in the convent. Other nuns came to visit Teresa's rooms. The Sisters could also leave the convent in order to take part in the social life of Avila and, as the need arose, they might reside outside the convent for longer periods.

Teresa was happy with life in the Convent of the Incarnation. She recalls that she found pleasure in everything that belonged to the religious life. "[I]t is true," she wrote, "that sometimes while sweeping, during the hours I used to spend in self-indulgence and self-adornment, I realized that I was free of all that and experienced a new joy which amazed me. And I could not understand where it came from."[35] A couple of years after her entrance into the Convent, everything changed when Teresa was affected by a serious illness. She fainted with increasing frequency and experienced frightening heart pains and many other illnesses. Care was arranged for her in the mountainous areas surrounding Avila, but the treatment did not do any good. Teresa recalls:

> After two months, because of the potent medicines, my life was almost at an end. The severity of the heart pains, which I went to have cured, was more acute. For sometimes it seemed that sharp teeth were biting into me, so much so that it was feared I had rabies. With the continuous fever and the great lack of strength . . . , I was so shriveled and wasted away (because for almost a month they gave me a daily purge) that my nerves began to shrink causing such unbearable pains that I found no rest either by day or by night—a very deep sadness.[36]

Teresa's father made sure that the treatment in the mountains stopped. He took her to a doctor who noted that her condition was hopeless. Teresa suffered terribly from the contraction of all her nerves at the same time. Having had a severe paroxysm, she was completely unconscious for almost four days. Her relatives kept watch by what they thought was her deathbed. Teresa received the anointing of the sick, and the creed was read to her continuously. On one occasion it was even thought that she was dead, but the Lord was pleased to recall her to consciousness.

---

34. Here I follow Bilinkoff, *Avila of Saint Teresa*, 112–16.
35. Teresa of Avila, *Book of Her Life*, 64 (4:2).
36. Teresa of Avila, *Book of Her Life*, 74 (5:7).

With her tongue bitten to pieces, and unable to move any part of her body except a finger, Teresa returned to the Convent of the Incarnation at Avila, carried there in a sheet.

For eight months, the body of this twenty-four-year-old Carmelite Sister was "worse than dead... The state of my weakness was indescribable, for I was then only bones."[37] Teresa's condition gradually improved, but she was paralyzed for almost three years. "When I began to go about on hands and knees, I praised God," she recalls.[38] During her convalescence, Teresa spent much time in prayer and silence. She went to confession and received communion increasingly often, and she says that during that time she commended herself to the care of the honorable St. Joseph.[39]

Eventually, Teresa recovered, and she could leave the infirmary and participate in convent life again. Her seven years of illness, however, had left their mark. Tomás Álvares describes in this way the struggle that Teresa now had to endure:

> What she read [during her period of illness], the hours spent on her own in stillness and her youthful enthusiasm had brought her into the world of prayer. The Castile and Andalusia, yes, the whole of Spain, lived in an age when interest in prayer was very highly valued. The call to "interior Christianity", to personal "prayer and meditation," was the yeast that permeated all religious groups and a movement that stretched across all strata of society... This seed took root in Teresa's soul, with a brilliant result to start with... But following the initial flame, her soul was covered over by ashes. The difficulties mounted. ... Finally, she succumbed. She gave up prayer and lost her joy in her life as a nun—yes, it went as far as resignation, and she was content to live "like most of them,"—that is, as one among those almost two hundred who populated the convent. That was a defeat. A kind of death.[40]

Teresa recalls that she certainly pulled herself together and resumed her prayers, but without any drop of devotion. For ten years she was in the captivity of the soul. She felt she was crucified between heaven and earth, unable to move in one direction or the other. This desert walk was

---

37. Teresa of Avila, *Book of Her Life*, 77 (6:2).
38. Teresa of Avila, *Book of Her Life*, 77 (6:2).
39. Teresa of Avila, *Book of Her Life*, 79 (6:6).
40. Álvarez, *Teresa av Avila*, 42–43 (translated by Gerd Swensson).

completed by the process of events that are usually described as Teresa of Avila's definite conversion. It is also possible to name what happened as Teresa's reformatory discovery. Teresa recalls:

> It happened to me that one day entering the oratory I saw a statue they had borrowed for a certain feast to be celebrated in the house. It represented the much wounded Christ and was very devotional so that beholding it I was utterly distressed in seeing Him that way, for it well represented what He suffered for us. I felt so keenly aware of how poorly I thanked Him for those wounds that, it seems to me, my heart broke. Beseeching Him to strengthen me once and for all that I might not offend Him, I threw myself down before Him with the greatest outpouring of tears.[41]

This breakthrough in the chapel took place in 1554, when Teresa was in her 40s; but Tomás Álvarez underlines that Teresa's definitive conversion should not be limited to this single occasion.[42] Just as in the case of Luther, Teresa's reformatory discovery was a process that lasted for many years. Soon after the incident in the chapel, Teresa read about the conversion of St. Augustine, in which he describes how God's voice reached him in a very clear way. Teresa also speaks of divine messages that had life-changing importance.

The first time that Teresa heard Jesus speak to her in a particularly remarkable way, she was reciting a hymn. She says that "while saying it, a rapture came upon me so suddenly that it almost carried me out of myself." Then she heard the Lord speak. "This experience terrified me because the movement of the soul was powerful and these words were spoken deep within the spirit."[43] During the years that followed, Teresa received many auditions (revelations of hearing) and visions (revelations of images). The extra-ordinary experiences that affected Teresa have led philosophers of religion—and many other people as well—to regard her as an unusually interesting mystic.

TERESA OF JESUS AND MYSTICISM

Reading Teresa's descriptions of her auditions and visions, it is hard to avoid being struck by the warmth of the relationship between her and

---

41. Teresa of Avila, *Book of Her Life*, 100–101 (9:1).
42. Álvarez, *Teresa av Avila*, 44.
43. Teresa of Avila, *Book of Her Life*, 211 (24:5).

Jesus. Teresa is sometimes scared, sometimes irresolute in view of the unusual experiences that she has. Her anxiety increases when she has to encounter confessors and Church authorities who think she is possessed by the devil. When she is subjected to tests by people who simply do not understand, Jesus comes to her aid. He comforts her and encourages her. He also has the good sense to reveal himself to her one bit at a time. In that way he avoids scaring the shaken-up Carmelite nun out of her wits. Teresa describes her first visions of Jesus in the following way:

> This vision caused me great fear; any supernatural favor the Lord grants me frightens me at first, when it is new. After a few days I saw also that divine face which it seems left me completely absorbed . . . I couldn't understand why the Lord showed Himself to me in this way, little by little, until later I understood that His Majesty was leading me in accordance with my natural weakness . . . One feast day of St. Paul, while I was at Mass, this most sacred humanity in its risen form was represented to me completely, as it is in paintings, with such wonderful beauty and majesty.[44]

In Teresa's day, people operated according to another categorization of religious experiences than that which Richard Swinburne has developed.[45] It was assumed that there were auditions and visions of three different kinds. First of all, a person might have corporeal visions or auditions, in which the person sees Jesus with their earthly eyes or hears him speak in the same way that they hear other people speak. Second, a person might have imaginative visions or auditions, in which they see Jesus with "the eyes of the spirit" or in their imagination, and they hear him speak with "the ears of the spirit" or the imagination, as if the soul had been given other ears by which to hear. Third, a person might have intellectual visions or auditions, in which they experience the presence of Christ without seeing any person and hear him speak a heavenly language without articulated words.

There was a ranking order to evaluate the different types of visions and auditions. In Teresa's day, intellectual visions or auditions were considered to be closer to perfect than imaginative ones. In turn, imaginative visions and auditions were considered more important than corporeal ones. Teresa noted that she had never had any corporeal visions or

---

44. Teresa of Avila, *Book of Her Life*, 237–38 (28:1, 28:3).
45. Cf. Teresa of Avila, *Book of Her Life*, 230–31 (27:8).

auditions: her visions and auditions usually belonged to the imaginative category.[46] In her autobiography she describes an intellectual vision that preceded her first imaginative visions:

> Being in prayer on the feast day of the glorious St. Peter, I saw or, to put it better, I felt Christ beside me; I saw nothing with my bodily eyes or with my soul, but it seemed to me that Christ was at my side. I saw that it was He, in my opinion, who was speaking to me. Since I was completely unaware that there could be a vision like this one, it greatly frightened me in the beginning; I did nothing but weep. However, by speaking one word alone to assure me, the Lord left me feeling as I usually did: quiet, favored, and without any fear. It seemed to me that Jesus Christ was always present at my side; but since this wasn't an imaginative vision, I didn't see any form. Yet I felt very clearly that He was always present at my right side and that He was the witness of everything I did. At no time in which I was a little recollected, or not greatly distracted, was I able to ignore that He was present at my side.[47]

Teresa's visions and auditions made her think. She reflected on what she could do for God, and she concluded that she would follow very seriously the vocation to the religious life that she had received. She began to think that life in the Convent of the Incarnation was far too comfortable. She and a few other nuns talked about how a monastic life that better reflected the original rule of the Carmelite Order might be shaped. One day, when Teresa had just received Communion, Christ told her to found a new convent to be called the Convent of St. Joseph. Teresa says that she suffered greatly as a result of that exhortation, because she could imagine what hardships that assignment might bring her. She thought that a great burden had been laid on her shoulders and, when she thought of the alarming state of the Church, she was gripped by doubts. However, Jesus did not give in. He returned with his exhortation and, following various negotiations within the ecclesiastical power system and a number of significant financial investigations, it was decided that the Convent of St. Joseph should be established at Avila.

---

46. Teresa of Avila, *Book of Her Life*, 238 (28:4).
47. Teresa of Avila, *Book of Her Life*, 228 (27:2).

LOVE AT THE HEART OF THE CHURCH

Teresa bought a few dilapidated buildings on the outskirts of Avila and engaged builders to restore them. She bought a church bell at half price because it had a hole in it. She received the money from her bother Lorenzo, who in their childhood had been prepared to travel to the Land of the Moors to be beheaded. The Convent of St. Joseph, the first reformed convent of the Carmelite Order, was dedicated in August 1562. Teresa moved there together with twelve nuns from the Convent of the Incarnation and she became the first prioress of the new convent.

The Sisters who accompanied Teresa were "a small group of poor but determined girls."[48] That was no coincidence. That was how Teresa wanted it. In the new convent they would live in radical simplicity, like the hermits on Mount Carmel. There would be no class differences among them. Everyone would help with the work that needed to be done, and they would all gather daily for the liturgical offices of prayer. They would also gather twice daily for an hour at a time for inward prayer together, and they would have two hours' shared recreation. Life in the convent was to be a common life with an eremitical character. There would be around twelve Sisters living in the convent at any time. Each Sister would have her own cell with a wooden plank bed, devotional pictures on the walls, and a jug of water so that she could wash in the morning. Otherwise, she would have no possessions. The community, on the other hand, would have two assets of importance for the life of the Sisters: a library of devotional literature, and a beautiful garden.

When Thérèse of the Child Jesus entered the Carmelite Convent at Lisieux just over three hundred years later, she joined a community life that was ordered in accordance with Teresa of Avila's instructions and vision. For Thérèse of the Child Jesus, Teresa of Jesus was an example. She was "the Great Teresa," while Thérèse remained "the Little Teresa." In their conversations, Thérèse and her Sisters often made connections with the thoughts and parables found in Teresa's writings and, like Teresa, Thérèse was encouraged to write autobiographical notes that described the history of her soul. In a text that Thérèse wrote to her sister Marie, who in the religious life was called Sister Marie of the Sacred Heart, she eloquently summarized a discovery that Teresa had also made: both of them wanted to be "everything" in the Church, and they both concluded

---

48. Álvarez, *Teresa av Avila*, 57.

that they could be that as Carmelite nuns. Thérèse explained her longing and her insight in the following way:

> To be Your *Spouse*, to be a *Carmelite*, and by my union with You to be the *Mother* of souls, should not this suffice me? And yet it is not so. No doubt, these three privileges sum up my true *vocation: Carmelite, Spouse, Mother,* and yet I feel within me other *vocations.* I feel the *vocation* of the WARRIOR, THE PRIEST, THE APOSTLE, THE DOCTOR, THE MARTYR. Finally, I feel the need and desire of carrying out the most heroic deeds for *You, O Jesus.* I feel within my soul the courage of the *Crusader,* the *Papal Guard*, and I would want to die on the field of battle in defence of the Church . . . O Jesus, my Love, my Life, how can I combine these contrasts? How can I realize the desires of my poor *little soul*?[49]

Thérèse meditated on St. Paul the apostle's description of the Church as the body of Christ.[50] The body has many different members, all of which are needed for the body to function. The eye cannot say to the hand that the hand is not needed. The foot should not despair about not being a knee. Each member of the body has its own function to fulfill. St. Paul's description of the Church moves on to the song in praise of love that we often read at marriage services in the Church of Sweden.[51] Thérèse recalls how her meditation on the Bible led her to find her vocation and her place within the Church. She wrote:

> *Charity* gave me the key to my *vocation.* I understood that if the Church had a body composed of different members, the most necessary and most noble of all could not be lacking to it, and so I understood that the Church *had a Heart and that this Heart* was BURNING WITH LOVE. *I understood it was Love alone* that made the Church's members act, that if *Love* ever became extinct, apostles would not preach the Gospel and martyrs would not shed their blood. I understood that LOVE COMPRISED ALL VOCATIONS, THAT LOVE WAS EVERYTHING, THAT IT EMBRACED ALL TIMES AND PLACES . . . IN A WORD, THAT IT WAS ETERNAL!

---

49. Letter to Sister Marie of the Sacred Heart, September 8, 1896. Thérèse of Lisieux, *Story of a Soul*, 192.

50. Cf. 1 Cor 12:12–31.

51. 1 Cor 13.

Then, in the excess of my delirious joy, I cried out: O Jesus, my Love ... my *vocation,* at last I have found it ... MY VOCATION IS LOVE!

Yes, I have found my place in the Church and it is You, O my God, who have given me this place; in the heart of the Church, my Mother, I shall be *Love.* Thus I shall be everything, and thus my dream will be realized.[52]

During the first period in the reformed Convent of St. Joseph at Avila, it dawned on Teresa of Jesus that the reason why she and her Sisters locked themselves up within the strict enclosure was not only because they wanted to live like hermits.[53] You could say that she realized that the Sisters had been given an assignment to be love in the fragmented heart of the Church. The Sisters should contribute to arousing and keeping aflame in the Church the love for Christ and the love for fellow human beings. Like Thérèse of the Child Jesus, Teresa assumed that everything in the Church was held in common—the hardships and the intercessions. She was deeply distressed by the ravages of the Lutherans. Teresa recalled that she had heard talk about the "the havoc the Lutherans had caused" on the other side of the mountain ranges "and how much this miserable sect was growing." "What is the matter with Christians nowadays?" she asked herself. "[H]elp your Church," she beseeched God. "Don't allow any more harm to come to Christianity, Lord. Give light now to these darknesses."[54]

An extensive reformatory program emerged from Teresa's dialog with Jesus and her conversations with her colleagues and her superiors. Teresa was given the task of founding one more convent for Carmelite nuns who wanted to live in accordance with the original ideals of the order. In *The book of her foundations,* she speaks about the seventeen convents for Carmelite nuns in Spain that she founded. This book is probably the most entertaining work that you can find on the library shelves reserved for so-called devotional literature. Teresa's sense of humor permeates her description of her everyday life as a reformer in the sixteenth century. The book is full of amusing episodes that are recorded in such a lively way that the mire on the muddy roads almost oozes through the covers. I would think that anyone who has experience of parish life

---

52. Letter to Sister Marie of the Sacred Heart, September 8, 1896. Thérèse of Lisieux, *Story of a Soul,* 194.

53. Cf. Álvarez, *Teresa av Avila,* 59–63.

54. Teresa of Avila, *Way of Perfection,* 41–42, 52 (1:2, 1:3, 3:9).

might recognize at least some of the activities and challenges that filled Teresa's days. She spent her time on budget work, on ordering supplies, on property management, and in worship. She negotiated with reluctant secular authorities who were very skeptical of the religious activity that she wanted to undertake. She received strange directives from higher up in the Church hierarchy to which she needed to relate in a creative way. Within the convents, there arose workplace conflicts that needed to be resolved. In the evenings and at night she wrote letters, books, and biblical discourses. She often suffered from a lack of time, and she did not always find time for her prayers. Her confessors seemed to worry that she might be overworked and/or undernourished, and as penance she was ordered to eat and sleep properly. Her Sisters could see how Jesus gave her superhuman powers.

Higher up in the ecclesiastical hierarchy of power, not everyone was as fascinated with Teresa of Avila's advances as her Sisters and confessors were. The Papal Nuncio, Felipe Sega, the pope's man in Spain, was very upset about "this restless, wandering woman, disobedient and obstinate who, under the cover of devotion, dreams up unsound teaching, roams around outside the enclosure at variance with the Tridentine Council and the Order of the Prelates, and who even presumes to teach as a master in conflict with what St. Paul has taught when he ordered that women should not teach."[55] Teresa talked with Jesus about that biblical text and the objections that other people besides the Nuncio had bought up in support of the view that she should keep silent. Jesus helped Teresa out of her predicament. He answered her, "Tell them they shouldn't follow just one part of Scripture but that they should look at other parts, and ask them if they can by chance tie my hands."[56] Strengthened by the words of Jesus, Teresa continued her work of reformation.

REFORMING WOMEN

Unlike Martin Luther and many of the reformatory models we highlight in the Church of Sweden, Teresa of Jesus was a woman. That meant that she sometimes encountered challenges and questionings that male reformers hardly ever had to face. The Carmelite Sisters in the reformed Convents also met with occasional opposition. Their lifestyle was questioned by those who thought that women ought to live differently.

55. Felipe Sega, quoted in Álvarez, *Teresa av Avila*, 72.
56. Teresa of Avila, *Spiritual Testimonies*, 393 (section 15).

Teresa's writings include several exhortations that her Sisters and other women should not lose heart. Instead, with boldness and "holy daring," nuns should strive for "the greater service of the Lord in His favor" like "strong men" during war (or like purposeful mountaineers). Then the Lord would make them so strong that they will astonish men.[57] We should not listen to those who say that women do best by keeping to their sewing: "they don't need these delicacies," since the ordinary oral prayers such as "the Our Father and the Hail Mary are sufficient."[58] Jesus did not despise women when he was among us in the world, nor does he do so now when he is leading his Church.[59] Learned men should therefore not be surprised or say that it is impossible that "a useless woman like me" has been given power to do such great works in the service of God, or that "the Lord makes a little old woman wiser, perhaps, in this science than he is, even though he is a very learned man."[60]

Teresa exhorts the Sisters to rejoice that they are free of the limitations that marriage would mean for them. God has freed them "from being subject to a man who is often the death of them and who could also be, God forbid, the death of their souls."[61] In one place Teresa likened marriage to slavery for a woman. She wrote: "They say that for a woman to be a good wife towards her husband she must be sad when he is sad, and joyful when he is joyful, even though she may not be so. (See what subjection you have been freed from, Sisters!)"[62]

In the Protestant Reformation movements that gained ground north of the Alps and the Pyrenees, the monastic life and marriage were not seen in the same way as Teresa of Avila viewed them. Martin Luther stopped wearing the habit of the Augustinian Brothers and married Katharina von Bora. Katharina had grown up with nuns ever since she had been placed in a Cistercian convent at the age of five. Luther helped her and some other nuns to run away from the monastic life; and then he tried to find suitable men whom they could marry. It was forbidden for anyone who had already made their solemn profession to leave their monastery or convent, and it was also a criminal offence to assist run-away nuns. So

57. Teresa of Avila, *Way of Perfection*, 47–48, 69–70, 98 (3:1, 7:8, 16:12).
58. Teresa of Avila, *Way of Perfection*, 118 (21:2).
59. Teresa of Avila, *Way of Perfection*, 50 (3:7).
60. Teresa of Avila, *Foundations*, 245 (27:11) and Teresa of Avila, *Book of Her Life*, 298 (34:12).
61. Teresa of Avila, *Foundations*, 306 (31:46).
62. Teresa of Avila, *Way of Perfection*, 134 (26:4).

not many people were willing to help women who left their convents as a result of the Protestant Reformation. However, Luther, who had reflected a great deal on the opportunities and limitations of monastic life, supported the former nuns' attempts to start a new life outside the walls of the convent.

The Luther scholar Bernhard Lohse stresses that, for a long time, Luther viewed the monastic life as one vocation among others.[63] God needs farmers and shoemakers as well as priests and nuns. The foot should not say to the hand that the hand is not needed in the Church of Christ. But Luther took the view that monastic vows must be voluntary, since eternally binding vows lack biblical warrant and militate against the freedom of faith. It should be possible to leave the monastery or convent if that form of life does not suit your personality. He also stressed that nuns and monks do not live a life that is more pleasing in the eyes of God than how other people live. You do not become more righteous or holy just because you choose to live in poverty, chastity, and obedience. In line with the criticism that Luther directed toward the pilgrimage movement, he warned against justification by works in the monastic life, and stressed that living in a monastery or convent could mean that the monk or nun neglects the love of neighbor that God commands.

The church historian Kirsi Stjerna has investigated how Luther's views on the monastic life affected the conditions of women in the sixteenth century. Both monks and nuns left their monasteries and convents because they were impressed by Luther's teaching about justification by grace through trusting faith in Jesus Christ. Former monks could become priests, but former nuns did not have that opportunity. Some of them became clergy wives, just like Katharina von Bora. Others made a life for themselves outside the convent walls. In the past, their life's work had been to study and to worship. Stjerna stresses that, when marriage was more highly valued as the central form of life for all people, it led to the "domestication" of women's activities: they should look after the home and the children. Developments also led to the perception that unmarried women were an anomaly and a potential threat to the social order. An unmarried woman was considered to be available on the marriage market, whether or not she wanted to marry, and it was easy to suspect her of indecent activities—or to seek to lure her into such behavior.[64]

---

63. The following is based on Lohse, *Martin Luther's Theology*, 137–43.

64. Stjerna, *Women and the Reformation*, 23, 31, 33–35, 38.

Stjerna stresses that not all women felt liberated by the dismantling of the monastic life that the Protestant Reformation brought. She describes how Marie Dentière was received when she sought to convince Franciscan Sisters to leave their convent.[65] Dentière was a former Augustinian nun who became a leading reformer in Geneva. She was the wife of a priest and an expounder of the Bible who preached publicly, which was something that women did not normally do at that time. Dentière visited the Sisters of St. Clare in Geneva and tried to persuade them to leave the religious life behind. She produced a good advertisement for marriage by telling them about her five children. She described how happy the Sisters might become if they could have "a handsome husband" at their side. But the Sisters were not convinced by Dentière's argument. Rather, they spit and screamed at her, and banged the convent porch shut. Jeanne de Jussie, the Sister who particularly polemicized against Marie Dentière, thought that it implied a restriction on women's rights to deprive them of the possibility of choosing the religious life. Just like Teresa of Jesus, she viewed marriage as captivity, while she saw the religious life as a sought-after freedom.

Jeanne de Jussie's argument is in line with the answer that the alpinist Alison Hargreaves gave when she was asked how it had come about that she had decided to ascend K2, even though there were critics who thought that she ought to stay at home with her family. Hargreaves gave a concise answer: that it is a woman's right to make her own decisions.

CHRIST'S REAL PRESENCE IN THE EUCHARIST

When Teresa worried about the advance of the Lutherans, the reason was not the dismantling of the monastic life. She had a far more pressing problem that she needed to deal with. There was a risk that the Calvinist Huguenots, whom Teresa mistakenly called "Lutherans," might come and steal the Blessed Sacrament before which the Sisters prayed in their chapel.[66] Some Protestants wanted to convince others forcibly that there was nothing special about the consecrated host by showing that they treated it as any other kind of bread. They thought that Christ was symbolically present in the bread when the Eucharist was celebrated, but that, when the service ended, the bread was again just ordinary bread.

---

65. I follow Stjerna, *Women and the Reformation*, chapter 9.

66. The bread and wine over which the priest has spoken the words of institution of Holy Communion are described as consecrated.

Teresa of Avila and Martin Luther thought differently. Teresa believed that Christ was not only tangibly present in her visions and auditions alone: he was also quite specifically present in the consecrated host, since that bread is the body of Christ. Therefore, when Teresa founded new convents, she always began by letting Jesus move into the convent by placing the blessed sacrament in the chapel. In connection with the dedication of the Convent of St. Joseph at Medina del Campo, she had to suffer a few dreadful days and nights because of the "Lutherans" (who were actually Huguenots, who held a purely symbolic view of the Eucharist). The house that had been purchased for the Sisters was so dilapidated that Teresa did not know what to do; but "[i]t pleased the Lord, who wanted the place [the Convent] to be prepared immediately." Floors were swept, tapestries arranged, some old nails found, and the bell hung up, and everyone "worked so quickly that when dawn came the altar was set up." Then Mass was celebrated, and the Most Holy Sacrament was put in place.[67] Teresa continues:

> Up to this point I was very happy because for me it is the greatest consolation to see one church more where the Blessed Sacrament is preserved. But my happiness did not last long. For when Mass was finished I went to look a little bit through a window at the courtyard, and I saw that all the walls in some places had fallen to the ground and that many days would be required to repair them. Oh, God help me! When I saw His Majesty [in the form of the Blessed Sacrament] placed in the street, at a time so dangerous, on account of those Lutherans, as this time in which we now live, what anguish came to my heart! . . . This made me suffer through very painful nights and days. Even though I put some men in charge of always keeping watch over the Blessed Sacrament, I was worried that they might fall asleep. So I arose during the night to watch it through a window, for the moon was very bright and I could easily see it . . . And His Majesty, as one who never tires of humiliating Himself for us, didn't seem to want to leave it.[68]

A couple of decades earlier, Martin Luther had had similar problems with certain priests who, in his view, treated the consecrated host in the wrong way.[69] At Friesnietz, a priest by the name of Adam Besserer had

---

67. Teresa of Avila, *Foundations*, 109 (3:8–9).
68. Teresa of Avila, *Foundations*, 109–111 (3:10, 3:13).
69. The following paragraph is based on Jolkkonen, "Eucharist," 129–32.

suffered a mishap. All who wished to receive communion had to let the priest know this in advance. Besserer therefore knew exactly how many wafers should be put out to be consecrated. He consecrated the correct number; but, when he distributed the body of Christ, he found that he was one host short. He solved the problem by taking a new (unconsecrated) wafer from the wafer box and distributing that instead. Later, however, he found the consecrated host, and put it back among the wafers in the box that had not been consecrated. When Luther and the other reformers at Wittenberg heard about what had happened, they made sure that Besserer was defrocked because he had shown by his action that he did not believe that Christ was really present in the consecrated host.

Another priest, Wolferinus at Eisleben, was not defrocked, but received a serious reprimand from Luther because Wolferinus believed that the bread and wine that was used during Mass (and thus was consecrated) ceased to be the body and blood of Christ at the end of the service, and that it could be dealt with just like any bread and wine. Wolferinus therefore replaced the surplus (consecrated) hosts in the box where wafers that had not been used for Mass were kept. Luther thought that this was unacceptable, since neither Wolferinus nor anyone else could know whether, or when, Christ ceased to be present in the consecrated host. Wolferinus and others, Luther argued, ought to follow the practice at Wittenberg and consume any leftover bread and wine. In that way people could receive bread and wine in confident faith that Christ would unite himself with them.

It has often been emphasized that Luther rejected the so-called doctrine of transubstantiation. That doctrine is a philosophical answer to the question of *how* Christ is present in the consecrated bread and wine. Luther—and those who shared his view of the Eucharist—believed that we should not try to explain *how* Christ is present in the bread and the wine of the Eucharist, nor waste any energy on unnecessary discussion about *when* he might leave the consecrated bread and wine. We should rather believe *that* he really is present there, and help other people to do the same.

Luther's understanding of the Eucharist has been described as a doctrine of consubstantiation. He himself did not use that concept, but it still has some value as an explanation. Luther believed that the consecrated Eucharistic bread is simultaneously bread (with all the substance of bread) and the body of Christ (with all the substance that Christ has). We could say that the consecrated Eucharistic bread is a "bread-body" entity with (*con-*) two substances. Inserted into the philosophical system of thought on which the doctrine of transubstantiation is built, this is a logical somersault. Within that framework, it is impossible for something to possess more than one substance at the same time. We must therefore conclude that the bread changes its substance (it is transformed) when it is consecrated. However, Luther did not think that philosophy should be allowed to limit theology. He believed that, for the sake of Christ, we might sometimes need to do logical somersaults.

In the Evangelical-Lutheran tradition, the *Augsburg Confession* (*Confessio Augustana*) is a normative confessional document. It was worked out by Philipp Melanchthon in dialog with Luther and other reformers and presented by the Protestant princes at a national assembly, the Diet at Augsburg, that the Emperor Charles V summoned in 1530. The Emperor wanted to put an end to the religious struggles that caused disorder in his empire. The *Augsburg Confession* was a serious attempt to restore peace and to protect Christian unity. It stresses the agreement that exists between Roman Catholic doctrine and the Evangelical-Lutheran tradition. Against the background of what unites, the signatories of this confessional document sought to achieve a constructive dialog.

The tenth article of the *Augsburg Confession* states that those who adopt it believe that Christ is really present in the consecrated bread and wine. Faith in this so-called real presence in the Eucharist is thus not something that separates Evangelical-Lutheran Christians from Roman Catholic Christians.[70] There are, however, practices or abuses that are linked to the eucharistic gifts from which Evangelical-Lutherans distance themselves. *The Formula of Concord,* the agreement that was written for the purpose of ending a number of doctrinal conflicts that had caused divisions within the Evangelical-Lutheran tradition, clarifies that those who adopt that confessional document distance themselves from the view "[that] one ought to adore the outward visible elements of the bread and the wine in the Blessed Sacrament."[71]

On that point, Teresa of Jesus held a different view. Her starting point was that there is a correspondence between the real presence of Christ in the consecrated eucharistic bread and Christ's real presence in

---

70. *Svenska kyrkans bekännelseskrifter,* 60. With regard to the significance of the real presence, see Grane, *Confessio Augustana,* 90–103; Braw, *För Kristi ära,* 45–48; Gassman and Hendrix, *För Kristi skull,* 155–70.

71. *Svenska kyrkans bekännelseskrifter,* 522: The Formula of Concord, VII, Contradictory Doctrines, point 19.

human persons; and, against the background of that correspondence, adoration of the Blessed Sacrament may be a form of devotion that reminds us of something essential. Christ is present in the hosts that are kept in the Tabernacle. He is also present in the hearts of believers. Teresa describes that presence with the aid of the image of a castle.

CHRIST'S REAL PRESENCE IN PEOPLE

"A safe stronghold our God is still" (English Hymnal 362) has become something of an Evangelical-Lutheran national anthem. When Luther wrote that text, he probably thought of the safety that he had experienced in the stronghold of Wartburg soon after the pope and the Emperor had rejected him. When Teresa of Jesus wrote *The interior castle*, she probably thought of Avila and the walls that surround the city center. As a child she had run through the gates in the city wall, and as a nun in the Convent of the Incarnation, she had the same panoramic view of that impressive structure that modern day tourists seek to capture with their mobile phone cameras.

Teresa was given the assignment by her superiors to write a book about prayer. She did not have the strength, the inclination, or the time to spend on that task. She talked with Jesus about this problem and asked him to speak in her place. Soon after that, things began to happen in her work on the book project. An image came to Teresa. She realized that we can "consider our soul to be like a castle." The castle is "made entirely out of a diamond or of very clear crystal, in which there are many rooms, just as in heaven there are many dwelling places." The various dwellings in the castle can be described as concentric circles. You can imagine that, inside the outer wall, there is yet another wall that is surrounded by the previous one. Inside that wall, there is the next circular wall that is surrounded by the first two walls. Between the walls are rooms or dwellings at different levels. At the very center is the main dwelling place "where the very secret exchanges between God and the soul take place."[72]

Once Teresa had made a start on the book project, it was easy for her to write. She spoke enthusiastically about how God, by grace, can lead a person further and further into the interior castle toward the most intimate union with Jesus.

---

72. Teresa of Avila, *Interior Castle*, 281, 283–84 (prologue, point 1; the first dwelling places, 1:1, 1:3).

You could say that *The interior castle* is a guidebook for pilgrims who travel through their interior landscape. Teresa describes seven different dwellings, which can be likened to the spaces between the walls that surround the bridal chamber. When she describes the first dwelling, or the first space, Teresa reminds the reader that the image of a castle should not be interpreted too literally. She does not want us to think of the castle as having just a few rooms, but as a million rooms. Nor should we imagine that the sun, Jesus Christ, only shines in the innermost dwelling. Rather, all the rooms, all the various parts of the soul, are in connection with "the sun that is in this royal chamber." It shines in all of the parts, but the rooms that are closer to the sun are brighter.[73]

Teresa often reminds her readers that not everyone can travel along the same route through the castle. She stresses that God leads people along different pathways, through different rooms; and so a single information board cannot help everyone to find the right way. Jesus draws us further and further into the castle, but our conversations with him might differ. They can vary between different dwellings and, because we are on the move on our pilgrimage through the castle, we do not live our whole life in one dwelling. Our dialog in prayer can be more or less wordy. Sometimes it is surrounded by tumults and disorder. Sometimes it will take place in greater stillness and concentration.

"Insofar as I can understand," Teresa writes, "the door of entry to this castle is prayer and reflection."[74] A person enters the castle by talking with God about what happens to them on the journey of life, and by reflecting on those existential issues that every person must face now and again. God has given life to every person, and God wants to save every one of us for eternal life. Teresa wants to help us to have the courage to allow ourselves to be brought further into the castle, even if we cannot see the goal toward which we are moving, and even though we might sometimes be affected by claustrophobia or be horribly surprised by the new discoveries that we make. The journey through the castle can be likened to the underground travel in an elevator that Thérèse of the Child Jesus describes. We must have the courage to let go, to listen to the voice of Jesus, to take his hand and walk in trust that he knows where we are going. For Teresa, Jesus is not only the bridegroom who is waiting

---

73. Teresa of Avila, *Interior Castle,* 291, 293–94 (the first dwelling places, 2:8, 2:12, 2:14).

74. Teresa of Avila, *Interior Castle*, 286 (the first dwelling places, 1:7).

in the innermost chamber. He is also the close friend, the "buddy" who accompanies us every step of the way. With him we can share everything.

MARTIN LUTHER AND SPIRITUALITY

When Martin Luther describes how people become united with Jesus Christ through faith in just as intimate a way as a bride and a bridegroom become united with one another, it might seem, at first sight, that he rejects the thought that there are six dwellings that the person must pass through before reaching the bridal bed in the innermost chamber. Luther's perspective is actually more complicated than that. You could say that in his view the union takes place at the same time, both at the gate into the castle and inside the innermost chamber.[75] Sometimes he stresses that, through faith, a person is completely righteous because she is completely united with Christ through faith. At other times he stresses instead that a person is partly righteous and partly unrighteous—a sinner. Then he stresses that Christ can permeate a person more and more by uniting himself with them.[76] When Luther chooses that perspective, he can discern different stages or steps that a person's love story with Jesus can go through. He can also highlight that, in collaboration with the grace of God, a person can contribute to developing the relationship in the right direction.[77] Kirsi Stjerna focuses on such aspects of Luther's theology when she takes an interest in the question of how we can develop Lutheran spirituality today. She also stresses that Luther reckons with the possibility that, as human beings, we can "act in such a way that we grow spiritually," becoming increasingly gripped by the Spirit of Jesus Christ. Stjerna thinks that it is important to hold out that possibility in our time, which is so interested in spirituality. The sixteenth-century Reformation was a reformation of the devotional practices that were current at that time. Inspired by Martin Luther and other reformers, we need to reflect on the devotional practices of our own time and reform them. We need to preserve and develop a spirituality that can help us who are alive today to become more and more gripped by the Spirit of Jesus Christ.[78]

Teresa of Jesus perceived the lack of spirituality as the greatest problem facing the Lutherans. She stressed that "what the devil did among

---

75. Cf. Braw, 199, 158 on the two types of righteousness that Luther describes.
76. Cf. Hägglund, *De homine*, 283–84, 338–39, 348–61.
77. Braw, *Mystikens arv hos Martin Luther*, 111, 158.
78. Stjerna, "Introduction," 6; Stjerna, "Luther, Lutherans, and Spirituality," 33, 36.

the Lutherans was take away all the means for awakening love, and so they went astray."[79] The aids or devotional practices that encourage us to enter the castle and that give us the desire to walk onwards, the Lutherans threw on to the garbage heap because they connected them with the prison cells of justification by works and not with the act of love in the bridal chamber. That led to a kind of paralysis of action, or to secularization from within, of which Teresa could see the traces not only in "the sect of the Lutherans," but also in Carmelite convents and monasteries. The fighting flame of the desert hermits and the martyrs seems to have been blown out. Individual people's attempts to live as followers of Christ were presented by "the experts" as "folly."[80] The secularization from within in the Carmelite convents was the impetus that led Teresa to become a reformer. She felt that there were so many people who did not love Christ for the simple reason that they could find no place to do so.[81] She wrote *The interior castle* in order to help us to discover how our love story with Jesus finds its shape.

It is possible to discern a load-bearing beam in the architecture of the interior castle with the help of a distinction between two theological perspectives that were taken for granted in the seventeenth century.[82] In the field known as *spiritual theology*, a distinction was made between *ascetic theology* and *mystical theology*. Ascetic theology studies the dwellings or stages of development in the human love story with Jesus that is characterized by the human ability, in collaboration with grace, to contribute to the strengthening and deepening of that relationship. Mystical theology studies instead those dwellings or stages of development that are characterized by God's complete take-over of the initiative. We could say that the first three dwellings in the interior castle that Teresa describes belong to ascetic theology, while the final three dwellings belong in turn to mystical theology. The fourth dwelling is expounded somewhat differently by different interpreters. The Carmelite nun Ruth Burrows suggests that parts of the fourth dwelling could belong to ascetic theology, whereas the other parts should be perceived instead from the perspective of mystical theology.[83]

79. Teresa of Avila, *Spiritual Testimonies*, 399 (section 26).

80. Cf. Teresa of Avila, *Foundations*, 258 (28:23).

81. Cf. Teresa of Avila, *Spiritual Testimonies*, 387 (section 6).

82. This distinction and its significance is summarized in *New Catholic Encyclopedia*, Vol. XIII, "Spiritual Theology."

83. Burrows, *Prayer and Practice*.

ASCESIS AMONG VIPERS AND WILD ANIMALS

Teresa begins her description of the interior castle by noting that we frequently find ourselves on the perimeter of the castle.[84] We are unaware of the precious things that can be found in our souls, or of our soul's high value. So we make little effort to preserve its beauty. "All our attention is taken up with the plainness of the diamond's setting or the outer wall of the castle; that is, these bodies of ours." In the first dwelling, there are so many bad things such as snakes and vipers and "poisonous creatures" that have entered the castle. Some of them are our excuses that we make in order to avoid giving priority to prayer. Other sharp teeth that keep us from focusing on God are our preoccupation with worldly things, possessions, honor or business affairs, and appreciation. In the first dwelling, the person must fight against the demons just as the desert hermits did. Gossip, slander, jealousy, begrudging envy, and pride bite us all from time to time. We need to install mosquito nets in the windows of the interior castle.

In the second dwelling, determination is required, Teresa thinks.[85] When the demons that want to draw us away from God intensify their attacks, there is a risk that we might follow their exhortations. Teresa pleads with us not to turn away or to run out of the castle just because it is tough. We should rather trust in God, not in ourselves, and wait for the help of Christ because "without it one can do nothing." Against the difficulties that beset us in the second dwelling, there is no other cure than continuously to begin again. Teresa emphasizes that "[t]he whole aim of any person who is beginning prayer—and don't forget this, because it's very important—should be that he work and prepare himself with determination and every possible effort to bring his will into conformity with God's will . . . Let us strive to do what lies in our power and guard ourselves against these poisonous little reptiles." Teresa frequently returns to the importance of our determination. Sometimes only "a little determination" is needed, but sometimes a more robust act of the will is required, "a determined determination." Teresa also points out that, even when she does not expressly state that everything in our relationship with God takes place by grace, she implies that this is the case. It is

---

84. The first dwelling places is introduced in Teresa of Avila, *Interior Castle*, 283–96. I quote from 284 and 294 (1:2 and 2:14).

85. The second dwelling places is introduced in Teresa of Avila, *Interior Castle*, 297–303. I quote from 300–301 (1:6 and 1:8).

clear, however, that, in Teresa's view, people can collaborate with grace in the ascetic dwellings in a way that is in line with Erasmus of Rotterdam's understanding of human free will. What happens is the work of the Lord, "and we ourselves do almost nothing," but we need to say "Yes" to God.[86]

In the third dwelling, we need help to see through our "holy illusions."[87] Many of us live with the mistaken view that the third dwelling is the highest point of our spiritual life or the goal of our pilgrimage. We imagine that anyone who has arrived here has reached the top; and so people in the third dwelling are by and large satisfied with themselves and with their relationship with God.[88] Teresa describes people in the third dwelling as "fond of doing penance and setting aside periods for recollection; they spend their time well, practicing works of charity toward their neighbors; and are very balanced in their use of speech and dress and in the governing of their households—those who have them." You could say that they are "sterling Christians" whose major obstacles on their continued journey are their lack of humility and their unwillingness to let go of their own world of imagination. Wilfrid Stinissen notes that what is typical for a third-dwelling person is that they overestimate themselves. They have, with some success, built up an ordered life (with a family, a job, monthly donations to the Red Cross, and their duties as churchwarden on Sundays). This person has exercised their spiritual muscles (for example, in the church's meditation group) and has gained a certain spiritual strength (which makes them reasonably resistant to gossip and undeserved criticism). You could say that a person in the third dwelling is satisfied with life as being both a sinner and justified. What is needed for them to take the step into the fourth dwelling is for God to intervene and to give the self-centered person a new center, so that they can become even more Christ-centered. They must, as Wilfrid Stinissen puts it, be christened at a deeper level.

In the fourth dwelling, "supernatural experiences begin," Teresa of Jesus stresses.[89] What happens at the beginning of the mystical life can best be described by the childhood story that Thérèse of the Child Jesus

86. Cf. Teresa of Avila, *Book About Her Life*, 190. (21.11).

87. The third dwelling places is introduced in Teresa of Avila, *Interior Castle*, 304-15. I quote from 306 (1:5). My exposition is largely based on Stinissen, *Inre vandring*, 44-59. Stinissen speaks of "holy illusions" on 46.

88. Cf. Burrows, 28, 30.

89. The fourth dwelling places is introduced in Teresa of Avila, *Interior Castle*, 316-34. I quote from 316 and 331 (1:1 and 3:9).

tells, mentioned earlier in this book, of how her sister Pauline took their father's cup and Thérèse's little thimble and filled them both with water. There was more room for water in the cup because there was a greater emptiness in it. Teresa of Avila believes that, in the fourth dwelling, God enlarges or extends the human soul and grants the person a new form of prayer, "the prayer of quiet" or deeper recollection. Teresa writes that it is like "a fount whose water doesn't overflow into a stream because the fount itself is constructed of such material that the more water there is flowing into it the larger the trough becomes." In the fourth dwelling, God integrates the person at a deeper level and draws her toward the center of the bridal chamber, just as a magnet attracts iron filings.[90]

MYSTICISM AMONG POTS AND PANS

You could say that Teresa of Avila, like Martin Luther, democratizes mysticism. She understands mysticism as the calling of all Christians, and she notes with confidence that many souls arrive at the fourth dwelling, the first mystical dwelling.[91] Teresa is convinced that, as long as we do not cease from prayer, we will be drawn forward by God on our pilgrimage, further and further into the castle. Sooner or later, we will reach the innermost chamber, in heaven if not before.[92] Anders Arborelius believes that it is particularly important that, in our time, we should let Teresa teach us that God is calling all people to a mystical transformation. He sees that the Church today runs the risk of "producing more papers than saints, and of drowning in documents, commissions and symposia."[93] Then it is easy for us to forget the overall purpose of all these meetings.

Just like Martin Luther, Teresa of Jesus personalizes mysticism by giving it a clearly Christocentric focus. Many people today are seeking interior stillness through various meditation techniques. Several popular forms of meditation are linked to what we call mental exercises. Sometimes the purpose is that thoughts should fade away and that the person should make contact with pure being. Sometimes it is positive thinking or being in the present moment that is sought instead.

Grethe Livbjerg stresses that Teresa thinks along different lines. The prayer that she describes is an "I-Thou" relationship, a conversation

---

90. Cf. Stinissen, *Inre vandring*, 63.
91. Teresa of Avila, *Interior Castle*, 334 (3:14).
92. Teresa of Avila, *Book of Her Life*, 170 (19:12).
93. Arborelius, *Förord in Betraktelser över Guds kärlek*, 11.

with Jesus Christ.[94] Teresa does not connect mysticism primarily with supernatural experiences of the kind that she herself was granted, but with an increasingly intimate union with Christ. In that sense she thinks in more Lutheran terms than most of us do. When Teresa reflects on the question of how we can know whether or not visions, auditions, or other supernatural experiences come from God, she notes that "a locution bears the credentials of being from God if it is in conformity with Sacred Scripture."[95] The Christocentric anchoring is thus combined with a biblical foundation that makes it appropriate to describe Teresa of Avila's view of mysticism as a mysticism of the Word of God. Teresa applies the Lutheran principle to allow *Holy Scriptures alone* to be the basic authority.[96]

Both Teresa of Avila and Martin Luther understood the mystical union between people and Jesus Christ as sacramentally founded. Kirsti Stjerna focuses on that anchoring when she stresses the central importance that baptism and Holy Communion have in Lutheran spirituality.

Both the Evangelical-Lutheran tradition and the spirituality of Carmel underline that the spiritual life of a person is not only an interior reality that affects that person: it also has an indispensable outward foundation in God's work with a person. In baptism and Holy Communion a person is united with Jesus Christ in a very specific and real way. Martin Luther emphasized that this union bears fruit through the good that we do for our fellow human beings and for God's creation. We live out this mystical union, so to speak, in our everyday life.[97]

The Carmelite scholar Donald Buggert presents Teresa of Avila's view of mysticism in a similar way when he stresses that her mysticism is an incarnate, everyday mysticism. Buggert notes that some mystics link the stories about the life of Jesus on Earth with an "ordinary Christian life." They believe that, when a person becomes "an authentic mystic," they are brought to "higher states of spiritual development," and they think that the earthly stories about Jesus then lose their importance in favor of a "higher vision."[98] Teresa does not share that view at all. She stresses that Jesus's human nature and his earthly life experiences are of decisive importance for all Christian life, and thus also for all mystics.

94. Livbjerg, *Teresa of Avila*, 185.
95. Teresa of Avila, *Book of Her Life*, 218–19 (25:13).
96. Cf. Teresa of Avila, *Interior Castle*, 371–72 (the sixth dwelling, 3:4).
97. Stjerna, "Luther, Lutherans, and Spirituality," 43–44.
98. The following is built on Buggert, *Christocentrism of the Carmelite Charism*, 21–25.

The mysticism that she describes is not about people rising above the earthly reality to meet God; rather, it is the case that God descends into our everyday life in order to become human here on Earth, even in us.

Like Martin Luther, Teresa also stresses that ordinary Christians have as much great value and as much access to communion with Jesus as monks and nuns do. Jesus is not like "those we have as lords here on earth, all of whose lordship consists in artificial displays: they have to have designated times for speaking and designated persons to whom they speak." If some poor little creature or those "who don't belong to the nobility" have any business matter to take up, they may not speak to this lord. Jesus, on the other hand, does not have his place in a palace, because there you cannot be yourself.[99] Christ does not grant audiences only to certain chosen people. Everyone is welcome to speak to him, just as they are, about their worries.

To speak to Christ without any frills is what Teresa of Jesus describes as engaging in interior prayer. She presents interior prayer as something very uncomplicated when she writes, "[M]ental prayer in my opinion is nothing else than an intimate sharing between friends; it means taking time frequently to be alone with Him who we know loves us."[100] Time for interior prayer is a mark of daily life in a Carmelite convent or monastery; but it is not only monks and nuns who have the advantage of having regular conversations with Jesus. Teresa believes that we, all of us, in the midst of occupations, sometimes need to withdraw into ourselves. And she stresses that, "[a]lthough it may be for only a moment that I remember that I have that Company within myself, doing so is very beneficial."[101] To her Brother Lorenzo, who complained that he did not have time to pray as much as he would want to, she wrote that the time that is spent on other useful things does not hinder prayer. She also stressed that God does not reward people according to how much time they have set aside for prayer, and notes that "Jacob did not become less a saint for tendering his flock."[102] Even when she turned to her Carmelite Sisters, Teresa pointed out that there is no conflict between daily occupations and prayer. She wrote: "Well, come now, my daughters, don't be sad when obedience draws you to involvement in exterior matters. Know

---

99. Teresa of Avila, *Book of Her Life*, 325 (37:5).

100. Teresa of Avila, *Book of Her Life*, 96 (8:5).

101. Teresa of Avila, *Way of Perfection*, 147 (29:5).

102. Letter to Don Lorenzo de Cepeda, January 2, 1577. Teresa of Avila, *Her Life in Letters*, 143.

that if it is in the kitchen, the Lord walks among the pots and pans helping you both interiorly and exteriorly."[103]

Teresa often underlined that the surest sign that something comes from God is that it makes the person love their fellow human beings.[104] The gifts of grace that God gives us—and this includes visions, auditions, and a deeper life of prayer—should be for the benefit of our neighbor. A mystic is not a passive person who enjoys remarkable mental states in their own private chamber. A mystic is an active person, one who is involved in Christ-formation. Christ takes hold of a person more and more from the center of their personality, from the heart, from the innermost chamber.[105] He lets the person become a Christ for their neighbors.

To walk through the interior castle and the interior life is not always a matter of dancing on a bed of roses. We often encounter sufferings and difficulties, just as Jesus did. Teresa knew that, and in the light of this she described the movement toward the gradually more intimate union with Jesus as a walk "always with the cross," even as the intimacy continues to grow rapidly.[106] She stresses that "embracing the cross, come what may, is an important thing."[107] Thus Teresa did not link mysticism with any kind of unshakable harmony, which is quite often done today. She stressed instead that all people, including mystics, have their crosses to bear. If anyone were to come to her and tell her that, ever since this great thing happened to them, they had lived in peace and joy, she would have concluded that "the great thing" had in fact not happened to that person at all.[108] A life in faith is not a static condition in a harmonious existence above the tribulations of this world. Quite often, the life of faith is at least as demanding as the ascent of an 8,000-meter peak. That theme was developed further by another Carmelite, John of the Cross.

---

103. Teresa of Avila, *Foundations*, 119–20 (5:8).

104. See, for example, Teresa of Avila, *Interior Castle*, 374, about the mystical life (The fifth dwelling, 3:8).

105. Buggert, *Christocentrism of the Carmelite Charism*, 24.

106. Teresa of Avila, *Book of Her Life*, 189 (21:10).

107. Teresa of Avila, *Book of Her Life*, 196 (22:10).

108. Teresa of Avila, *Interior Castle*, 344–45. (The fifth dwelling, 2:9).

4

John of the Cross and Faith

GERLINDE KALTENBRUNNER WAS SITTING alone in her tent, drinking water.[1] The night had been cold and clear, but toward morning a storm had blown up on Dhaulagiri, "the white mountain"—the seventh highest in the world and one of the hardest of the 8,000-meter peaks to ascend. Strong wind often ravages that area.

At an altitude of 6,800 meters, Gerlinde Kaltenbrunner was accompanied by three Spanish climbers. In a tent some five meters higher up, Santi and Ricardo were waiting for the winds to calm down. In another tent, fifteen meters away, Javi was asleep. Suddenly an avalanche tumbled down the mountain. Gerlinde recalls how she was yanked away by an enormous force and buried alive in the snow. When she regained consciousness, she was lying with the tent cloth pressed tight over her face, and she had no idea in which direction the sky lay.

About a month earlier, Gerlinde and Ralf had got married. During their honeymoon they had walked in Nepal together with relatives and friends. Now Ralf was on another 8,000-meter peak. The knife that he had once given Gerlinde was fastened as usual to her climbing harness with a snap-hook. Since Gerlinde had planned to leave her tent as soon as the winds calmed down, she was wearing her harness inside the tent. That saved her life. About forty-five minutes after she had been buried in the snow, she managed to get hold of the knife, cut the tent cloth, and dig herself out of the half-a-meter thick snowdrift. She stood there in her

---

1. The following narrative is taken from Kaltenbrunner, *Mountains in My Heart*, 209–21.

socks, her eyes searching the snowdrifts. She could see no trace of Santi's and Ricardo's tent.

Gerlinde dug up her tent: she needed her boots so that she did not get frostbite in her feet. Then she started to dig where she thought Ricardo's and Santi´s tent would be. Some two meters below the surface of the snow, her shovel came across something hard. Gerlinde dug out enough of Santi's and Ricardo's bodies to establish that they were both dead. Then she and Javi, who also tuned out to have survived, buried them in the snow again.

The questions came afterwards. Why did I survive but not those two? Were there any signs of the approaching danger that we ought to have noticed? Gerlinde Kaltenbrunner also examined herself. She is a strong alpinist, to whom other climbers have given the affectionate nickname "Cinderella Caterpillar," since she is able to plough a path through the snow that others can follow. She has no air of self-importance, and she has shown that she is able to break off an attempt to reach the top or to call a halt to an expedition when she can see that the risks are too great. The place for the tent on Dhaulagiri was sensibly chosen. It was comparatively secure, and neither her common sense nor her gut feelings had protested when she pitched her tent; but still, the catastrophe happened. Ricardo and Santi were experienced mountaineers, but they had had no chance against the avalanche. Gerlinde asked herself how much you should trust your own strength, your common sense, and your gut feelings when you set out on a life-threatening adventure such as ascending an 8,000-meter-high mountain peak, weather forecasts and health checks notwithstanding. Avalanches do not always follow predictable paths, so it is hard to know what to believe or who is trustworthy.

PUZZLEMENT AND GUT FEELINGS

In the year 1996, the singer Marie Fredriksson, who also was part of the Swedish pop rock duo Roxette, was on the Swedish Top of the Pops list with the ballad *Tro*. The Swedish word "tro" covers the meaning content that in English is represented by the words "belief" and "faith" respectively. The two English terms are thus translated with the same Swedish term. Since Marie Fredriksson's success, innumerable groups of confirmation candidates have joined in singing her lines, "Faith, I want to feel faith, I want to feel tomorrow's coming, here and now, in peace and quiet.

In a wintry world, is there any faith? I want to feel a desire for a future as bright as freedom."

Today, many people want to have faith, but we do not want to be limited by any religious faith. This ambivalence is hardly caused by any conceptual confusion; but even so, a couple of remarks about concepts might still be relevant. They can explain what we long for when we are caught by Marie Fredriksson's hit song.

The Swedish concept "tro" (belief) can be used in several different senses. Sometimes we say that we believe that something is happening when we are not entirely sure whether it is really true. We might answer, for example, that we believe that the neighbor's new-born baby will be called Alma (because a proud older brother said so; but he is not old enough to be considered a reliable source). We might also say that we believe that there is life on other planets (but so far, nobody really knows what the facts are). Many people describe beliefs of this kind as the very lifeblood of the work of the natural sciences. Scholars investigate the truth of more-or-less probable hypotheses that they believe in. And if it turns out that they have believed correctly, they might receive the Nobel Prize.

Marie Fredriksson and the confirmation candidates do not sing about the probability that so-far unproved hypotheses will turn out to agree with reality. They use "tro" in another sense (faith). They want to feel trust, confidence, and hope for the future. To believe in oneself and one's own opportunities is a form of trust; and we can call that "faith." A similar kind of faith may be present in a passionate supporter who says that she believes that Washington Capitals will win The Stanley Cup. She is not only saying that it is probable that Washington Capitals will win, but also that she hopes that this will be the case.

Religious faith is often described as a mixture of holding something to be true and trust-filled confidence. Like the beliefs that many scholars of the natural sciences hold, many religious people also reckon with that there is a content of faith (or a belief content) that in some sense might be better or worse. It might, for example, be true or false, valid or invalid, fruitful or destructive. The content of faith can be defined precisely and be investigated, just as it is possible to be specific and to test the assumption that the neighbor's child will be called Alma. That statement may be true or false. By asking the parents, you will find out the facts.

But religious faith is not only a matter of holding more-or-less probable hypotheses to be true. Such faith is also a trusting attitude, a hopeful confidence that is woven into the content of your faith that you hold to be true. This confidence affects the person's actions and their attitudes to everything that happens in their life. To believe in Jesus can mean, for example, to hold true that he is risen from the dead. The content of that belief might be linked to a confident attitude, a trusting faith, that makes that person happy to speak with Jesus in prayer. Exactly how the weaving together of holding something to be true and having faith, as trusting confidence, is constructed is a much-debated issue among philosophers of religion. In theology, an attempt has been made to clarify this relationship through a distinction that has gained ground in the Evangelical-Lutheran tradition. Theologians distinguish between *fides quae*, the content of faith, what is believed, and *fides qua*, the trusting position, the attitude of faith, what it means to live in faith.[2]

For Martin Luther, just as for many other people, faith is not a separate religious sphere of existence, but something that concerns life as a whole. You can therefore say that, from the perspective of religious faith, everything in the whole world is about religious faith, including the text of Marie Fredriksson's song. When Luther stresses that people are justified by faith alone, the concept of "faith" includes both the content of that faith (*fides quae*, certain doctrines) and the trusting attitude or view with which the content of that faith is connected (*fides qua*). In real life, the content of faith can rarely be separated from the trusting attitude, although it is possible to make that distinction at a theoretical level. With the help of this theoretical distinction, like Luther we can clarify that, while the devil is convinced about the existence of God, since the devil is fighting against God, the devil does not have any trust in God, but instead hates God. That is why we cannot say that the devil *has faith* in God, even though the devil is more convinced about the existence of God than any doubting humans can ever be. In the faith that justifies, the content of faith and trust always belong together.

The Swedish Luther scholar Birgit Stolt stresses that Martin Luther did not separate the cognitive side of faith (the content of faith) from its affective side (the trusting attitude).[3] However, such a distinction is sometimes made in the Evangelical-Lutheran tradition, whether consciously or unconsciously. Learning Luther's *Small Catechism* by heart,

---

2. Cf. *Nordisk teologisk uppslagsbok* (*Nordic Theological Encyclopedia*), "tro," where Hjalmar Lindroth gives a good summary of the development of this distinction and its importance in the Evangelical-Lutheran tradition.

3. Stolt is a good, easy-to-read summary of ground-breaking research. Stolt, "Luther's Faith of 'The Heart.'"

for example, has put the emphasis on the content of faith in a way that has not always helped people to see Jesus as a loving life-long friend. Even today, well-meaning educational measures that aim to increase our knowledge of the Christian faith and tradition (the content of the faith) might be too one-sided, unless they also include practices that will facilitate our human ability to live in a trust-filled dialog with Christ (the trusting attitude). Good teaching about the faith includes both dogmatics ("What does the Christian tradition say about Jesus?") and spirituality ("Now we speak together with Jesus, and trust that he listens to us").

When we as Church or as individuals seek to hand on our faith to children or young people, we usually adapt our doctrinal presentations and our spiritual practices to the cognitive and emotional development level of the children or young people. With regard to adults, we are not equally aware that a fruitful transmission of faith must be both flexible and multifaceted. The Swedish psychotherapist Göran Bergstrand reminds us of this when he highlights the model of faith development developed by the American scholar James W. Fowler. Bergstrand and Fowler stress that both children and adults are able to believe, but differently, since they are at different stages of maturity. These differences are important in relation to our opportunities to develop fruitful strategies to pass our faith on. The faith must be allowed to mature with us—and we with the faith.

SUCKLING CHILDREN AND DEEP-THINKING TEENAGERS

James Fowler's model belongs in the psychology of religion. It clarifies how our cognitive abilities and our affective resources shape our faith throughout our lives, in the sense of both *fides quae* and *fides qua*. Fowler distinguishes seven different stages of development that our potential to believe and our way of believing can go through.[4]

The first, foundational faith, or *primal undifferentiated faith*, as Fowler calls it, is a form of faith that can be described as a preliminary stage to faith. That which will become faith is not yet clearly set out, but we know from observation that the quality of the relationships with those who care for the young child determines that child's ability to feel trust. Fowler emphasizes that a child's foundational faith and first trust develops when the child is not yet able to use language. He thinks that the significant mark of this stage of development is the tension between trust and mistrust.

---

4. The following is based on Bergstrand, *Från naivitet till naivitet*. Cf. Fowler, *Stages of Faith*.

That which in the long term will become the person's image(s) of God grows from the young child's experiences of those who care for it during the early years of life.

When a child has reached the age of two, it has often developed two decisive abilities that change its perspective on life. First, the child has learnt to walk and run; and second, the child has begun to speak. These abilities cause the child to have faith in another sense. Fowler calls this second stage *intuitive-projective faith*. Initially, the child's speaking is dominated by a number of new observations that it makes. At this stage, the child cannot think from any other perspective than its own, and it has not yet learnt to distinguish between fantasy and reality. Fowler stresses that stories are important as meaning-creating contexts at this age. Faith communities that want to pass on their faith to young children therefore do well to tell narratives from their own tradition. Those stories give the children maps that they can use to orient themselves as they discover more about the world and deal with challenging circumstances, such as the insight that all will eventually die.

Fowler suggests that most people leave the second stage of faith development behind at about the age of seven, when a new development stage of life and of faith begins. The child is now formed by *mythic-literal faith*. Fowler stresses that, at this stage of life, the child takes a greater interest in how things are in reality, because it improves its ability to distinguish between fantasy and reality. Thinking about reality also develops through the fact that, in this stage, the child masters the basic Kantian categories of thought: time and space. The child's ability to listen and to use stories also develops further. Now the child begins to be able to look at reality from perspectives other than its own; and that provides new richness to its narrating. The possibility of taking up different perspectives means that questions about fairness comes to the fore. With regard to images of God, Fowler underlines that, previously, the child was able to alternate between human, anthropomorphic, and non-anthropomorphic images of God; but in this third stage of development, the images of God are invariably anthropomorphic. According to Fowler, a child in this stage lives in a world that is characterized by "justification by works" and by a longing for perfection. The child identifies people primarily according to their surface appearance, which they reveal by their actions; and that surface should preferably be faultless. Fowler notes that there are individuals who never leave this faith development stage behind; but most of us will gradually abandon mythical literal faith.

The fourth stage, the *synthetic-conventional faith*, is typically found during the teens, when the human ability to think in abstract terms develops. In this stage a person can integrate their own thoughts into more overarching systems. This abstracting ability provides new perspectives on one's own person; it is now possible to observe oneself from other people's perspectives, and that creates a kind of anxiety. How do others actually view me? During our teenage years, many of us easily end up in what Fowler describes as "the tyranny of the others." To a major extent, life is governed by a desire to fit in and to be appreciated by those whose function is to create ideal styles that we wish to emulate. Even though this superficial adaptation is considerable, we also discover during this stage of development that there is more to people than the surface that they show us. We begin to suspect that there may be hidden depths, both within ourselves and within other people. Our images of God will be affected by that insight. God is perceived by many teenagers as a great mystery. However, that is no obstacle to the ability that many teenagers have to provide answers to questions about what they believe with great certainty. Many can describe the content of faith that they embrace ("I do not believe that there is a God," or "I believe that everyone comes to God when they die"), and Fowler thinks that those descriptions are often presented as if they were taken for granted. Few teenagers can explain why they believe as they do. Many teenagers believe like their classmates, like the cool priest who works with young people, or like that famous rock star.

REFLECTIVE STUDENTS AND IRRESOLUTE RELATIVISTS

The most difficult step to take in the development of faith is the step from synthetic-conventional faith into the fifth stage of development, your own, thought-through faith—what Fowler calls *individuative-reflective faith*. That transition normally takes a long time to complete. Fowler thinks that it would be easier if that transition took place while people were in their twenties. What characterizes the shift from conventional faith to a person's own thought-through faith is that the authority is moved from "others" to oneself. Now it is no longer parents, friends, the congregation, or secular society that are permitted to decide what people think about their faith. Now a person reflects more independently on various issues of life and meaning.

Many university students are somewhere in the transition between the fourth stage and the fifth stage of development in Fowler's model. They like to reflect, systematically and intensely, on what is reasonable to believe. From about the age of twenty, many of us can develop "the perspective of the third person." We can reflect on reality from abstract or hypothetical starting points. We can investigate the expectations that other people have of us and decide what goals in life we ourselves want to realize. That affects our ability to scrutinize our views about faith. It is hard work to engage with existential issues and to examine views in which you have previously put your trust. The fifth kind of faith is therefore marked by tensions. While a person longs to appear as their own individual person, they do not want to lose community with others. While a person's critical thought tells them that it seems improbable that there is a God, they can have a deep sense that there is, in spite of everything, a God behind it all.

The sixth stage of faith development, Fowler calls *conjunctive faith*. He believes that not many people arrive at this stage. However, some middle-aged people can find a new kind of security in their own faith, which Fowler describes as a new stage of faith development. Previously, during the fourth stage of development (*the synthetic-conventional faith* of the teenage years), people showed no great tendency to change. Rites, symbols and views of faith should preferably remain as they were when a person first met them. In the fifth stage of development (*individuative-reflective faith*), a relativist attitude was cultivated instead. People realized that others might think differently, and that they might have good reasons for their views. Your own personal faith no longer appears as the only truth, even though it continues to be a personal truth. The relativism of the thought-through faith can, for example, be expressed in the view that my faith may be true for me while at the same time your faith may be true for you.

In the sixth stage of development, an open-hearted stability appears in the person's own perspective. This new security has to do with the fact that the person has now discovered more of their own unconscious aspects and is able to relate to them in a fruitful way. In the fifth stage, a person trusted to a great degree in their own cognitive abilities. By contrast, *the conjunctive faith* involves much more of their total personality. When the human personality develops, a person's opportunities to live in faith also change. The sixth stage of development, therefore, is marked by a greater ease in living with paradoxes and by the ability to unite opposites. That ability makes a person genuinely interested in what is strange and in those who do not believe and think in the same way. At this stage a person is well aware that other perspectives can transmit truths that might enrich their own perspective, and they will be keen to discover more of them. Reality is complicated, and it can be described in a number of different ways; but that does not mean that all perspectives are equally good or that they relate to the truth in the same way. Aided by the truths to which my perspective and my faith give me access, I can discover new truths in other contexts. My own context, with its advantages, is the key that opens up that possibility. Fowler and Bergstrand describe the faith that binds everything together as "a second naivety," as a trusting confidence that leads our thinking to the little child that rests securely in the arms of its parents. The joy in the resources of your tradition, and the ability to use them, makes a person unaffectedly curious to find out what they can learn from other traditions and from the people who live according to them.

The seventh stage of faith development, *the universalizing faith*, is what Fowler connects with exceptional people who live their vision without compromises. In the sixth stage, a person is affected by a degree of ambiguity: the truths and the connections that a person discovers give birth to visions of a better world and a better Church, but reality does not permit itself to be transformed in any simple way, and that makes a person ambivalent. Most of us relate to that ambiguity by compromising. We reduce our expectations and lower our goals and our ambitions so that we do not have to live with the ambivalence to which the differences between vision and reality lead. People who live in the seventh stage of all-embracing total faith, however, do not choose solutions that involve compromise. Instead they develop strategies that make it possible for them to transform reality together with others on the basis of their vision. Göran Bergstrand points to Martin Luther King, Mother Teresa, and Dag Hammarskjöld as examples of people whom we can place in this seventh stage of development in Fowler's model. Fowler in turn stresses that religious fanatics do not have an all-embracing total faith, even though they might identify themselves as heroes of the faith. What distinguishes people with an all-embracing total faith from fanatics is that those who are in the seventh stage of faith development fight for the rights of all people and of the entire creation, and not only for those who share their own perspective.

Fowler's model is an academic mapping out of how our faith can develop in tandem with our growing intellectual intelligence (our cognitive abilities) and the emotional intelligence that we develop throughout our life (our affective abilities). The process that Fowler describes underlines both the development of the body (the ability to walk, to speak, and to think in more abstract terms) and our ability to interact with other people (to see what they do, to listen to what they say, to converse trustingly with them, and to view the world from their perspective).

Scientific descriptions of our human potential to believe can add highly relevant knowledge that we might find useful when we reflect on handing on the faith and on faith development. In order to fulfill this function in the context of the Church, however, such descriptions do need to be complemented by theological models that present God as actively at work in the faith development of a person. If secular models are allowed to reign supreme, there is a major risk that they will contribute to the Church's secularization from within, rather than helping us to avoid that.

As Christians, we have access to a rich supply of spiritual literature, written for the purpose of helping us to grow and mature in our trust in Jesus. Both Martin Luther and John of the Cross have contributed influential descriptions of how God deals with us human beings for the purpose of developing our faith. They add a theological dimension that goes beyond those observations from the psychology of religion that Fowler has published. Paradoxically enough, Luther's and John's most important contributions are about the significance of *nothing* (*nihil* in Latin, *nada* in Spanish). When a person becomes more and more *nothing*, Christ can more and more become everything in them.

CHRIST'S REAL PRESENCE IN FAITH

In current research on Luther, lively discussions continue about the understanding of Luther's theology that the Finnish professor Tuomo Mannermaa and the scholars who have been inspired by him have contributed. The so-called Mannermaa school is a new paradigm in research on Luther, which, among other things, describes how Luther viewed the development of faith.[5] Tuomo Mannermaa was a professor of ecumenical

---

5. I describe, analyze, and discuss the interpretation of Luther according to the new Finnish paradigm and Tuomo Mannermaa's work in Johannesson, *Helgelsens filosofi*. The following is based on that work and on the textual material to which I refer there. Mannermaa, *Christ Present in Faith*, is an important source for this discussion.

theology at the University of Helsinki. Within the framework of ecumenical dialog between the Evangelical-Lutheran Church in Finland and the Russian Orthodox Church, Mannermaa was commissioned to investigate whether there was any correspondence in Luther's theology with the Orthodox view of the divinization of human beings. Mannermaa discovered that there is such a correspondence, but that this aspect of Luther's theology has been left in the background, since the Evangelical-Lutheran tradition has stressed other aspects of Luther's theology at the expense of his views on the divinization of human beings. Mannermaa's scholarly work focuses to a large extent on the insight that we need to rediscover Luther's views on the divinization of human beings and the central role that they play in Luther's thinking if we want to understand and expound his theology correctly. The discussions that take place today about this new Finnish paradigm in Luther research focus in turn on the issue of how central Luther's views on the divinization of human beings actually are. Mannermaa believes that the divinization of human beings is in fact the structuring principle in Luther's theological thought, while other Luther scholars think that it plays a less important role in Luther's theology.

Mannermaa stresses that Luther trusts that Christ's presence in faith is real; consequently, Christ is present in the believer. He uses the philosophical concept of "real-ontic" to describe this presence. By using that concept, Mannermaa wants to underline that the presence of Christ in the believer, according to Martin Luther, is an ontological presence—in other words, a real presence. The real presence of Christ in the believer is similar to the real presence of Christ in the Eucharist. Just as the consecrated host has all the qualities of the bread while at the same time it has all the qualities of Christ, so the believer has both their own human qualities as well as Christ's qualities. Luther used the concepts of bridal mysticism to underline that Christ and the believer possess all things in common.

That Christ and the believer have all things in common turns our thoughts to the incarnation. Jesus was both God and human. In a similar way, the believer is both human and made divine through Christ's (who is God) real presence in faith.

Mannermaa stresses that, according to Luther, the divinization of human beings is an ongoing process. A person becomes righteous when the righteousness of Christ becomes theirs as they are united with Christ through faith. Like many other Luther scholars, Mannermaa stresses that Luther alternates between two different theological perspectives when he describes a person's relationship with God. Sometimes he describes people as *either* justified through faith *or* sinners. Within the framework of that perspective, there is little room for the thought that a person can be more or less believing, faith-influenced, or righteous. However, there is room for that thought in the other perspective that Luther uses. Within the framework of this second perspective, Luther stresses that the believer is *simultaneously* a sinner and justified. When Luther moves within this framework, he is able to observe that the proportions of sin and righteousness can vary between different people or during a person's lifetime. It is against that horizon of understanding that Tuomo Mannermaa describes Luther's perceptions of the divinization of human beings. Mannermaa believes that Luther presented divinization as a gradually more intimate union with Christ through faith. The conclusion is that divinization is a process of faith development that can be described as growth in righteousness or holiness. The Evangelical-Lutheran tradition does not normally use the concept of "divinization," but instead describes a person's growth in faith and righteousness by using the concept of "sanctification" or "holiness." Objectively, the two concepts refer to the same reality—that is, to a person's growth in the communion with Jesus Christ that faith implies.

In Luther's presentation of divinization (or the process of sanctification), the cross plays a very particular role. We could say that Luther agrees with Teresa of Avila's statement that the main aspect of the process of growing in faith, or of the sanctification of a person, is that person's embracing of the cross. When Luther and Teresa of Jesus speak of "the cross," that concept denotes not only the cross of Christ, but also many forms of suffering, worry, misfortune, challenge, and difficulty that we mortals may have to face during our lives. The basic thought is that God can form us by helping us to carry the crosses that we must shoulder during our pilgrimage here on Earth. God lets us grow in faith, righteousness, and holiness through our cross-bearing. To embrace the cross means not running away from it, but rather running to God whenever we encounter suffering and difficulty.

THE THEOLOGY OF THE CROSS AND THE THEOLOGY OF GLORY

An important aspect of Martin Luther's thought is the distinction between the theology of the cross and the theology of glory, which he introduced during a theological debate in Heidelberg in 1518. In that gathering, Luther presented 28 theses as background to the discussion.[6] In the theses, Luther described the difference between a theologian of the cross who is able to know, or to get to know, God through suffering, and a theology of glory that abhors the cross and suffering. The primary characteristic of the theology of glory is its confidence in human abilities. Theologians of glory believe that we can grow in faith and come closer to God through our own efforts. In that sense they hold to an objectionable belief in justification by works. They think that we can climb up to God by using some ladder that we ourselves can use to ascend heavenward.

Some theologians of glory seek to approach God and the heavenly world through intellectual effort. Among them we can count, for example, some philosophers who, like certain scholastics, develop rational arguments in favor of God's existence. Other people choose other ladders that they think make it possible for them to climb up toward God. Some, for example, focus on the scholastic perception that there is a deep spiritual dimension in every person. Then they try to deepen that dimension further by doing spiritual exercises of various kinds. Luther objects to the glory theologians' confidence in people's natural abilities. His rejection is linked to his understanding of the fall into sin. Luther believes that the fall has had such all-pervading consequences that the image of God in humanity has been completely destroyed. Human beings have become the image of the devil. They cannot use their human abilities, which since the fall have been marked by sin and the devil, in order to turn to and approach God. To enable people to do that, God must take the initiative and convert a person by uniting them with God through faith.

Tuomo Mannermaa describes Luther's understanding of a person's sanctification, her growth in holiness, in the light of his theology of the cross.[7] Mannermaa stresses that Luther imagines that God must in certain senses first "annihilate" a person in order to be able to unite them with God. You could say that God creates a space within a person, and then fills that space with God. God creates that space, that empty place,

---

6. Luther, *Heidelberg Disputation*, 31:39–70.

7. Mannermaa discusses the distinction between the theology of the cross and the theology of glory in Mannermaa, *Two Kinds of Love*, chapter 3. The following is also built on Mannermaa, "Why is Luther so Fascinating?"; Mannermaa, "Justification and *Theosis* in Lutheran-Orthodox Perspective"; and Kärkkäinen, *One with God*, 40–45. Valuable perspectives are also given by Peura, "Christ as Favor and Gift," 93–94, and Juntunen, "Luther and Metaphysics."

by showing the person that, in themselves, they are "nothing" (*nihil*). Luther described this process of destruction as God's alien or annihilating work. That breaking down is a tool that God uses in order to realize that which Luther describes as God's real work, God's purpose: the sanctification of the human being.

Mannermaa underlines that God's annihilating work does not mean that God destroys or breaks down a person or their personality. What God destroys or breaks down, rather, is a person's justification by works, their glory-related theological trust in their own ability. God reveals to a person how little they understand of themselves and breaks down their wrongly directed trust in themselves and their unrighteous self-love. God can use a number of misfortunes and sufferings to achieve such a breakdown. The characteristic mark of God's annihilating work is that it somehow punctures a person's attempts to make themselves God.

Mannermaa stresses that Luther thinks that a person's love determines their entire existence. We can summarize that thought in a witty phrase: "Tell me what you love, and I will tell you who you are!" The purpose of God's annihilating work is to "destroy" a person's love for that which draws them away from God. God makes a person receptive to God (*capax Dei*) by breaking down their wrong faith in their own capacity and their misdirected trust in human security systems. The empty space that emerges as a result of the annihilating work, God fills with God. In that way a person is granted the opportunity to love God with the love that God gives them.

Even though God's annihilating work is an expression of love, we do not experience this work as building us up. We feel anxiety, pain, and terror when we are subjected to divine care of this kind. We think that we have lost the ground under our feet, and maybe our faith as well. We do not understand anything, and we do not know what to do. Mannermaa stresses that Luther's message is that we should not actively attempt to understand or do anything. Our attitude instead should be one of waiting and trusting, just like the attitude of a happy little child in the arms of a safe adult.

An infant will die unless an adult takes care of it. In the same way, a person's sanctification will die unless God takes care of it. Luther believes that Christ's real presence in faith is something that God grants them continuously. To put it simply, people do not walk about as believers who are justified and divinized by themselves. People do not carry around any kind of spiritual form of existence that they can keep if they run away from God. Rather, a person becomes a believer, justified and divinized in every new moment, by being in contact with God. Just as the water in a little pool in the mountains is drinkable only if there is a fresh flow of water into that pool, so a person becomes divinized through the contact with Christ that flows into them through the well-spring of faith.

Luther describes a Christian person's desirable basic relationship with God as *passio*, passive. Since we have a hard-to-overcome tendency to want to be active in our relationship with God, God must continuously carry out God's annihilating work in us. We need to be made into "nothing" again and again, and we need to be emptied of our warped trust in ourselves. Only then will God have room to act in our lives.

Luther thinks that even things that we regard as evil in themselves can be an expression of God's love. In relation to that thought, he entangles himself in an argument that is in line with the book that Nicholas Wolterstorff was given when his son died in the Alps. Wolterstorff found no comfort in the idea that God sometimes shakes mountains so that climbing accidents occur, maybe for the purpose of helping people to grow and mature in their faith; but, with hindsight, he could see that his son's death had in some respects made him, Nicholas, a better person. His faith and his relationship with God had also been affected and had matured. Wolterstorff questioned more seriously the homages that successful climbers receive when they reach the summit. He discovered how often we neglect the little people who populate the valleys. There are large crosses on the highest peaks in the Alps. Following his son's accident, Wolterstorff imagined small, invisible crosses along the mountain slopes. Those crosses remind us of all those who never made it all the way up, or who never came down again after successfully reaching the summit.

Wolterstorff could not believe that God sends all accidents and sufferings. God does not want to deprive us of our lives—but God can sometimes use larger or smaller crosses to realize God's life-giving purposes. Martin Luther expressed that thought as well, as we can see in his pastoral letters.

MARTIN LUTHER'S PASTORAL LETTERS

A few years ago, the Australian priest Stephen Pietsch presented his doctoral dissertation on the letters that Martin Luther wrote to people living with depression. This dissertation is not primarily a work in the field of the history of ideas, but rather a study of pastoral theology. Pietsch highlights the structures of the pastoral care that Luther gave depressed people, and he discusses how we can use Luther's insights today.[8] Pietsch notes that, in the past, depression was called *melancholy*; and in the days of Luther, this was a blanket term for several very common conditions that were linked with depression, anxiety, and suicidal thoughts. He describes the sixteenth century as a melancholic culture, since there are clear signs that people were affected by melancholy more frequently during that century than in previous ages. Thus, the causes of melancholy and its diagnosis and forms of treatment were keenly discussed in the sixteenth century.

Pietsch stresses that the condition that today we describe as depression is a growing problem of public health in many parts of the world. Recent statistics from Sweden show that every fifth person states that they have been diagnosed with depression at some stage in their life. Pietsch wants to investigate how Martin Luther's teaching of the faith could help depressed people today. Like other scholars who are interested in the history of psychiatry, he is careful to emphasize that it is not at all easy to translate concepts from the sixteenth century into contemporary medical terminology. The vocabulary to which people had access in the sixteenth century when they wanted to describe feelings and various conditions of the soul was more intensely colorful and more nuanced than ours. Pietsch pays attention to the poverty of vocabulary in the field of the interior life against the background of Birgit Stolt's research into "the rhetoric of the heart" in Luther's linguistic usage.

In his dissertation, Pietsch analyzes twenty-one letters of comfort that Luther wrote to people who had been affected by melancholy. He summarizes the content of the pastoral care that Luther provides in those letters and relates it to a number of different methods of treatment that are used today to help people who have been affected by depression. When Pietsch motivates his method, he stresses that Martin Luther was primarily a pastor of souls. In his ninety-five theses, Luther protested against poor pastoral care. Developing his teaching about how a person is justified by grace through trusting faith in Jesus Christ, his ambition was not to create a coherent theological system to impress the authorities of that time, but to offer people better pastoral care. We should therefore approach the doctrine of justification as a resource for pastoral care.

When a person suffers from depression, both their feelings and their thoughts are affected. They feel downcast, anxious, and hopeless.

---

8. The following is based on Pietsch.

They might think that life is meaningless, that no one can love them, and that it might be just as well to die. Depression has both affective and cognitive symptoms. Thus both a person's understanding of the content of her belief (*fides quae*) and their ability to have faith (*fides qua*) are affected. That means that certain aspects of Luther's teaching about justification through faith appear primarily in his letters to depressed people. When Luther comforts people who have been affected by melancholy, he describes trusting faith in Jesus Christ as much more—and much deeper—than what can be found in our thoughts and feelings. You could say that the mystical aspects of faith come to the fore. A person is united with Christ through faith, even though it does not feel like that, and even though they are not able to hold it as a truth.

Pietsch highlights the central aspects of the treatment for depression that Luther recommends in his letters. Among other things, Luther stresses that he values the medical resources that are available in his day. Luther's view is that the pain should be alleviated by the means that are available. When Luther diagnoses a condition as somatic rather than mental or spiritual, his view is that a visit to a pharmacy might be appropriate. He often recommends various activities that he imagines might help a person to overcome this melancholy. In his letters, for example, he encourages contact with good friends, play, games, and sports. Humor and good meals are also important aspects of the treatment for depression that Luther promotes. Pietsch often returns to the obvious similarities between the pastoral care that Luther offers in the letters he has studied and various behavior-focused forms of therapy that we use today.

Luther's basic view is that, if possible, melancholy should be relieved. He often stresses that melancholy comes from the devil. Pietsch therefore discusses Luther's demonology. Like Teresa of Avila and other sixteenth-century people, Martin Luther regards the devil as a real evil power that acts in this world. Birgit Stolt emphasizes that we cannot understand Luther's theology correctly if we neglect the function that the devil serves in his world of ideas.[9] Today we tend to ignore Luther's very specific experiences of the devil, since the devil does not fit into our "enlightened" worldview. Pietsch thinks that it is possible that we might have to take ideas about the devil more seriously than we usually do in pastoral conversations with people who suffer from mental illnesses. People do

---

9. Cf. Stolt, *Martin Luther*, 17–18.

not cease to experience the struggle against evil forces just because we think it is unfashionable to speak of the devil.

Luther often begins his letters to a depressed person with a prayer that God will liberate them from melancholy. Then he might note that melancholy is of the devil and that, by taking refuge with Christ and the Bible, the person must try to stand firm against demonic thoughts and feelings. If the thoughts come nevertheless, "like fiery serpents," the person should not care about those serpent-like thoughts. They should rather turn to gaze upon Christ who has given his life for us. Then things will get better, if that is God's will.[10]

You could say that Luther encouraged depressed people to fight courageously against the demons, just as the desert hermits did. "[A]void getting into an argument with the devil when those deadly thoughts come" is a good piece of advice that he often repeats.[11] "Continue thinking about and remembering other things, and say: 'Alright, devil, leave me alone. I have no time for your thoughts. I must eat, drink, ride, travel, or do this or that.'"[12] Since the devil cannot abide joyful thoughts, the melancholic person should first of all try to rejoice by spending time on whatever they find brings joy. In a letter to a melancholic man, Luther described the attitude that he encouraged with a parable from married life: "Be like the fellow who, whenever his wife began to nag and gnaw at him, pulled his flute out from under his belt and played soothingly until she got tired of it and left him in peace." Ending his letter, Luther summarized in a few pregnant lines the pastoral care that he gave to melancholic people. If the depressed person can be sure that these thoughts come from the devil, they have already won the victory. To anyone who is weak in the faith, Luther gives the following advice:

> [B]ecause your faith is still fragile, listen to us, who by God's grace, know it, and lean on our staff until you learn to walk by yourself. And when good people comfort you . . . try to believe that God is speaking to you through them. Pay attention to them and don't doubt that it is most certainly God's word coming to you, in line with God's command, through men, for your comfort. May the same Lord who has bidden me, and whom I

---

10. Letter to Barbara Lisskirchen, April 30, 1531. Pietsch, *Of Good Comfort*, 271.

11. Letter to Jerome Weller, July 1530. Cf. Pietsch, *Of Good Comfort*, 282–83.

12. Letter to Jonas von Stockhausen, November 17, 1532. Pietsch, *Of Good Comfort*, 279.

must obey, give all these things to you in your heart and enable you to believe and confess them. Amen.[13]

It is well-known that Martin Luther himself periodically suffered from severe melancholy. Pietsch notes that Luther sometimes shared his own experiences in his letters to other depressed people. On some occasions, he used the word "temptation" of the melancholy that had affected the addressee of the letter.

In that context, Pietsch notes an interesting shift of perspective in Luther's attitude toward temptations. When he was younger, he only used the word "temptation" to describe a person's terror before a judgmental God. Temptations were only evil. But when he was older, he could also describe other difficulties or trials as temptations. This indicates that, over time, the concept took on a deeper theological meaning for him; it also came to include difficulties and challenges that God could use to help people to mature in faith. Birgit Stolt's research is the foundation for Stephen Pietsch's observations. Stolt notes that Luther occasionally uses the German word *Anfechtung* (temptation) as virtually synonymous with the Latin concept of *tentatio*, which means a trial that God sends.[14] Following the shift of perspective that Luther's understanding of temptation went through, he thought along similar lines to those of another theologian of the cross, John of the Cross.

A LOVE STORY BEYOND THE USUAL

Juan de Yepes Álvarez was born in Fontiveros, a village some 70 miles from Avila, that in the sixteenth century had a population of about five thousand.[15] Juan's father, Gonzalo de Yepes, was an aristocrat who had become an orphan early in life. He was employed by his rich uncles in Toledo, where they traded in silk. Gonzalo made regular business trips to the major market town of Medina del Campo. On his way there, he usually stayed overnight with a widow at Fontiveros. The widow owned a small silk weaving company, where she employed Catalina Álvarez, a young and very poor girl who, like Gonzalo, was an orphan. Gonzalo and Catalina fell deeply in love with each other. The widow tried to prevent this romance, since she knew how the rich uncles would react; but her efforts had no result. Gonzalo and Catalina married—and the reaction

13. Letter to Matthias Weller, October 7, 1534. Pietsch, *Of Good Comfort*, 287.
14. Stolt, *'Laßt uns fröhlich springen!'* 66–67.
15. The following is based on Arborelius, *Allt och intet*.

of the rich relatives was not slow in coming; they rejected Gonzalo completely and disinherited him. They thought that he had insulted the family and violated their honor by marrying Catalina.

His relatives' reaction meant that Gonzalo had no money and no job. He did not manage to find a new job within the trading profession, so he learnt Catalina's profession and they worked together in the widow's weaving company. When the widow died, Gonzalo and Catalina opened their own weaving company in their home. They struggled on and worked hard to support themselves and their three children. The oldest son, Fransisco, was born in 1530. Twelve years later the youngest son, Juan (or John, as we call him in English) was born. Somewhere in between the two, the middle son Luis was born. Soon after the birth of John, Gonzalo was taken seriously ill. Catalina had to stop working in order to look after her husband. For two years she nursed the seriously plague-ridden Gonzalo before he died. She was then left on her own with no savings and three children to support.

There was a famine in Castile at that time. When John was about six years old, the poverty in Fontiveros had become a source of great misery. Catalina decided to move to the large trading town of Arévalo to find better opportunities to support her family. At that time Luis died, probably from being undernourished.

Fransisco was eighteen when the family moved to Arévalo, and he soon found new friends. With them he hung around the streets and squares at night, dancing, playing, and singing. Another entertainment that this gang of youngsters engaged in was to plunder fruit gardens. On one occasion they stole almonds from a garden that probably belonged to the church, because someone called out to them that, if they were stealing from that garden, they would be excommunicated. That incident abruptly ended Fransisco's wild youthful pursuits. Rather than hanging around the streets and squares, he started to spend much time in prayer. Catalina also made a decisive effort to help Fransisco to sort out his life. She made sure that he married Ana Izquierdo, a young woman from a neighboring village. Ana soon learnt weaving, and she became just as involved in the care of the poor as Fransisco was. Between them they made sure that many foundlings were given food and shelter.

When John was nine, the family had to move again because of their poverty. Now Catalina, Fransisco, Ana, and Juan went to the commercial center of Medina del Campo. They found a home on the street called Calle de Santiago. In many respects, that street became "mother's street" in the life of John of the Cross. The Convent of the Augustinian Sisters, where John was allowed to help in the sacristy, was also in that street; so too was the Jesuit College where John was educated. Calle de Santiago also became home to the convent of the Reformed Carmelite Sisters that Teresa of Avila founded in that city. It was there that Teresa and John were to meet for the first time.

The nine-year-old John was accepted as a student at a boarding school for orphaned and poor boys, where he learnt to read and write. The school also trained their students in some or other craft so that they would be able to support themselves later in life. John managed the reading and writing extremely well, although Fransisco recalled that John's education in crafts was not good. John tried to become a carpenter, a tailor, a woodcarver, and a painter, but none of those professions suited him all that well. Having finished his education, John was employed at a hospital that cared for people with syphilis and other venereal diseases. In those tasks he did very well. He had a great and deeply founded compassion for suffering people. It is recalled that he used to cheer up the downcast by telling them little stories and by singing to them. While working at the hospital, John continued his studies. At the Jesuit College, situated some two hundred meters from the hospital, he received a thorough education in the humanities. He studied grammar, rhetoric, and logic, he learnt Latin and Greek, and he read the classical masters in their original languages. When he had time, he could visit his family, who lived close by.

AN UNUSUALLY SUCCESSFUL RECRUITMENT

In the year 1563, John entered the Carmelite Monastery of St. Anne in Medina del Campo. The twenty-one-year-old John, who now got the name Brother John of St. Matthias, was immediately accepted as a novice. The quick process suggests that the Prior of the monastery knew with whom he was dealing. It is recalled that John was encouraged by others to become a monastic Brother. Several other orders seem also to have been interested in recruiting him. However, the contemplative ideals of the Carmelite Order attracted John, which was why he went there.

Having made his monastic vows, John was given permission to follow the original rule of the Carmelite Order rather than the milder variant of the rule that had been ratified by the pope in 1432. He was sent to the university city of Salamanca to continue his studies. John was a brilliant student, but first of all a monastic Brother. He spent much time in prayer before the Blessed Sacrament. He wanted to follow the suffering Christ in a very tangible way. He slept on a plank bed with a piece of wood for a pillow. He fasted frequently and wore a hairshirt next to his body. His monastic Brothers appreciated and respected him, even though he stuck to his principles rather more than the average Brother. John himself began to question his life as a Carmelite and struggled with the question of whether he should transfer to the Carthusians, an even more contemplative and radically eremitical monastic order.

In August 1567, the then fifty-two-year-old Teresa of Jesus founded a Reformed Carmelite Convent for Sisters in Medina del Campo. That was when Teresa and John met for the first time. Teresa had managed to gain permission to found two monasteries for Reformed Carmelite Brothers, and she was looking for suitable candidates who could establish them. In Medina del Campo she spoke to the prior of the Carmelite monastery, Antonio de Heredia. He had also been thinking about a transfer to the Carthusians, since he was longing for a more contemplative life. Furthermore, Teresa spoke to the twenty-five year-old John. He had just been ordained to the priesthood and was visiting Medina del Campo to say his first Mass in his home city. Teresa managed to convince John not to leave the Carmelite Order. She wanted him instead to become involved in the work of reform that had just started. Teresa's efforts were successful. When she left Medina del Campo, she was very happy with her visit from many perspectives. She had, as she herself expressed it, managed to recruit one full-length monastic Brother, the tall Brother Antonio, and a half-length monastic Brother, the considerably shorter John of St. Matthias. Within a year, Teresa had procured a small house at Duruelo, which would become the first reformed monastery for Carmelite Brothers.

John arrived at Duruelo in early October 1568, together with a bricklayer who had worked at Teresa's convent at Valladolid. The bricklayer and John started to clear out the dilapidated house, working purposefully and intensely. The monastery was ready to be dedicated a couple of months later. At the time of the dedication, John took the monastic name John of the Cross. Antonio, who took the name Antonio of Jesus, was appointed the Prior of the Brothers, while John became the Novice Master. Together with a third Brother, José de Jesus, Antonio and John constituted the first community of Reformed Carmelite Brothers.

The little community of Brothers grew, and after two years they already needed a larger house. When the Brothers were offered an opportunity to move to a better building in a neighboring village, they took it. However, John did not remain in the new monastery for very long. Teresa needed him elsewhere. When she reluctantly accepted the appointment as Prioress of the Convent of the Incarnation at Avila, she called John there. Teresa had been commissioned to sort out certain shortcomings in the convent that she had entered as a twenty-year-old. Her commission is evidence that the Carmelite Order was not yet divided into one branch for "the calced" (those wearing shoes, to which the Sisters in the Convent of the Incarnation belonged) and another branch for "the discalced" (those without shoes, who were involved in Teresa's work of reform). However, at that time, the different ideals of the calced and the discalced began to cause deep tensions within the monastic community. Sometimes severe conflicts led to something that could be likened to a civil war. The life of John of the Cross was marked to a great extent by such internal conflicts.

In the year 1577, a new Papal Nuncio for Spain, Felipe Sega, was appointed. Unlike his predecessor, he was not friendly toward Teresa of Jesus and the reform that she had initiated. When the Sisters in the Convent of the Incarnation were about to elect a new Prioress, he threatened that whoever voted for Teresa would be excommunicated. Even so, the Sisters did elect Teresa. The calced Carmelites suspected that it was John of the Cross who had encouraged the Sisters to do so. One night in December 1577, some calced Carmelite Brothers came to John's home at Avila, accompanied by armed men who abducted him and took him secretly to the Carmelite Monastery at Toledo. Here they tried to convince him to give up the work of reform that he was part of. John refused; so, the Brothers locked him in a little cupboard that had been hewn out of the wall and that was normally used as a toilet for the guestroom next door. There was no window in that space, only a small slit in the ceiling that let in some light. John was kept locked in there for nine months. The Brothers brought him bread and water, but John found it difficult to eat, not least because he feared that the Brothers would try to poison him through his food. He was never allowed to wash, in spite of lice and persistent diarrhea. Eventually he managed to escape from his prison. He sought the protection of the discalced Carmelite Sisters in Toledo, who were able to admit a priest into the enclosure on the grounds that there was a seriously ill Sister who needed a confessor. The calced Carmelites could only search the chapel, the parlor, and the outer parts of the Convent. The Sisters took care of the dirty and emaciated John of the Cross.

They sorted out his badly worn habit and managed to get him to eat some pears fried with cinnamon.

THE NIGHT AND NATURE

When John had escaped from his monastic prison, he could once again engage in one of his favorite occupations—praying outdoors in nature. For the rest of his life, he was sent here and there throughout Spain to assist Reformed Carmelite Sisters in recently founded convents or eremitical Carmelite Brothers who lived in places where no one thought it possible to live. For a period, he assisted young Carmelites who were studying in the university city of Baeza. As a monastic Brother and priest, John helped as confessor and pastor, and also as bricklayer, woodcarver, washer-up, vine-grower, and gardener. Sometimes he was elected to positions of trust within the Order, and sometimes he lost them. Some loved him, others loathed him. It seems that he left nobody unaffected. John of the Cross had integrity and civil courage. He was not a fighter, but he did speak up when he thought that something was deficient or if someone else had landed in a fix. His heart was full of compassion for the little ones and the poor; no honorable potentates should be allowed to oppress them.

On his travels throughout Spain, John walked barefoot across breathtakingly beautiful mountain ranges. In the city of his birth, Fontiveros, he could sometimes glimpse the snow-covered mountains of Sierra de Gredos on the horizon. As a prisoner on his way to Toledo, John was brought across the Sierra de Guadarrama, and after his escape from his prison, he walked through the inhospitable mountain pass of Despeñaperros in the majestic mountain range of Sierra Morena.

Many climbers and mountain hikers are struck by the overwhelming insight that we are part of a larger context when they admire an imposing valley or stand below a towering peak. The mountains have such a long history that our concepts of time become puny. The beauty of what you see cannot be captured by the camera. The mountain slopes in photos are never as impressive as they are in reality. So, it is wise to put away the mobile phone on mountain peaks, even if the signal is strong. It is not possible to share this experience in a picture and post it on Facebook. It is easy, however, to be affected by a spring-fresh joy in life—even in the autumn—when you walk in a beautiful landscape.

When I do a mountain hike, I often hum a poem by John of the Cross. In a strict sense, it is not a poem, but a prayer that is written in the form of a long, continuous text. John is a uniquely and divinely talented poet. He is able to express himself poetically even when he is not writing poetry. In the prayer that I sing, he puts into words the sense of freedom that many of us connect with uplifting times spent in nature. When you are allowed to breathe deeply for a while and enjoy all this beauty, you might feel that you have everything you need. For John of the Cross, that sense includes the same insight that the reformatory discovery did for Martin Luther: a person owns everything that God owns because they live in a communion of ownership with God through Jesus. In John's poetry and writings, grace and nature communicate with one another. The happiness that you can feel when you discover a spring flower outside your house or when you take a coffee break below a majestic mountain top is linked to the happiness of the reformatory insight that all God's assets belong to us through Jesus. Therefore, John can rejoice alternately over nature and grace as he writes:

> Mine are the heavens and mine is the earth. Mine are the nations, the just are mine, and mine the sinners. The angels are mine, and the Mother of God, and all the things are mine; and God himself is mine and for me, because Christ is mine and all for me. What do you ask, then, and seek, my soul? Yours is all of this, and all is for you ... Go forth and exult in your Glory! Hide yourself in it and rejoice.[16]

When John was the Superior of the Carmelite Monastery at El Calvario, he often took the Brothers out into nature. There they prayed together and enjoyed one another's company while the birds sang, and pleasant scents wafted around them. Whenever a Brother was downcast or depressed, John handled the situation in a way that is reminiscent of the treatment that the mountaineer Edurne Pasaban was given after her suicide attempt, when she was encouraged to continue climbing mountains. John would take the melancholic person with him out into nature so that he could again admire creation.

John's treatment of melancholy and depressive conditions is often noted when his name is mentioned in Sweden today. John not only wrote poetry: he also wrote two books about how "dark night" periods in life

---

16. John of the Cross, *Sayings of Light and Love*, 87–88 (prayer of a soul taken with love, 27).

can help us to grow and mature in faith. Those books are commentaries on one of John's poems, and were collated gradually over several years. One of them is *The Dark Night of the Soul*. In that work, John primarily illuminates everything that God does in a person's life with the purpose of uniting them with God. In the other book, *The Ascent of Mount Carmel*, John describes what attitude a person should take and how they should act on the way to a deeper union with God. In both these works, John discusses how we should diagnose different sorts of depression.

John's basic view is that there are melancholic conditions that are fruitful stages of development in a person's relationship with God. There are also melancholic conditions that are not beneficial. John wants to help us distinguish between different sorts of depression, because he is keen to ensure that melancholic people are given the right treatment. Some forms of depression can be treated medically, while other forms cannot necessarily be treated in the same way. Simply put, we could say that John wants to distinguish between sickly depression and healthy depression. He describes healthy periods of melancholy as significant but very tiresome aspects of a person's development in faith and in the life of prayer.

John uses the night as a metaphor to describe the depression that he is interested in. In *The Dark Night of the Soul,* he distinguishes between two different nights: the night of the senses and the night of the spirit. He describes how both nights express themselves and how God, through them, leads a person into an ever more intimate relationship with God. In *The Ascent of Mount Carmel*, John reckons with three different nights. The first can be described as the night of the senses, because it touches the life of perceptions and emotions. The second night John describes as the night of faith. That night is a process of purification that affects a person's way of thinking. During the third night, additional human abilities are purified in a corresponding way. The description of the third night is incomplete, since *The Ascent of Mount Carmel* ends very abruptly. Nobody knows whether John left the book unfinished or whether the last few pages have been lost. In my view, the presentation of the third night might have been clearer if John had divided it into two separate nights that might run in parallel. Had he also described these nights as the night of hope and the night of love, the links between the second night (the night of faith) and the third (the night of hope/love) would have been clearer. John's point is that faith, hope, and love, which are divinely granted gifts of grace, theological virtues, or spiritual abilities that people have received through creation and baptism, develop further through the night of faith and the night of hope/love.

IN THE SPIRITUAL SPORTS SHOP

The first few chapters of *The Dark Night of the Soul* are the most entertaining ones. John describes with warmth and humor "the imperfection of beginners" in the spiritual life. It is easy to recognize oneself, and that is also the point of those chapters. John imagines that, by reading those chapters, we will feel a longing for God to lead us into the night of the senses so that we become somewhat easier to deal with.[17]

John describes how spiritual pride, spiritual avarice, spiritual gluttony, and other cardinal or deadly sins can express themselves in us when we try to deepen our faith and our following of Christ. When we begin to take our faith seriously, we behave much as we do when we have discovered how wonderful it is to hike in the mountains on holiday. We rush to the outdoor sports shop and buy new walking boots and a very expensive tent. We test all the rucksacks on the market in order to find the best carrying equipment. We freeze-dry food, we subscribe to at least two periodicals on outdoor pursuits, and we test which type of gas works best in the new burner for our hiking kitchen. Meeting other people who also love mountain-hiking, we become very enthusiastic, and immediately want to share our best touring tips. This generosity is often linked to a poorly disguised competitive instinct. As a beginner, one would like to appear as somewhat more experienced than other beginners in the field.

John describes how beginners in the spiritual life like to receive special attention from spiritual guides or ecclesiastical high-ups. In devout language, they express their longing to speak of spiritual matters. However, they find it difficult to be honest—for example, in the context of confession—since they would like to appear holier than they really are. Beginners are very rarely content with their spiritual life. Instead they become "unhappy and peevish because they don't find the consolation they want in spiritual things." They buy many books that contain spiritual counsel and regulations, and they "weigh themselves down with over-decorated images and rosaries . . . And they prefer one cross to another because of its elaborateness."[18]

---

17. John of the Cross, *Dark Night of the Soul*, 361 (book one, 1:1).
18. John of the Cross, *Dark Night of the Soul*, 365–66 (book one, 3:1).

John emphasizes that beginners usually have a strong desire for spiritual gratification. "When the delight and satisfaction procured in their spiritual exercises passes, these beginners are naturally left without any spiritual savor. And because of this distastefulness, they become peevish in the works they do and easily angered by the least thing, and occasionally they are so unbearable that nobody can put up with them."[19] The beginner's gluttony and over-consumption of spiritual activities and items is caused, according to John, by the fact that they "strive more for spiritual savor than for spiritual purity and discretion."[20] "All their time is spent looking for satisfaction and spiritual consolation; they can never read enough spiritual books, and one minute they are meditating on one subject and the next on another, always hunting for some gratification in the things of God."[21] When they do not feel at home or included in any specific church context, they immediately become over-critical, and want everyone else to adapt to their desires and inclinations.

John describes beginners as being affected by both exaggerated enthusiasm and spiritual gloom. The gloom is linked to the fact that they so easily become jealous of others. John accurately notes that many "experience sensible grief in noting that their neighbor is ahead of them on the road to perfection, and they do not want to hear others praised . . . They cannot bear to hear others being praised without contradicting and undoing these compliments as much as possible."[22] For many beginners, the basic problem is that they "want God to desire what they want."[23] They want God to help them get what they want and to make them feel well. John argues that a person cannot overcome all the imperfections of the beginner's stage on their own by converting or by making an even greater effort. God must intervene; and God does this by leading the person into the night of the senses—a process of faith development that John describes as terribly difficult and yet extremely fruitful. What happens in the night of the senses is that God pulls the carpet out from under all the person's attempts to build up a nice, devout, and refreshing spiritual life.

---

19. John of the Cross, *Dark Night of the Soul*, 370 (book one, 5:1).
20. John of the Cross, *Dark Night of the Soul*, 371 (book one, 6:1).
21. John of the Cross, *Dark Night of the Soul*, 373 (book one, 6:6).
22. John of the Cross, *Dark Night of the Soul*, 374 (book one, 7:1).
23. John of the Cross, *Dark Night of the Soul*, 374 (book one, 7:3).

SPIRITUAL AND MENTAL TROUBLES

In *The Dark Night of the Soul,* John provides three signs that God is leading a person into the night of the senses.[24] Wilfrid Stinissen points out that John is not the first to have noted these three signs. They can also be found in the works of earlier authors—for example, John Tauler, a fourteenth-century mystic who significantly influenced Martin Luther's understanding of God's hiddenness and God's hidden work.[25] According to John, the first sign that God is leading a person into the dark place of faith in order to call forth a deeper union with God is that they "do not get satisfaction or consolation from the things of God, they do not get any from creatures either. Since God puts a soul in this dark night in order to dry up and purge its sensory appetite, he does not allow it to find sweetness or delight in anything."[26] John quickly notes that this sign is also a symptom that appears in melancholic people. He therefore stresses that the second sign is necessary so that we can know that God has brought a person into the dark night of the soul. John writes:

> The second sign for the discernment of this purgation is that the memory ordinarily turns to God solicitously and with painful care, and the soul thinks it is not serving God but turning back, because it is aware of this distaste for the things of God. Hence it is obvious that this aversion and dryness is not the fruit of laxity and tepidity, for lukewarm people do not care much for the things of God nor are they inwardly solicitous about them.
>
> There is, consequently, a notable difference between dryness and lukewarmness. The lukewarm are very lax and remiss in their will and spirit, and have no solicitude about serving God. Those suffering from the purgative dryness are ordinarily solicitous, concerned, and pained about not serving God. Even though the dryness may be furthered by melancholia or some other humor—as it often is—it does not thereby fail to produce its purgative effect in the appetite, for the soul will be deprived of every satisfaction and concerned only about God. If this humor is the entire cause, everything ends in displeasure and does harm to one's nature, and there are none of these desires to serve God that accompany the purgative dryness.[27]

24. John of the Cross, *Dark Night of the Soul,* 377–80 (book one, 9).
25. Stinissen, "Företal." Wrede, *Unio mystica* analyzes Tauler's theology.
26. John of the Cross, *Dark Night of the Soul,* 377 (book one, 9:2).
27. John of the Cross, *Dark Night of the Soul,* 378 (book one, 9:3).

John's description of the second sign and his statement that the faith development of the dark night can be going on at the same time as a person is affected by melancholy or other forms of illness is eagerly discussed by scholars who investigate what John can teach us today. Some believe that it is important that we distinguish between the dark night of the soul (which is a spiritual stage of development) and depression (which is a sickness of another kind). If we do not maintain that distinction, there is a major risk that a person may be given the wrong treatment. People who are searching spiritually and who wonder whether they have made the right choices in life might be put on the sick list, while deeply depressed people might never be given the medication that could save their lives. Regina Bäumer and Michael Plattig represent that view.[28] Martin Lönnebo also reasons along those lines when he notes that there is an equally major difference between the dark night of the soul and depression as there is between a patient file recorded at a psychiatric clinic and a psalm in the Psalter.[29]

Wilfrid Stinissen, Iain Matthew, and Kevin Culligan are examples of contemporary Carmelites who emphasize instead that it is important that what we describe as mental ill health can become fruitful spiritual processes of purification in a person's life. Their view is that God can use a number of different dark rooms in God's work of development. God can use divorce, depression, career setbacks, involuntary childlessness, or the processes of mourning to achieve an increasingly intimate relationship with a person. Even though God is not the origin of every dark night that happens to us, and does not want it to happen to us, God can turn evil into something good. Therefore, we cannot make any strict distinction between the dark night of the soul and other dark periods that we are forced to suffer.

Iain Matthew notes that John's own night included his months of imprisonment in Toledo. Regarding others, he can use 'night language' about the most non-mystical inflictions: financial difficulties, loneliness, friends' betrayals; misjudgments by the authorities; community conflicts.[30] Wilfrid Stinissen reasons along the same lines when he stresses that, to some extent, it is up to a person to determine how they want to understand the difficulties that they are going through. Even though not

---

28. Bäumer and Plattig, "Dark Night and Depression."
29. Lönnebo, *Religionens fem språk*, 100.
30. Matthew, *Gud berör och förvandlar*, 139.

every kind of suffering can be regarded as a dark night, there is in fact some liberty of interpretation. Stinissen writes:

> It happens that a pained person asks me: "Is this the dark night?" The answer is: It is you who must decide. If you are bitter and revolt, it is a suffering that is by and large in vain and that will destroy your life. But if you say "Yes" and willingly allow that to happen that must happen, then this can become an element in your dark night. You will meet *God* in this. You will get to know him in a new way, you will understand that he is other than you thought, that his love is not sentimental, but that he has a completely different significance than what you had sensed. One and the same thing can become a blessing or a curse, depending on how you receive it.[31]

Stinissen notes that it would be absurd to comfort all who find themselves in mental distress by telling them that they are going through the dark night of the soul. Psychological suffering is not always a dark night of the kind of which John speaks; but sometimes it might be an element of the dark night. For the suffering to function as a dark night, the suffering person must be consciously on their way to God, Stinissen believes. They must also choose to see the suffering in the larger context of faith if it is going to be meaningful to speak of a dark night.[32]

Kevin Culligan shares Stinissen's perspective. He notes that the most common question he is asked when he lectures on spiritual guidance is how one can distinguish spiritually fruitful periods of depression from damaging conditions of illness. Today many Carmelites are very well-educated in psychiatry and psychology. This interest in medicine and medical information is nothing new, however. It was found in both Martin Luther and the Carmelites who lived in the sixteenth century. In a letter to the Prioress of the Convent at Valladolid, Teresa of Avila writes about a syrup that "relieved me of that torment of melancholy."[33] Cullingan stresses that, for Christians who are affected by mental ill-health, an aspect of the dark night might be to seek and receive help from other contexts besides spiritual exercises in the church context.[34]

---

31. Stinissen, *Natten är mitt ljus*, 50–51.
32. Stinissen, *Natten är mitt ljus*, 74–75.
33. Letter to Mother Maria Bautista, May 14, 1574. Teresa of Avila, *Collected Letters*, Letter 63.
34. Culligan, "Dark Night and Depression," 119, 132.

Cullingan verbalizes an important insight with which scholars with different perspectives on the relationship between the dark night and depressions can agree. People do not consist of only body and soul. There are spiritual dimensions within us as well. The Spirit, and the life of the Spirit in a person, God, collaborate with a person's physical health and spiritual development in a number of different ways. We can only understand a small part of this intricate collaboration.

One thing that we can understand is that a person's life of prayer is affected by the state of their body, soul, and spirit.[35] John of the Cross highlights the life of prayer particularly when he notes that the third sign that a person is being brought into the dark night of the soul is that they are no longer able to pray in the same way as in the past. They are no longer able to meditate, no matter how much effort they put into it.[36] In *The Ascent of Mount Carmel*, John expands the third sign into three different signs, all of which indicate that God makes it possible through the purifying process of the night for the person to pray in a new way: God lets the person discover contemplative prayer. In this prayer, the person "likes to remain alone in loving awareness of God, without particular considerations, in interior peace and quiet and repose."[37] John believes that the growth of contemplative prayer is connected to what he describes as the night of faith in *The Ascent of Mount Carmel*.

THE DIVINE COMPUTER SUPPORT

Like Martin Luther, John of the Cross assumes that faith is the proper way for the soul to find union with God.[38] Sometimes he describes faith as the only way to experience union with God.[39] When John elaborates his thoughts concerning this union in *The Ascent of Mount Carmel*, he distinguishes between two different types of union with God.[40] He describes

---

35. Culligan, "Dark Night and Depression," 135.

36. John of the Cross, *Dark Night of the Soul*, 380 (book one, 9:8).

37. John of the Cross, *Ascent of Mount Carmel*, 189–90 (book two, 13:4. The three signs are summarized in 13:2, 13:3, 13:4).

38. John of the Cross, *Ascent of Mount Carmel*, 173 (book two, 8:1). Cf. Stein, *Science of the Cross*, 65.

39. John of the Cross, *Living Flame of Love*, 692 (stanza 3, point 48); John of the Cross, *Spiritual Canticle*, 515 (twelfth stanza, point 1); John of the Cross, *Ascent of Mount Carmel*, 262 (book two, 30:5).

40. The following is based on John of the Cross, *Ascent of Mount Carmel*, 154–78. (book two, chapters 1–9); and on Pulkkanen, *Dark Night*, 50–51, 96–97.

the first as a substantial union or a union by being. In that context, he stresses that everything is connected to God, since God has created everything. If God were to withdraw God's assistance, the world would fall to pieces because it would lack substance. The second union John describes as a union by likeness, which corresponds to what Martin Luther describes as the sanctification of a person. John of the Cross thinks that God draws a person through this union by likeness into an ever more intimate relationship with God. In that process, God sometimes makes use of the difficulties and sufferings that afflict a person. Besides these two forms of union with God, which John defines in *The Ascent of Mount Carmel*, he also believes that a person can be united with God by other means—for example, through the sacraments.[41]

A person's union by likeness is affected by the nights through which God leads them. What happens in the dark night that John describes as the night of the senses is that God makes sure that the person's faith will have a strong root system. God allows the seed of faith to grow, just like a growing plant, whose leaves begin to shoot up above the surface of the soil. Through the night of the senses, God changes the preconditions for a person's potential to believe. They can believe at a deeper level of the personality and in a more fruitful way.

The Carmelites like to use images from nature to explain how faith grows and develops through the dark night of the soul. However, I take the liberty of using a metaphor from engineering. When Thérèse of the Child Jesus describes a person's relationship with Jesus, she uses the image of an elevator. With reference to the development of technology in our own time, you could say that what is happening in the dark night of the soul is that a person's faith is updated by undermining their own attempts to grow in faith. Simply put, John of the Cross assumes that everyone has what we could describe as a first version of faith (faith 1.0), since every person is part of creation. All people are in touch with God, who is the source of faith. When a person is baptized, their faith is updated (they are given faith 2.0) by receiving the Holy Spirit. Through the dark night of the senses, a person's faith is updated yet another time (they are given faith 3.0). That updating is usually fairly complicated to carry out, since diverse system faults occur regularly in connection with that transformation. There are many bugs in the human system that can cause malfunctions. A person can therefore receive many messages that

---

41. Cf. Matthew, *Gud berör och förvandlar*, 172.

things are wrong during the updating, but once it has been carried out, the system can be re-started, and then it functions more adequately. For most people, subsequent updates are not so complicated to carry out. We can receive faith 3.1, faith 3.2, faith 3.3, and so on, without needing to re-start the system.

The updating of the entire system of faith that the night of the senses implies can be described as God's taking command of a person's relationship with God, somewhat like computer support taking command of my desktop in order to sort out what I have messed up. During the dark night, a person discovers that God acts independently, and that God's will does not permit itself to be adapted to that person's own will. People often feel scared when God takes the initiative. With increasing anxiety and worry, a person sees how God moves around the documents on the desktop and sorts them out into a different order than they had chosen. God has put their own computer mouse out of order.

The purpose of the dark night is to teach a person to rest safely in God's hands, even though God might appear for the moment to be frightening, and even though the person cannot understand at all how this painful process of transformation could possibly be something good. In *The Dark Night of the Soul*, John stresses that a person should wait passively while God updates their faith. They should not disturb God's work by pressing this or that button on the keyboard—and, in particular, by ceasing to pray, which is like pulling out the plug. When John describes human inactivity in the process of updating, his descriptions are in line with Martin Luther's point that it is the Holy Spirit alone who awakens a person's faith and enables their growth in faith.[42] John writes that, if the souls who are in the state of updating in the dark night "know how to remain quiet, without care or solicitate about any interior or exterior work, they will soon in that unconcern and idleness delicately experience the interior nourishment."[43] The nourishment that John speaks of is the contemplative prayer that God gives people. Through contemplative prayer, a person believes, hopes, and loves at an interior level that is more fully illuminated by the sun. Further dimensions of a person's existence will also be shaped and divinized by God's sunlight.

---

42. Luther, *Bondage of the Will*; *Luther's Works*, 33:242–43.
43. John of the Cross, *Dark Night of the Soul*, 379 (book one, 9:6).

In the Carmelite tradition, the contemplative prayer that God grants a person through the dark night is often linked to mysticism.[44] It therefore seems natural to place the process that John describes as the night of the senses alongside the same part of the journey that Teresa of Avila calls the fourth dwelling. In the fourth dwelling, the person finds the turning point between their own attempts to sort out their spiritual life and the mystical life that God grants them.

If we want to fit the night of the senses into James Fowler's model, we should first of all note the difficult transition between one's own *individuative-reflective faith* and *conjunctive faith*. John has a message that can be particularly liberating for adults who in various ways are forced to realize that they need to mature further in order to come to terms with life. It may be that a divorce or an illness puts a spoke in the wheel. Existential issues come to the fore. Family therapists and doctors are brought in. John underlines that God is there as well to help those who are affected. We cannot achieve full human maturity on our own, however much we might work at it ourselves. God must come to our aid. With the help of God, we can be more thoroughly healed or made whole.

In the thought-through stage of faith, people rely on their own ability to think. They might even, with some ambiguity, seek to decide what it feels right for themselves to believe. *Conjunctive faith*, in turn, is characterized by the fact that a person's more unconscious aspects have been drawn into the life of faith. During the development of *conjunctive faith*, a person has realized that they are more than what they think and feel. They have a deeper identity, which John of the Cross would describe as a union with God by likeness.

BRIDES, MOTHERS, SISTERS, AND WIDOWS

Like Martin Luther, Teresa of Jesus, and Thérèse of the Child Jesus, John of the Cross also uses the image of the intimate union of love between bride and bridegroom to describe a person's union with God by likeness. Both in the poem that begins with the stanza, "The living flame of love" and in the commentary with the same title, the soul/the bride sings praise to the bridegroom whom she loves so passionately and for whom she longs. John wrote that poem for Ana del Mercado y Peñalosa, who was a devout widow under his pastoral guidance. He also wrote a commentary on another poem that has become a classic in the tradition of bridal

---

44. See further Johannesson, "Kön och bön."

mysticism, *The spiritual canticle*. That book he gave to another woman under his guidance, Anna of Jesus. She was a Carmelite Sister and one of Teresa of Avila's closest assistants. (It was one of Anna's relics that Thérèse of the Child Jesus asked the Sisters to fetch when she was dying.)

In *The spiritual canticle*, John describes how the bridegroom/God/Jesus inflicts a wound of love on the bride/soul/person that only God can heal. He tells how the bride/soul/person, through union with the bridegroom/God/Jesus, reaches a deeper knowledge of the faith. He has the bride sing the praise of her bridegroom in the following lines:

> There he gave me his breast;
> there he taught me a sweet and living knowledge;
> and I gave myself to him,
> keeping nothing back;
> there I promised to be his bride.[45]

John's use of the bridal metaphor is extensive and thought-provoking. With regard to the dark night of the soul and the process of maturing faith, however, a different metaphor sticks out. John describes how God, like a nursing mother who brings up a child, helps a person to grow and develop by letting them pass through the night of the senses.

John highlights how the human desires for pleasure, success, and possessions that he believes must be purified through the dark night of the soul "resemble little children, restless and hard to please, always whining to their mother for this thing or that, and never satisfied."[46] In his view, a person's own effort to develop a relationship with God in accordance with their own inclinations "resembles a little boy who kicks and cries, wanting to walk when his mother wants to carry him; thus he neither allows his mother to make any headway nor makes any himself."[47] John also uses the metaphor of a mother when he discusses the difficulties caused by pastors who try to make people whom God has brought into contemplative prayer to begin to pray by again using words and images. He describes those problems in figurative language that circles around some very strange breastfeeding routines. For a person engaged in contemplative prayer, meditation exercises are just as wrong as feeding a suckling child by hand would be. The experience of such forced meditation "resembles that of a suckling child who finds that the breast is

---

45. John of the Cross, *Spiritual Canticle*, 475 (stanza 27).
46. John of the Cross, *Ascent of Mount Carmel*, 132 (book one, 6:6).
47. John of the Cross, *Living Flame of Love*, 701 (stanza 3, point 66).

taken away just when it is beginning to taste the milk that was gathered there for it. As a result it is forced to renew its efforts of grasping and squeezing."[48] Even when John describes how God deals with beginners and helps them to grow in faith through the dark night, he likens God to a nursing mother. For the good of the child, a mother must sometimes abstain from satisfying needs that would stop the child from growing and developing. John writes:

> God nurtures and caresses the soul, after it has been resolutely converted to his service, like a loving mother who warms her child with the heat of her bosom, nurses it with good milk and tender food, and carries and caresses it in her arms. But as the child grows older, the mother withholds her caresses and hides her tender love; she rubs bitter aloes on her sweet breast and sets the child down from her arms, letting it walk on its own feet so that it may put aside the habits of childhood and grow accustomed to greater and more important things. The grace of God acts just as a loving mother by re-engendering in the soul new enthusiasm and fervor in the service of God. With no effort on the soul's part, this grace causes it to taste sweet and delectable milk and to experience intense satisfaction in the performance of spiritual exercises, because God is handing the breast of his tender love to the soul, just as if it were a delicate child.[49]

We could say that the person who is in the dark night experiences this as though God has rubbed the breast with bitter aloe juice and put them down on the floor, where they discover that they cannot manage on their own. That discovery gives them a new perspective on what is important in life. John writes that, after the dark night, a person lives in a faith that can be described as a second naivety, a new form of childhood. Now the person will no longer try to squeeze out the milk by hand; now God allows that person to sink back on to the mother's breast and drink again. Teresa of Jesus makes a link to the same metaphors when she stresses that, in the final dwelling of the interior castle, it seems that God continuously provides nourishment for the soul. In the seventh dwelling, "from those divine breasts where it seems God is always sustaining the soul there flow streams of milk bringing comfort to all the people of the

---

48. John of the Cross, *Ascent of Mount Carmel*, 192 (book two, 14:3).
49. John of the Cross, *Dark Night of the Soul*, 361–62. (Book one, 1:2).

castle."[50] We could say that a person comes into the second period of breastfeeding by God bringing them through the dark night of the soul.

John's bridal mysticism and his "mother" metaphors were not overly challenging in his own time. However, his view that the independence of the Reformed Sisters of the Carmelite Order should be preserved was a challenge. In John's day, influential Carmelite Brothers wanted to carry out a change of structures that would mean a loss of power and influence for the Sisters. John opposed such a reorganization, and for that he was punished. He lost all his appointments within the Carmelite Order and was sent to an isolated monastery in the mountain range of Sierra Morena. One of his monastic Brothers, Diego Evangelista, even started a campaign of slander in order to discredit John's good name.[51]

John was abused within his own Order because he cared too much about the Sisters of the same Order. And then he was taken seriously ill. In December 1593 he died in the Carmelite Monastery at Úbeda, where he had been cared for during his final days. Ana de Mercado y Peñalosa, the widow who had been given the manuscript of *The Living Flame of Love,* made sure that he was later buried at Segovia.

Anna of Jesus, who had been given the manuscript of *The Spiritual Canticle,* had not only that manuscript in her possession: she had also been given a copy of one of John's most famous drawings. Anna of Jesus was the Prioress in the convent at Beas de Segura at the same time as John was the Superior in the nearby monastery. The Sisters in that convent were particularly close to John. On their behalf he had drawn a sketch of Mount Carmel that summarized his teaching.[52] That sketch is a kind of map or guide that shows how one can reach the top of the mountain. John made sure that every Sister in the convent at Beas was given her own copy. So, it was not only the Prioress who received that gift of grace.

THE WEIGHTLESS RUCKSACK

Anyone who has ever undertaken a mountain hike for several days knows how important it is not to pack too many things or any heavy equipment in the rucksack. What we bring with us is particularly important if we have to walk a long way or up steep slopes. Nothing vitally important should be missing, and nothing unnecessary should be included. When

---

50. Teresa of Avila, *Interior Castle,* 435 (seventh dwelling, 2:6).
51. Arborelius, *Allt och intet,* 168.
52. John of the Cross, *Ascent of Mount Carmel,* 110–11.

John was the Superior in the Monastery of El Calvario, he walked eight to ten kilometres across the mountains every week in order to visit the Sisters at Beas. Iain Matthew tells us about the hike and the drawings that the Sisters were given. He writes:

> Retracing the journey, one can follow a meandering route which takes hours, leaving one hot and slightly irritated. There is, apparently, a more direct route. John would probably have made it his business to find this one, and take it. To keep the sisters going while he was away, John wrote cards for each one of them. One which he spread fairly widely . . . was a sketch of a mountain, with wide paths leading to dead ends, and one narrow path going direct to the summit. (Add the scrunch of sand and stones and we are with him on his route to Beas.) On the central path is the word 'nada'—'nothing.' It is repeated all the way up—*nada, nada, nada, nada, nada, nada,* and at the broad, spacious, sun-kissed summit, *nada*.[53]

The wide paths that do not lead anywhere are called "the way of the imperfect spirit with regard to earthly things" and "the way of the imperfect spirit with regard to heavenly things" respectively. We walk along the path of the imperfect spirit with regard to earthly things when we believe in and behave as if possessions, pleasures, successes, and honors were goals worth striving for. God leads us through different nights in order to show us that pleasant dinners, beautifully furnished flats, or exotic travel are not the meaning of life. We walk along the path of the imperfect spirit with regard to heavenly things when we believe and behave like those beginners whom John so lovingly describes in the introductory chapters of *The Dark Night of the Soul*. Along the path of the imperfect spirit we might, for example, engage in devotions, since we enjoy appearing a little better as Christians than the great majority. Someone might want to stand in high favor with the rector. Someone else might apply for the post as rector because it is a greater honor to be the rector than to be the curate. Just as with earthly matters, God needs to purify our desires and inclinations with regard to heavenly matters. God does that by pulling away the carpet from under our devotions and ambitions. However, that does not mean that God clears away all forms of spiritual exercise.

In *The Ascent of Mount Carmel*, John illuminates the significance of fruitful *ascesis* in a person's life. We could say that he contributes to the list of what we need to pack in our rucksack so that we are not overcome

---

53. Matthew, *Gud berör och förvandlar*, 67–68.

along the road. A feverish debate in the Carmelite Order in the sixteenth century focused on how demanding the ascetic exercises that the Brothers and Sisters would be permitted to undertake should be. John is regularly described as an advocate of common-sense moderation; but to many of us who read his writings today, he seems like an excessively radical desert hermit who always recommends the most troublesome and painful exercises. It is quite obvious that he himself did not follow the comfortable way. He would hardly have felt at home in the noisy fellowship around Martin Luther's dinner table. However, in the final chapters of *The Ascent of Mount Carmel,* John describes at least one form of *ascesis* that is in line with the criticism of the devotional life at that time that was the driving force of the Protestant Reformation.

John reflected on how we can use the things around us in a way that furthers our growth in faith rather than endangers our devotional life. When he discusses rosaries and images of the saints, he presents an *ascesis* that aims actively to counter our turned-in focus on ourselves and our own activities in relation to God. We might then counteract our own justification by works. If, for example, we become too attached to a particular rosary, we might begin to believe that God will hear our prayers better if we use that particular rosary. Then our spiritual exercise might consist of replacing that rosary. In the same way, we can use images of the saints in the wrong way. Sometimes ignorance about images of saints and icons goes so far, John writes, "that [people] trust more in one statue than in another and think that God will answer them more readily through it, even when both statues represent the same person, such as those of our Lord or our Blessed Lady."[54] John regards that sort of attitude to items that can help us to grow in faith as wrong.

Based on the same premises, John criticizes pilgrimages, sermons, and ceremonies that have the wrong focus. Among the ceremonies, he highlights some liturgical habits and practices that "are used by many today with indiscreet devotions." John explains what the problem is with such unwise devotions when he writes:

> These people attribute so much efficacy to methods of carrying out their devotions and prayers and so trust in them that they believe that if one point is missing or certain limits have been exceeded their prayer will be profitless and go unanswered. As a result they put more trust in these methods than they do in the living prayer, not without great disrespect and offense toward

---

54. John of the Cross, *Ascent of Mount Carmel,* 333–34 (book three, 36:1).

God. For example, they demand that the Mass be said with a certain number of candles, no more nor less; or that it be celebrated at a particular hour, no sooner nor later; or that it be said after a certain day, not before; or that that the prayers and stations be a particular number and kind and that they be recited at certain times and with certain ceremonies, and neither before nor after, nor in any other way; and that the person performing the ceremonies have certain endowments and characteristics. And they are of the opinion that nothing will be accomplished if one of these points is lacking. What is worse—and intolerable—is that some desire to experience an effect in themselves: either the granting of their petition or the knowledge that it will be granted at the end of those superstitious ceremonies.[55]

John criticizes not only the effect-seeking liturgical formalism that becomes solemn in a fraudulent way. He also criticizes a wrong focus on Church ceremonies that could best be described as the opposite kind of trap. Far too often we celebrate Church feasts as if the church were an actor in the entertainment profession. When there is a solemn festivity in some location, we sometimes care more about other things than the real reason for the celebration. John writes:

> Many are usually happier because of the recreation derived from the celebration—by seeing or being seen, or by eating, or by some other means—than because of God's pleasure. In these inclinations and intentions they do not please God. This is especially so with those who in organizing the religious festivals invent ridiculous and undevout things to incite laughter among the people, which only adds to the distraction. Others design displays meant to please the people more than to arouse their devotion.[56]

John's criticism of distorted church festivities, and the *ascesis* that he recommends, aims to liberate people from all the things that hamper their faith development. John encourages us to cut the bonds that stop us from flying free into the sky. Today, for example, he would encourage us to abstain from buying a new mobile phone, since we need to learn that a mobile phone is *nada* from the perspective of eternity. In the same way, we might have to force ourselves to go to church, even though it might not be our favorite priest who is preaching, since we need to learn that

---

55. John of the Cross, *Ascent of Mount Carmel*, 344–45 (book three, 43:2–3).
56. John of the Cross, *Ascent of Mount Carmel*, 338 (book three, 38:2).

it is all right to pray and to celebrate Mass, even if the preacher is awful. John expressively describes a person's *ascesis* as a work of liberation. The *ascesis* creates the empty space that is necessary for God to give even more of God to each person.[57] In that sense you could say that the *ascesis* that John values is the sort that protects the freedom of the Christian person.

The visit by the relics of Thérèse of the Child Jesus gave us in Sweden a reason to deepen our reflection on what characterizes a sound and liberating *ascesis*. Sometimes Thérèse of the Child Jesus is described as the prime disciple of John of the Cross. Thérèse realized that everything is grace—even a person's ascetical exercises. She stressed that God grants the believer the grace to collaborate with God so that faith, hope, and love may permeate that person and the whole world more and more. In John's language, we could say that Thérèse discovered that, by realizing more and more of her own smallness, a person can become everything, since that person shares everything with God, and God is everything.

Thérèse can also help us to deepen our reflection on the significance of the night for the development of our faith. In the early 1990s, the Church of Sweden celebrated a great jubilee: the four hundredth anniversary of the adoption of the Augsburg Confession by the Uppsala Meeting.[58] In view of that jubilee, the Carmelite Brother Anders Arborelius asked us whether "a Lutheran 4th centenary, the one that remembers the Uppsala Meeting in 1593, might give reason to find certain points of contact between the night of John of the Cross and the night of Martin Luther."[59] That question was brought up again when the relics of St. Thérèse of the Child Jesus visited the Nordic countries.

During her final days here on Earth, Thérèse of the Child Jesus not only suffered from tuberculosis. She was also affected by the dark night of faith. She thought that she had to eat the same dry food as atheists. She also said that, during that difficult period of her illness, she would have committed suicide if she had not had her faith. That she did not commit suicide—even though the strong medication was within her reach—shows that God preserved Thérèse in the faith, even though she herself was not able to believe, either intellectually or on a more emotional level. Faith might rest deeper than that.

57. John of the Cross, *Ascent of Mount Carmel*, 166 (book two, 5:11).

58. The Uppsala meeting in 1593 marks the final confirmation and consolidation of the Lutheran Reformation in Sweden.

59. Arborelius, *Allt och intet*, 9.

Like many Church of Sweden parishes that sing songs from the ecumenical community at Taizé, Thérèse of the Child Jesus testifies to a vitally decisive insight that many of us think of spontaneously when we hear John of the Cross mentioned. In the dark night of the soul, God lights a fire that never goes out.[60] In another much-loved song, the Swedish hymn "Närmare Gud till dig" (Nearer My God to Thee), the same night metaphor that John of the Cross has developed is used. In the fourth verse there is a line that puts into words an experience that many people who have been affected by something as dark as night can agree on afterwards: "This dark night has brought me / nearer my God to thee" (Swedish Hymnal 271:4). The faith grew when the person's trust in God matured. When the person was brought through the darkness, the night brought them closer to God. That is an insight that makes me hopeful. I believe that God can bring even churches and denominations through dark periods and risky challenges. With the help of God, the hard things can bear good fruit.

---

60. I allude to the Taizé song "Dans nos obscurités" (In Our Darkest Night).

5

The Compass Direction

EVEN DURING HIS LIFETIME, George Mallory was virtually canonized around the British Empire. Newspapers reported on his hardships on Mount Everest, and the lecture tours that he carried out between his attempts to reach the peaks gathered large audiences. Mallory's halo did not slip when he lost his life on the highest mountain in the world. Today he is a cult figure far beyond the small circle of committed mountaineers. His attitude to demanding tasks is regularly used as an inspiring example within the framework of leadership training. Rock bands and stage artists have articulated his philosophy of life.

Mallory had received his degree from the University of Cambridge. He had just been appointed to a prestigious teaching position when he set off on what was to become his last Everest expedition. At the altitude of 8,200 meters above sea level, he wrote his final message—in perfect British English—to the geologist Noel Odell. Mallory told him that he and Andrew Irvine had lost their compass somewhere in their tent. "[F]or the Lord's sake, rescue it," he exhorted Odell.[1]

When Mallory was asked why he wanted to ascend the highest mountain in the world, he not only gave the laconic answer for which he has become so famous. "Because it's there" was not the only thing he had to say about his driving forces. Mallory explained his passion in greater detail and reflected on its importance in his writings. He stressed that the point of ascending Mount Everest was not to put his hands on something valuable. We cannot find gold, silver, pearls, or new supplies of coal or iron on Mount Everest; so, it is not dreams of wealth that drive us toward

---

1. There is a photo of Mallory's note in Hemmleb et al., *Ghosts of Everest*, 15.

the skies. We can of course learn something about how the human body reacts to the lack of oxygen from our attempts to reach the summits; but that knowledge is not the most important aspect. What is central is what happens inside a person when they outwardly face a mountain. Mallory is believed to have said that "if you cannot understand that there is something in man which responds to the challenge of this mountain and goes out to meet it, that the struggle is the struggle of life itself upward and forever upward," then you cannot understand why we walk in the mist in order to reach heights that are not marked on the inadequate maps that are available to us.

As a student at Cambridge, George Mallory was associated with the artist Duncan Grant. Grant used Mallory as a stylish nude photo model. Mallory noted that he wanted to explore his own naked self, who he was, beyond all the various roles that he had and the achievements for which he received so much attention. In Duncan's photos, Mallory is posing in a studio. There are photos from the Everest expeditions that show Mallory's agile body, and at least some of his nakedness, in more natural positions. In the Himalayas, George Mallory not only had the chance to make history: he also had the opportunity to get to know more about himself and the conditions of life that we share with one another.

GOD AND THE NAKED PERSON

In the mountains, a person's naked self often appears very clearly. If you need to use your hands in order to have the courage to continue the route across a windy ridge toward the top, you feel your vulnerability very keenly in both body and soul. If you have to wade through an ice-cold torrent from a glacier with the water streaming around your thighs, you will not think of anything else besides how easy it would be to lose your footing and be swept away. That is why mountains in the world of the Bible are connected to people's honest and life-changing encounters with God. On a mountain, a person stands naked before God in a very particular way. If all goes well, the mountain winds will blow away a person's excessive trust in their own ability and their unjustified confidence in that over-expensive equipment from the sports shop.

The Bible speaks of several different kinds of mountains. They all fulfill the role of stripping people of the distorted ideas and attitudes that hide their true selves and so prevent an open-hearted dialog with God. In the mountain deserts, both Jesus and the desert hermits of the early

Church fought the demons. Here they could not avoid the temptations that most people do not discern in everyday life as life-threatening. It became clear that fatal pride and the deadly summit fever had to be overcome so that they—and the whole of humanity—would not perish. The prime cause of death on high mountains is exaggerated ambitions. Many desert hermits would say that the same applies to life in general.

In the biblical world, the mountain of temptation and the mountain of transfiguration are much closer to one another than we might believe. We could say that both are part of the same mountain range. On the mountain of temptation, God lets us discover how little we can achieve on our own. The earthly ropes that we use when we ascend the peaks cannot hold the weight with which we load them. On the mountain of transfiguration, God lets us see God's back through the beauty of nature, or face-to-face in Jesus Christ. God lets us find the lost compass in the midst of the earthly mess by giving us commandments or assignments that enable us to journey on with confidence.

Most of us will never attempt to climb the highest mountains in the world; but we can still share the alpinist's hardships, dreams, and life experiences. We can feel the same dizzy happiness before the beauty of nature as a mountaineer who sees the sun's rays in the ice crystals when we smell the scent of the lilies of the valley; or when we discover a single autumn leaf on our balcony. Many of us feel that we encounter God in nature. A walk in the forest or in your own garden can be your mountain of transfiguration.

The mountain of temptation is also situated exactly where we are. The deadly summit fever that pushes us to continue in the wrong direction by telling us that it would be a shame to turn back can affect us in the most unexpected circumstances. There is just one more step on the career ladder, one more possession that you need, one more man or woman whom it would be exciting to conquer. Both the biblical authors and the early desert hermits testify that the mountain of temptation is very hilly. Behind every hill are yet further hills that you can strive to climb, even though they are in fact leading you in the wrong direction.

God leads us up on to the mount of transfiguration and down from the mount of temptation. God can also raise the dead when the mountains have fallen on us. Mountains can crush us without either ourselves or God being the cause of the accident. We might be affected by sorrow in the family or by a serious illness that, figuratively speaking, forces us to crawl on all fours across a narrow mountain ridge with steep slopes on either side. Maybe we will have to go through a divorce or a difficult reorganization at work. It might feel like a glacier torrent that risks sweeping our feet from under us.

Most of the mountains that we are forced to ascend we have not chosen for ourselves. If anyone were to ask us why we ascend such a mountain, the only meaningful answer is the laconic statement, "Because it is there." The mountain has affected me. The struggle that I have to go through is, in the words of George Mallory, "the struggle of life itself."

A MOUNTAIN SPIRITUALITY

On YouTube I found a couple of charming films with a Carmelite Brother called Robert Opala. Dressed in sportswear, he is sitting in an alpine landscape in the vicinity of Grossglockner, the highest mountain in Austria, where he lectures on Carmel's spirituality through the ages. Sometimes you see him with an ice axe and climbing rope on his way up to some peak in the area. Opala describes the Carmelite tradition as "a mountain spirituality." On mountains, we are very tangibly faced with the beauty of creation—and with our own limitations. Opala stresses that Carmelites explore how God can meet us through such life experiences.

Over the years I have been asked on a number of occasions why I am so interested in the spirituality of the saints of Carmel. Just like George Mallory, I have given many different answers when I have tried to say something clever about my driving forces. Sometimes I have stressed that there are remarkable similarities between the Evangelical-Lutheran tradition and the spirituality of the Carmelites. Usually, I have added that the spirituality of the Carmelites needs to be explored in our day and age, which is so interested in spirituality. Sometimes I have pointed out that all the philosophers of religion who are interested in mysticism write about the Carmelites. Now and then I have wondered whether I should give a laconic answer, just like George Mallory: "I am interested in the Carmelites because they are there." I grew up in Filipstad, and I regularly visited the Libris bookshop in Karlstad. On the shelf of spiritual classics there were, by and large, only books by Carmelites, and I read them because I was curious about everything that had to do with the Christian faith. When I grew older, I realized that the Carmelites had helped me to put words to experiences that I found hard to describe within the framework of any other system of language or thought.

Like George Mallory, I wanted to explore new areas that we have not yet had the opportunity to map out; and so I greatly valued having a compass. The Evangelical-Lutheran tradition is my compass when I explore the mountain spirituality of Carmel. I would very much like us to help one another to find that compass whenever it gets lost in the Church of Sweden's tent. My thought is that it might be easier to find that compass if we asked someone else to help in the search for it. I believe that the three Doctors of the Church of the Carmelite Order can help us to rediscover what it means that people are justified by grace alone through faith-filled trust in Jesus Christ. We can have a constructive dialog with them because they understand a person's life-giving relationship with God in a way that is in line with—and challenges—Martin Luther's theological thinking.

Just like Mallory, I am attracted to the adventure of walking beyond the edges of the map. The scholar in me would like to spend a few years in a library for the purpose of clarifying exactly how Thérèse of the Child Jesus's understanding of grace relates to Martin Luther's perspective on God's benevolent will and care. In the future, I hope to get the opportunity to explore in greater detail whether the Christology that Teresa of Jesus expresses is far too creation-based to attract Luther, and whether John of the Cross uses the concept of "faith" in the same sense as Martin Luther does. Right now, I am spending time on another project: I want to engage in receptive ecumenism for the purpose of describing how the three Doctors of the Church of the Carmelite Order can help us in the Church of Sweden to counteract the secularization from within. My conclusions can be summarized against the background of a clearer description of the secularization from within that challenges me.

THE SECULARIZATION FROM WITHIN AND THE INTEREST IN SPIRITUALITY

The philosopher Charles Taylor has written an influential and much-discussed book on what characterizes our secular and secularized age.[2] Taylor distinguishes between three different meanings of the concept of "secularization." First, we can use this concept to denote a development that separates Church and state to an increasing extent. The state becomes increasingly secular in the sense that it is increasingly possible to participate in social life without having to participate in activities that

---

2. The following is based on the introduction to Taylor, *Secular Age*.

are connected to religious denominations. When we use the concept in that sense, we can say, for example, that schools' end-of-term ceremonies that have no prayers or blessings are an expression of the secularization of society, as is the removal of morning prayer with hymn singing at the beginning of the school day. If we speak of the inner secularization of the Church in this sense, we might refer to a development that makes it possible to participate in the life of the church without engaging in activities that include prayer, blessings, and hymn singing.

Second, we can use the concept of "secularization" to describe a development in which fewer and fewer people state that they embrace religious perceptions of faith and/or participate in religious activities. On the basis of that understanding, we could, for example, describe Sweden as one of the most secularized countries in the world, since very few Swedes say that they believe in God when they respond to questionnaire surveys. Correspondingly, we could describe the secularization of the Church from within as a change that means that a smaller number of young people are confirmed. In the Church of Sweden, we follow very carefully the secularization from within in this sense, aided by our statistics. We know almost exactly how many people receive Holy Communion every year, and how many confirmands we have.

Taylor's primary contribution to the discussion of definitions is that he distinguishes a third meaning that the concept of "secularization" might have. Taylor believes that we sometimes speak of a development in which the preconditions for religious faith are changing radically as a form of secularization. The shift of perspective or of paradigm appears as a form of secularization against the background of established religious traditions of interpretation.

Taylor stresses that, today, secularization in the third sense is the most interesting area of investigation. He claims that the Western world is currently going through a stage of development that he describes as a subjective turn.[3] This change of perspective means, among other things, that people have less and less confidence in external authority in the form of holy scriptures, leaders, ideological convictions, or moral standards that are held in common and are widely accepted. Instead, our interior life emerges as the primary source of authority. Each person is encouraged to be their own authority, to think independently, to choose for themselves, and to follow the path that feels right for them. The individual person's

---

3. Cf. Heelas and Woodhead, *Spiritual Revolution*, 2–7, 78–82.

preference and taste becomes the norm in a way that affects their perception not only of humanity but also of God.

In one sense, this change implies increasing individualism. In another sense, this subjective turn emerges as a collective phenomenon. We live in and keep up a culture that holds out that the highest good, that which is really worth striving for, is to realize oneself. We no longer connect self-realization with fulfilling our function in building up society. Rather, we connect self-realization with harmony, with a job that feels meaningful, and with exotic experiences in our spare time. The subjective life of the individual thus comes to the fore at a collective level.

Charles Taylor believes that this subjective turn changes the preconditions for religious faith more thoroughly than the Protestant Reformation in the sixteenth century did. That which we experience today is a greater paradigm shift than the process of development in which Martin Luther and Teresa of Jesus were involved in their own times. The British scholars Linda Woodhead and Paul Heelas have investigated what these changes might mean for religious communities of various kinds.[4] They believe that this subjective turn in the area of religion expresses itself in a turn to the spiritual, or in a growing interest in spirituality. Just like so many others, they connect spirituality with a religious practice that stresses that people can encounter God—or something divine—within themselves. Within the framework of a Swedish research project, this development has been described as if God were about to move into human beings.[5]

Woodhead and Heelas predict that churches and congregations that do not manage to adapt to these changed preconditions will quite simply die out before long. That is how strong and thorough this spiritual turn is in the Western world today. Things will be particularly bad for churches and congregations of the kind that they describe as "congregations of humanity"—congregations that seek to represent all of humanity. Such congregations or churches are characterized by their stress on the importance of ethical choices rather than holding on to dogmatic truths.[6] Those who represent such churches or congregations like to speak of love and of the equal value of all people. They also stress the common responsibility of all people for society and for the survival of Planet Earth. Our vocation

4. Heelas and Woodhead, *Spiritual Revolution*.
5. Bäckström, *Religious Change in Northern Europe*, 101.
6. The description I summarize here can be found in Heelas and Woodhead, *Spiritual Revolution*, 18.

to take care of our fellow human beings is underlined, while what might be described as a heavenly reality must recede into the background. Unfortunately, the results sometimes become moralizing attempts to foster or educate those who think differently, and who, it is believed, must be schooled in one's own perspective. Such attempts do not attract independent thinkers who are interested in spirituality. Woodhead and Heelas pay attention to the Swedish context when they describe a future scenario in which the majority religion, and the denominations with which it is primarily linked, will continue to lose ground.[7]

I do not see the research of Woodhead and Heelas as a prophecy of disaster. They do not want to deprive those of us who are working in Christian denominations of our joy in working. Instead, they want to give us a greater understanding of the context in which we work and of the challenges that we need to handle. The reflections that Woodhead and Heelas contribute are in line with the insights and analyzes that are also available within the Church of Sweden, not least at the parish level, where trends and social tendencies emerge early. Today many parishes seek to offer Christian activities that attract people who live in the era of the subjective turn. In the Church of Sweden, for example, we arrange pilgrimages. We invite people to retreats, to holy dance and meditation groups. We celebrate Quiet Mass with different stations around the church that are intended to offer each person the opportunity to find some kind of religious practice that suits their taste. All this points to our ambition to attract spiritually interested people who are marked by the subjective turn.

Thérèse of the Child Jesus, Teresa of Jesus, and John of the Cross have something important to teach us in our attempts to connect to this interest in spirituality—namely, to think theologically in a way that can be described as *spiritual theology*. In the Roman Catholic context, spiritual theology is an established university subject.[8] Today some researchers stress that it is high time that Evangelical-Lutheran theologians developed a corresponding area of research that would illuminate what an Evangelical-Lutheran spiritual theology might mean.[9] What they look for could be likened to a theological reflection that is comparable to medical research. Doctors in the making go through an education that is built on

---

7. Heelas and Woodhead, *Spiritual Revolution*, 141.

8. Arborelius, *Spiritualitet*, 7–11, 13–23, introduces the subject in Swedish.

9. See, for example, Hanson "Christian Spirituality and Spiritual Theology," and Yeago, "Promise of God and the Desires of Our Heart."

scientific research and well-tested experience. When they begin to work, they should in practice be able to help people who suffer from various ailments. In a corresponding way, a spiritual theology should teach us who are involved in parish life to handle relevant pastoral problems with the aid of the dogmatic treasures and the well-tested experiences to which we have access.

I can see two major problems of pastoral care, or two significant challenges that we who work in the Church of Sweden today have to face in the encounter with the contemporary interest in spirituality. These challenges can be described with the aid of Teresa of Avila's image of the interior castle and the teaching of John of the Cross on the dark night of the soul. The first challenge appears at the entrance to the interior castle, or at the stage prior to that of beginners. The second challenge becomes relevant in the first dwellings of the interior castle, when the beginners have ended up in the damaging over-consumption that John of the Cross describes with such crystal clarity.

CHEAP GRACE

The first challenge has to do with the fact that we live in a culture that is deeply marked by the subjective turn and by an increasing interest in spirituality. That leads to numerous people seeking a context that can help them to interpret their lives and to deal with existential issues. Like many adventurous climbers, they want to explore more of the high points of life. They are curious about territories about which they do not know much. If people who are keen on expeditions encounter a church that prefers to forbid all attempts to ascend holy mountains just because people could lose their lives in the mountain ravines of justification by works, they will turn back at the gate.

It is important that, as a church, we do not proclaim what Dietrich Bonhoeffer calls "cheap grace" at the entrance to the interior castle, because then there would be a major risk that we were forcing people to shrink their lives.[10] Cheap grace is grace that leaves everything as it is. It brings no obligations and does not invite imitation. It proclaims that all is well, even when all is not well. Cheap grace is described by Bonhoeffer as a kind of theology of glory, since it is an escape from the cross and a poor excuse for a lack of conversion and struggle against the demons. To

---

10. Bonhoeffer, "Cost of Discipleship," 53–54; Johannesson, "Den billiga nåden som dyrköpt erfarenhet," 38–39.

proclaim cheap grace is to do people a disservice. It is just as damaging to live by cheap or false grace as it is to sustain ourselves on crisps and jellybeans: we become sick as a result of a poor diet, and we also miss out on many taste sensations by adopting eating habits that are too one-dimensional. There are dimensions of existence that we can only explore if we are set in divine motion by the heavenly bridegroom/God/Jesus. At the entrance to the interior castle, there is need for a church that will encourage searching people to pluck up the courage to take the first step across the threshold in undertaking the pilgrimage. Such a church would open the gates to that castle of crystal that every person is.

When Teresa of Avila introduces the final dwelling in the interior castle, she returns to how important it is that we actually enter the castle, and do not remain outside. At the same time, she urges the Sisters in the seventh dwelling to remember that, in some way, they are also still in the first dwellings. She also notes that there is something strange about the thought that a person might want to stay outside the castle, believing that it is meaningless to make any effort, since grace will achieve everything anyway. Love does not work like that, Teresa points out. God's love is in all people, and therefore there is a motivating or driving force that will make every person long, consciously or unconsciously, to enter more deeply into the castle. All people want to go further on this journey because God dwells within them. Teresa writes:

> If you do not strive for the virtues and practice them, you will always be dwarfs. And, please God, it will be only a matter of not growing, for you already know that whoever does not increase decreases. I hold that love, where present, cannot possibly be content with remaining always the same.[11]

Teresa assumes that it is God's indwelling love that is already in people from the beginning of the journey that attracts them and draws them further into the castle. So she does not imagine that a person wants to go further into the castle so that, at the end of the journey, they may at last be given a satisfactory relationship with God and become righteous. Instead, she believes that a person longs for God because God is already within them. For Teresa, it is unthinkable that any person would not want to grow in love for God. She is entirely convinced that everyone—deep down—wants to participate in the adventure of life.[12] For us as Church, it

---

11. Teresa of Avila, *Interior Castle*, 447 (Seventh Dwelling, 4:9).
12. Cf. Teresa of Avila, *Book of Her Life*, 1:5:11, 76, where Teresa says that she

is a challenge and a task to take that desire for adventure seriously, and to channel it so that the journey can head in the right direction.

SPIRITUAL SPA ACTIVITIES

The second challenge can be described as an aspect of the first dwellings of the interior castle. Here can be found the keen interest in spiritual exercises that John of the Cross believes characterizes those beginners whom God has not yet brought into the dark night. There is a risk that, in our well-meaning attempts to connect with the contemporary interest in spirituality, we do not permit beginners to be anything more than beginners. We do not challenge their or our own views about the excellence of the group on pilgrimage, or the decisive significance of meditation for a meaningful life. In the worst case, we might then contribute to the cultivation of a certain kind of justification by works or to a spiritual lust for pleasure of the kind that John of the Cross believes we should actively resist. We might end up running a spiritual SPA—a business that offers activities whose primary purpose will be to make people feel good in the context of the Church. Just like lecturers at other SPA establishments, we would then stress how important it is for our health to meditate regularly, to follow the advice on diet that is provided in the old spiritual classics, and to rinse out the bowels during a retreat at least once a year. Our proclamation might contribute to a problematic self-satisfaction in these devout circles.

The second challenge is to steer the spiritual enthusiasm in the right direction. In that context, the Carmelites remind us that the well-ordered spiritual life, the burning interest in pilgrimages, and the desire to meditate regularly are not the goal but a stage on the journey. There are further dwellings in the interior castle besides the first ones. Therefore, John of the Cross writes considerably more than seven chapters on the imperfect early stage in the spiritual life. He stresses that God and life will bring the person on pilgrimage into darkness and difficulties. Sooner or later the well-organized spiritual life that we ourselves have built up will, it should be hoped, break down. Maybe the pilgrimage group will come to an end, or the desire to meditate might decrease. If a person lives in the false perception that spirituality is something that they can achieve by themselves, it is easy to go wrong when the darkness increases. If they

---

would rather perish than cease to grow in love.

have only been told that God grants harmony and joy in life, it might be difficult to discern the activity of God in anxiety, worry, and defeat.

The Carmelites often warn against the self-satisfaction and the depression that regularly appear in the context of spiritual exercises. When we think that we are good Christians, or when we take pleasure in our devotions, we can easily become proud and arrogant. When we feel that we are too poor in our prayers, or when we become bored by our devotions, we can easily become excessively sad. John of the Cross stressed that we need help to overcome that attitude which Martin Luther would describe as being turned in on ourselves. While as Church we must encourage the pilgrimage through the interior castle and the adventure that the ascent of Mount Carmel implies, we must at the same time speak honestly about the vitally important defeat of self-sanctification. People cannot divinize themselves, however much they might try. They need grace, faith, and Christ in order not to lose their footing on the steep slopes of life. When God leads us spiritual beginners through the dark night, the purpose is for us to realize how dependent we are on God. The night forces us to embrace the cross. When we experience our own weakness, the insight grows that the cross must be the staff on which we support ourselves through our pilgrimage here on Earth.[13] We cannot build our spiritual life on anything less. In that sense, the night is a mountain of transfiguration that helps us to see Jesus in a clearer light.

Teresa of Avila stressed the importance of embracing the cross, or to use it as a walking staff, when she developed a line of thought that is reminiscent of an argument that Martin Luther presents. Luther likened a person to a horse that is ridden either by God or by the devil. He emphasizes that a person cannot want or do anything good unless they are governed by God.[14] Teresa likened a person to a slave when she described the basic conditions for their fruitful spiritual growth and maturity. That basic precondition is Jesus Christ, the crucified. Teresa writes:

> Keep in mind that I could not exaggerate the importance of this. Fix your eyes on the Crucified . . . Do you know what it means to be truly spiritual? It means becoming the slaves of God. Marked with His brand, which is that of the cross, spiritual persons, because now they have given Him their liberty, can be sold by Him as slaves of everyone, as He was . . . And if souls aren't determined about becoming His slaves, let them be convinced

13. Cf. John of the Cross, *Ascent of Mount Carmel*, 171 (book two, 7:7).
14. Hägglund, *De homine*, 177, 180.

that they are not making much progress, for this whole building, as I have said, has humility as its foundation. If humility is not genuinely present, for your own sake the Lord will not construct a high building lest that building fall to the ground.[15]

Eliseo de los Mártires (1550–1620), a faithful disciple of John of the Cross who became the first Provincial of the Discalced Carmelites in Mexico, collected some sayings of John's as evidence in the process of his canonization. He testifies that John developed another line of thought (which can also be found in Martin Luther) when he linked the genuine spiritual life with "the love for the good of one's neighbor."[16] According to Eliseo, John stressed that the most divine of all divine works is to help God to take care of other persons. He explains what that means:

> That is, that the supreme perfection of any soul in their rank and degree is to progress and grow, according to their talent and means, in the imitation of God, and the most wondrous and divine thing is to be a co-operator with Him in the conversion and conquest of souls . . . [I]t is clearly true that compassion for our neighbor grows the more according as the soul is more closely united with God through love; for the more we love, the more we desire that this same God should be loved and honored by all. And the more we desire this, the more we labor for it, both in prayer and in all other possible and necessary exercises.
> And such is the fervour and power of the love of God that those of whom He takes possession can never again be limited by their own souls or contented with them. Rather it seems to them a small thing to go to Heaven alone, wherefore they strive with yearnings and celestial affections and the keenest diligence to bring many to Heaven with them.[17]

We need to reflect on how we can best help the people who attend our services, turn up for our pilgrimages or participate in our meditation groups not to become stuck in those inward-turned perspectives that John of the Cross connects with the stage of beginners. We should not uncritically satisfy people's desires for spiritual pleasure. We should also challenge the limited perspectives of self-satisfaction and depression. God wants to transform people who are searching spiritually into evangelizing missionaries if we are to believe John of the Cross. Our task is to

15. Teresa of Avila, *Interior Castle,* 446 (Seventh Dwelling, 4:8).
16. John of the Cross, "Spiritual Sayings Attributed to S. John of the Cross," 312.
17. John of the Cross, "Spiritual Sayings Attributed to S. John of the Cross," 312–13.

give God a helping hand. Sometimes that can mean that we, like Thérèse of the Child Jesus, need to stress "the spiritual riches that *render one unjust,* when one rests in them with complacence and when one believes they are *something great.*"[18]

The Evangelical-Lutheran tradition stresses that a correct understanding of the justification of human beings is the doctrine by which the Church stands or falls. We could say that, in the Evangelical-Lutheran tradition, the teaching about justification is the magnetic pole toward which an accurate compass should point. When we seek to orient ourselves toward the future in a landscape marked by both secularization and an interest in spirituality, we need to find a reliable compass direction. I believe that the Carmelites can help us with that.

TO FIND THE COMPASS DIRECTION

If you look up "North Pole" in an encyclopedia and start reading the article, you will soon be quite confused. You will learn that compasses do not point to the geographic North Pole. They point to the magnetic North Pole, which is incidentally, a magnetic South Pole, since opposites attract. Furthermore, the magnetic North Pole is not situated where the North Pole is marked on our maps, but at a distance some 1,200 miles from that point. What should perhaps rightly be called the magnetic North Pole is in fact very close to the geographic South Pole that is marked on a map. Inspired by this complex information, one can draw the conclusion that everything seems to be not only upside-down, but also somewhat dislocated.

In a similar way, we could say that the generally accepted understanding of the Evangelical-Lutheran doctrine of justification shifts somewhat when it is expounded with the help of the Carmelite Doctors of the Church. The emphases become a little different. Sometimes the shift results in an upside-down perspective, since the Carmelites now and again sound like true Lutherans. They develop thoughts that are essential aspects of Luther's theology, but that have been moved into the background in the Evangelical-Lutheran tradition that emerged.

When I have engaged in receptive ecumenism in this context, I have chosen to emphasize the similarities between the teaching of the Carmelites and the theology of Martin Luther. I have emphasized that Thérèse

---

18. Letter to Sister Marie of the Sacred Heart, September 17, 1896. Thérèse of Lisieux, *Letters of St. Thérèse of Lisieux,* 2:999 (LT 197).

of the Child Jesus—just like Martin Luther—stressed that everything is grace. I have noted that Teresa of Jesus—just like Martin Luther—points out that we can never bypass Jesus on our way to God. I have made it clear that John of the Cross—just like Martin Luther—accentuates how the faith unites us with God in a cross-marked way.

I believe that the Carmelite Doctors of the Church can teach us who stand in the Evangelical-Lutheran tradition because they understand to a great extent the central tenets of the doctrine of justification—that is, grace, Christ, and faith—in a way that is in line with Martin Luther's theology. Within the framework of that understanding, they expound themes to which some of us think Luther ought to have paid much more attention—namely, how a person's growth and development in faith and holiness can be expressed. In our secularized and spiritually interested time, those themes are highly relevant. I believe that the Carmelites can help us in the Evangelical-Lutheran tradition to develop a spiritual theology that focuses on the question of how we can offer life-giving adventures in the mountains while at the same time avoiding the deadly justification by works.

There are a few essential differences between Luther's theological work and the teaching that the Carmelite Doctors of the Church contribute that are significant in this context. Thérèse of the Child Jesus, Teresa of Avila, and John of the Cross do not say exactly the same things as Martin Luther. That is why they can add something important to our reformatory conversations on where the magnetic North Pole of the doctrine of justification is actually located. They shift the perspective a little. The reason is that they can see connections, whereas Luther is primarily interested in clear differences.

When Luther developed his theological positions, to a large extent he reasoned dialectically. He formulated his opinions by investigating how opposites relate to one another. The law is opposed to but collaborates with the gospel. Sin and righteousness stand in a relationship of mutual tension while, at the same time, there is a significant interaction between them. In contrast, the Carmelites think synthetically, unifying, to a larger extent. Their writings do not emphasize opposites but continuity.

The exposition of grace by Thérèse of the Child Jesus, for example, lacks the opposition or tension between the grace of God and human activity that is so often prominent in the Evangelical-Lutheran tradition. Thérèse is not interested in the question of who does what in the love relationship between God and humanity. Martin Luther, on the other hand, is very interested in that, and he believes it to be the decisive issue. I believe that Thérèse of the Child Jesus's lack of interest can be liberating for us who stand in the Evangelical-Lutheran tradition. If we can perceive everything as grace—including our ascetic exercises—there is no need for us to proclaim any cheap grace out of fear of the horrors of justification by works.

Teresa of Avila's descriptions of a person's relationship with Christ correspondingly lack any clear distinction between people's relationship with God through creation and the relationship with God that is linked to salvation. In the Church of Sweden, we use the term "creation theology" remarkably frequently. By that concept we usually mean something that can affect all people—regardless of their faith. It suggests that there is another form of theology, "salvation theology," that to a greater extent—or even exclusively—concerns only certain persons. Teresa of Avila thinks along different lines. For her, creation theology is always salvation theology. Therefore, salvation is also proclaimed by creation. She assumes that a person can meet Christ through creation; and so she can present God's message through nature in a very Christocentric way. We not only see the back of God when we move in nature: we can also meet Christ and hear him speak through flowers, stars, and watercourses. I believe that we who stand in the Evangelical-Lutheran tradition have something to learn from Teresa of Jesus. Our dichotomizing between creation theology and salvation theology regularly makes us face the question of how we might squeeze Jesus into preaching that is aimed at a wider audience. We assume that people who do not see themselves as professing Christians find the message about Jesus difficult. Teresa does not share that starting point at all, since, in her world of perception, Jesus belongs to what we would call creation theology. That makes her very confident in her preaching. Christ dwells in every person—even if they do not know that. It is the task of the Church to help people to discover that they are not empty inside. Jesus can be found in every person. He knows everyone, and he wants every person to come to know him even better.

The continuity between creation and salvation is also found in John of the Cross's understanding of the growth of faith. John assumes that all people have at least an embryo of faith that can then grow and develop through baptism and the dark night of the soul. Martin Luther thinks instead that faith is a gift that God grants to certain chosen people when they hear the gospel of Jesus Christ. Here is a difference between Martin Luther's starting points and the teaching of John of the Cross. Another difference touches on their understanding of the significance of depression in our relationship with God.

John's theology of the cross does not include the same opposition between happiness and unhappiness that Martin Luther regularly expounds in his pastoral letters to melancholic people. Simply put, not all anxiety is the work of the devil, according to John of the Cross. He thinks that anxiety and worry can be *both* something that God does not want a person to suffer *and* something that God can use to lead a person closer to God. Martin Luther sometimes thinks along the same lines; but he often describes an "either-or" relationship instead. In Swedish church practice, this relationship can sometimes result in an excessive focus on us having a nice time. I have nothing against entertaining choir performances, a jumping castle in the church grounds, or humorous advertisements; but sometimes I wonder whether we undermine people's confidence in us as a church by continually sending the message that we can be happy in church—and that, if we are not happy, we can become so by participating in the activities of a church. Personally, I find it hard to be sad together with someone else who assumes that the divinely given normal state is to be happy. I therefore think that the churchy niceties sometimes scare people away. It needs to share the space with the insight that God can fill us with anxiety—and that is quite in order. I think we can learn something from the teaching of John of the Cross on the dark night of the soul. John can help us to reflect in greater detail on the growing mental ill-health of our day, since he stressed that what primarily stops us from finding a deeper joy in life is our spasmodic attempts to hold on to the superficial happiness that money and success can give us.

John often wrote about the person or the soul in the singular; but that does not mean that he thinks that the ascent of Mount Carmel is exclusively an individual matter. Teresa of Jesus illuminated the collective dimension when she stressed that the soul of every person is an interior castle. Against that background, we could say that every person is somewhere on Mount Carmel. For mountaineers, it is a matter of honor to assist other climbers on the highest mountains of the world. In the same way it is an honor for us to help one another on the steep slopes of the mountains of life.

The British Carmelite Iain Matthews also stresses that the ascent of Mount Carmel is not about individuals who manage the achievement of sinking a solitary flag-pole into the summit.[19] Instead, the ascent of Mount Carmel is about contributing to a common garden culture in an earthly landscape that can sometimes be barren and inhospitable. The English Carmelite nun Sister Mary of St. Joseph, in turn, points out that the produce of Carmel's garden is meant for all people. She stresses that the paths on Mount Carmel that the Carmelites have trod lead straight into the heart of humanity.[20] You do not have to be a Carmelite in order to use them.

The international book market has a rich supply of books that describe how the spirituality of Carmel can be applied in various contexts of life. One of my favorites is written by Carolyn Humphreys, an American occupational therapist who illustrates in a very specific way how we can deal with the stress and performance anxiety of our time with the help of insights and tools that have been developed in the Carmelite tradition.[21] She believes that the spirituality of Carmel can help us to counteract the mental ill-health of our time. In a similar way, I have reflected in this book on how we can deal with the secularization from within with the help of Carmel's three Doctors of the Church. How the Evangelical-Lutheran tradition could enrich Carmel's tradition I will leave for other people to investigate. Receptive ecumenism is a problem-based way of working, built on the investigation of how decisive challenges faced within one's own tradition can be handled with the aid of resources that someone else's tradition might provide. I am grateful for the compass direction that Carmel's Doctors of the Church have helped me to find, since, in my view, it points toward the future.

19. Matthew, *Gud berör och förvandlar*, 149.
20. Mary of St. Joseph, *På detta berg*, 56.
21. Humphreys, *Carmel, Land of the Soul*, 2004.

Appendix

Ten Themes for Reflection and/or Conversation

1. *Our mountain ascents—metaphorically speaking.* Which mountains do we strive to ascend (in the family, in society, at a personal level, or in the Church)? What risks and what opportunities are connected to our mountaineering attempts? Which aids do we use during our climb? When are our efforts worth the trouble?

2. *Children and the transmission of the faith.* Thérèse of the Child Jesus, Teresa of Jesus, John of the Cross, and Gerlinde Kaltenbrunner grew up in families that lived with many acts of devotion and biblical stories. How do we hand on the life of faith to children today? In what forms did you encounter the faith when you were growing up? How have those encounters marked you and your attitude to life?

3. *Role models.* Some people have mountaineers or other elite sports personalities as their role models. What characterizes a good role model? Both the Evangelical-Lutheran and the Roman Catholic traditions point to the saints as good role models. Which saints can be highlighted as good role models in the context of your life?

4. *Receptive ecumenism.* Which challenges or problems are relevant in your church context? How can those challenges be handled with the help of some other denomination? What is needed for your own church to receive that help?

5. *The night and mental ill-health in our time.* Why do so many people feel unwell in our welfare society? When would it be wise to describe depression as the dark night of the soul, and when might it be life-threatening? In what respects might contemporary mental ill-health be a spiritual concern?

6. *Faith and persecution.* In the third century there were several extensive periods of persecution against Christians in the Roman Empire. In the sixteenth century, Martin Luther was declared an outlaw as a result of a decision by Emperor Charles V. What opposition have you met because of your faith? Which kinds of ongoing religious persecution do you find particularly frightening? What can we do together to alleviate them or prevent them?

7. *Spiritual and religious experiences.* What characterizes a spiritual or religious experience? When did you last meet someone who told you about such an experience? What did you think while you listened to their story? What did you learn from that story and from your reflections on it?

8. *Body and spirit.* Many people connect spiritual experiences with physical movement (such as going on a pilgrimage) or with the lack of physical movement (such as concentrated sitting in silence). What would lead you to say that you have met God or that you have had a spiritual experience during a service of worship, a jog, or a moment of meditation?

9. *The Mass.* Is it easy to view the Mass as an encounter with God through Jesus Christ? Or do you find it difficult to do that? What makes it easier—or more difficult—for you to believe that Christ really does meet us in the Word (the readings and the preaching) and unites himself with us through the bread and the wine of the Eucharist?

10. *The growth of faith and personal sanctification.* Which devotions help us to grow in faith and holiness? Why do they work? Which devotions do we need to abstain from, and which ones do we need to develop? How can we make allowances for the fact that different forms of devotion suit different people?

Bibliography

Álvarez, Tomás. *Teresa av Avila: Guds vagabond.* Tågarp and Glumslöv: Karmeliterna, 2006.
Arborelius, Anders. *Allt och intet: Johannes av Korsets liv.* Tågarp and Glumslöv: Karmeliterna, 1991.
———. "Förord." In *Andliga redogörelser och Själens rop till Gud,* by Teresa of Avila (Teresa av Jesus), 9–11. Tågarp and Glumslöv: Karmeliterna, 2015.
———. "Förord." in *Betraktelser över Guds kärlek,* by Teresa of Avila (Teresa av Jesus), 6–13. Tågarp and Glumslöv: Karmeliterna, 2011.
———. *Spiritualitet: Andlig teologi.* Tågarp and Glumslöv: Karmeliterna, 1994.
Athanasios of Alexandria. *Antonios liv.* Skellefteå: Artos & Norma, 1991.
Aurelius, Carl Axel. *På helig mark: pilgrimen i historia och nutid.* Skellefteå: Artos & Norma, 2014.
Bergstrand, Göran. *Från naivitet till naivitet.* Stockholm: Verbum, 1990.
Bilinkoff, Jodi. *The Avila of Saint Teresa: Religious Reform in a Sixteenth-century City.* Ithaca, NY: Cornell University Press, 1989.
Bonhoeffer, Dietrich. "The Cost of Discipleship." In *Dietrich Bonhoeffer: Writings Selected with an Introduction by Robert Coles,* 53–64. Maryknoll, NY: Orbis, 1998.
Braw, Christian. *För Kristi ära: Hjärtat i Augsburgska bekännelsen.* Skellefteå: Artos & Norma, 2016.
———. *Mystikens arv hos Martin Luther.* Skellefteå: Artos & Norma, 1999.
Breashears, David, and Audrey Salkeld. *Last Climb: The Legendary Everest Expeditions of George Mallory.* Washington, DC: The National Geographic Society, 1999.
Buggert, Donald. *The Christocentrism of the Carmelite Charism.* Middle Park, Melbourne: Carmelite Communications, 1999.
Burrows, Ruth. *Prayer and Practice: Interior Castle Explored.* London: Sheed and Ward, 1981.
Bäckström, Anders, et al. *Religious Change in Northern Europe: The Case of Sweden. From State Church to Free Folk Church. Final Report.* Stockholm: Verbum, 2004.
Bäumer, Regina, and P. Michael Plattig. "Dark Night and Depression." *Carmelus* 61 (2014) 85–104.
Culligan, Kevin. "The Dark Night and Depression." In *Carmelite Prayer: A Tradition for the 21st Century,* edited by Keith J. Egan, 119–38. New York: Paulist, 2003.
Davidson Bremborg, Anna. *Pilgrimsvandring på svenska.* Lund: Arcus, 2010.
De Meester, Koen. *Med tomma händer.* Tågarp and Glumslöv: Karmeliterna, 1987.
De första munkarnas bok. Tågarp and Glumslöv: Karmeliterna, 2009.
Egeria. *Resebrev från det heliga landet.* Artos & Norma Bokförlag, Skellefteå, 2007.

BIBLIOGRAPHY

Erasmus. *On the Freedom of the Will*. In *Luther and Erasmus: Free Will and Salvation*. Edited by Gordon W. Rupp and Philip S. Watson. Philadelphia: Westminster, 1969.

Ficocelli, Elizabeth. *Shower of Heavenly Roses: Stories of the Intercession of St. Therese of Lisieux*. New York: The Crossroad, 2004.

Foley, Marc. *The Context of Holiness: Psychological and Spiritual Reflections on the Life of St. Teresa of Lisieux*. Washington, DC: ICS, 2008.

Fowler, James, W. *Stages of Faith: The Psychology of Human Development and the Quest for Meaning*. San Francisco: HarperCollins, 1995.

Gammelgaard, Lene. *Climbing High: A Woman's Account of Surviving the Everest Tragedy*. New York: Harper Collins, 1999.

Gassman, Günther, and Scott Hendrix. *För Kristi skull: Introduktion till de lutherska bekännelserna*. Skellefteå: Artos & Norma, 2017.

Geneviève of the Holy Face. *My Sister Saint Thérèse*. Rockford, IL: Tan, 1997.

Grane, Leif. *Confessio Augustana: Orientering i den lutherska reformationens grundtankar*. Stockholm: Verbum, 1979.

Hägglund, Bengt. *De homine: Människouppfattningen i äldre luthersk tradition*. Lund: C.W.K. Gleerups, 1959.

———. "Luther und die Mystik." In *Kirche, Mystik, Heiligung und das Natürliche bei Luther: Vorträge des Dritten Internationalen Kongresses für Lutherforschung*, edited by Ivar Asheim, 84–94. Göttingen: Vandenhoeck & Ruprecht, 1967.

Halldorf, Peter. "Öppning." *Pilgrim* 2 (2016) 4–5.

Hanson, Bradley. "Christian Spirituality and Spiritual Theology." *Dialog* (1982) 207–12.

Heelas, Paul, and Linda Woodhead. *The Spiritual Revolution: Why Religion Is Giving Way to Spirituality*. Oxford: Blackwell, 2005.

Hemmleb, Jochen, et al. *Ghosts of Everest: The Search for Mallory and Irvine*. Seattle: The Mountaineers, 2001.

Hoffman, Bengt. *Hjärtats teologi: Mystikens plats hos Martin Luther*. Delsbo: Åsak, 1989.

———. *Luther and the Mystics: A Re-examination of Luther's Spiritual Experience and His Relationship to the Mystics*. Minneapolis: Augsburg, 1976.

Humphreys, Carolyn. *Carmel, Land of the Soul: Living Contemplatively in Today's World*. New York: St. Pauls, 2004.

Iserloh, Erwin. "Luther und die Mystik." In *Kirche, Mystik, Heiligung und das Natürliche bei Luther: Vorträge des Dritten Internationalen Kongresses für Lutherforschung*, edited by Ivar Asheim, 60–83. Göttingen: Vandenhoeck & Ruprecht, 1967.

Jantzen, Grace M. *Power, Gender and Christian Mysticism*. Cambridge Studies in Ideology and Religion 8. Cambridge: Cambridge University Press, 1995.

Jensen, Roger. *Pilegrim: Lengsel, vandring, tenkning–før og nå*. Oslo: Novus, 2015.

Johannesson, Karin. "Den billiga nåden som dyrköpt erfarenhet." In *Nåd och åter nåd–en skrift för gemensamt delande*, 38–52. Uppsala: Uppsala Stift, 2018.

———. *God Pro Nobis: On Non-Metaphysical Realism and the Philosophy of Religion*. Studies in Philosophical Theology 37. Leuven: Peeters, 2007.

———. *Gud för oss: Om den non-metafysiska realismen och dess konsekvenser för religionsfilosofins uppgift och natur*. Stockholm: Thales, 2002.

———. *Helgelsens filosofi. Om andlig träning i luthersk tradition*. Stockholm: Verbum, 2014.

———. "Kön och bön." *Svensk Teologisk Kvartalskrift* 84 (2008) 108–21.

John Climacus. *The Ladder of Divine Ascent*. Translated by Colm Luibheid and Norman Russell. Mahwah, NJ: Paulist, 1982.

John of the Cross. *The Ascent of Mount Carmel*. In *The Collected Works of St. John of the Cross*, translated by Kieran Kavanaugh OCD and Otilio Rodriguez OCD, 110–349. Washington DC: ICS, 2017.

———. *The Dark Night of the Soul*. In *The Collected Works of St. John of the Cross*, translated by Kieran Kavanaugh OCD and Otilio Rodriguez OCD, 358–457. Washington, DC: ICS, 2017.

———. *The Living Flame of Love*. In *The Collected Works of St. John of the Cross*, translated by Kieran Kavanaugh OCD and Otilio Rodriguez OCD, 469–630. Washington, DC: ICS, 2017.

———. *The Spiritual Canticle*. In *The Collected Works of St. John of the Cross*, translated by Kieran Kavanaugh OCD and Otilio Rodriguez OCD, 633–715. Washington, DC: ICS, 2017.

———. "Spiritual Sayings Attributed to S. John of the Cross." In *The Complete Works of Saint John of the Cross*, edited by E. Allison Peers, 3:308–18. London: Burns, Oates & Washbourne, 1934.~%XJolkkonen, Jarl. "Eucharist." In *Engaging Luther: A (New) Theological Assessment*, edited by Olli-Pekka Vainio, 108–37. Eugene, OR: Cascade Books, 2010.

Juntunen, Sammeli. "Luther and Metaphysics. What is the Structure of Being According to Luther?" In *Union with Christ: The New Finnish Interpretation of Luther*, edited by Carl E. Braaten and Robert W. Jenson, 129–60. Grand Rapids: Eerdmans, 1998.

Kaltenbrunner, Gerlinde. *Mountains in My Heart: A Passion for Climbing*. Seattle: Mountaineers, 2014.

Kasischke, Lou. *After the Wind: Tragedy on Everest. One Survivor's Story*. Harbor Springs, MI: Good Hart, 2015.

Krakauer, Jon. *Tunn luft: En insidesskildring av tragedin på Mount Everest*. Köping: Forum, 1999.

———. *Into Thin Air: A Personal Account of the Mount Everest Disaster*. New York: Villard, 1997.

Kärkkäinen, Veli-Matti. *One with God: Salvation as Deification and Justification*. Collegeville, MN: Liturgical, 2004.

Lagercrantz, David, and Göran Kropp. *8000+*. Stockholm: Bokförlaget, 1999.

Livbjerg, Grethe. *Teresa av Avila: Vänskapens mystiker*. Skellefteå: Artos & Norma, 2015.

Lohse, Bernhard. *Martin Luther's Theology: Its Historical and Systematic Development*. Translated by Roy A. Harrisville. Minneapolis: Fortress, 1999.

Luther, Martin. *The Bondage of the Will*. In *Luther's Works*, edited by Philip Watson, 33:15–295. Philadelphia: Fortress, 1972.

———. *The Freedom of a Christian*. In *Luther's Works*, edited by Harold J. Grimm, 31:333–37. Philadelphia: Fortress, 1957.

———. *Heidelberg Disputation*. In *Luther's Works*, edited by Harold J. Grimm, 31:39–70. Philadelphia: Fortress, 1957.

———. *Ninety-five Theses or Disputation of the Power and Efficacy of Indulgences*. In *Luther's Works*, edited by Harold J. Grimm, 31:25–33. Philadelphia: Fortress, 1957.

———. *Treatise on Good Works*. In *Luther's Works*, edited by James Atkinson, 44:21–114. Philadelphia: Fortress, 1966.

Lönnebo, Martin. *Religionens fem språk: Om religionens mening och förnyelse*. Stockholm: Verbum, 1993.
——. *Själen: Lilla träningsboken för själen*. Stockholm: Verbum, 1999.
——. *Väven. Stora träningsboken för själen. Om fascinationen inför det inre livets rymder*. Stockholm: Verbum, 1999.
Mannermaa, Tuomo. *Christ Present in Faith: Luther's View of Justification*. Minneapolis: Fortress, 2005.
——. "Justification and *Theosis* in Lutheran-Orthodox Perspective." In *Union with Christ: The New Finnish Interpretation of Luther*, edited by Carl E. Braaten and Robert W. Jenson, 25–41. Grand Rapids: Eerdmans, 1998.
——. *Two Kinds of Love. Martin Luther's Religious World*. Minneapolis: Fortress, 2010.
——. "Why Is Luther so Fascinating? Modern Finnish Luther Research." In *Union with Christ: The New Finnish Interpretation of Luther*, edited by Carl E. Braaten and Robert W. Jenson, 1–20. Grand Rapids: Eerdmans, 1998.
Martling, Carl Henrik. *En sky av vittnen: En ekumenisk helgonkalender*. Skellefteå: Artos & Norma, 2010.
Mary of St. Joseph. *På detta berg: Bön i den karmelitiska traditionen*. Tågarp and Glumslöv: Karmeliterna, 2011.
Matthew, Iain. *Gud berör och förvandlar: Johannes av Korset i nytt ljus*. Tågarp and Glumslöv: Karmeliterna, 2007.
McGinn, Bernhard. "The Letter and the Spirit: Spirituality as an Academic Discipline." in *Minding the Spirit: The Study of Christian Spirituality*, edited by Elizabeth A. Dreyer and Mark S. Burrows, 25–41. Baltimore: Johns Hopkins University Press, 2005.
McGrath, Alister E. *Historical Theology: An Introduction to the History of Christian Thought*. Oxford: Wiley-Blackwell, 2013.
Murray, Paul D. "Receptive Ecumenism and Catholic Learning—Establishing the Agenda." In *Receptive Ecumenism and the Call to Catholic Learning: Exploring a Way for Contemporary Ecumenism*, edited by Paul D. Murray, 5–25. Oxford: Oxford University Press, 2008.
New Catholic Encyclopedia. New York: McGraw-Hill, 1967.
Nordisk teologisk uppslagsbok för skola och kyrka. Lund: Gleerups förlag, 1957.
Nyman, Magnus. *Förlorarnas historia: Katolskt liv i Sverige från Gustav Vasa till drottning Kristina*. Stockholm: Veritas förlag, 2002.
Oberman, Heiko A. "Simul gemitus et raptus. Luther und die Mystik." In *Kirche, Mystik, Heiligung und das Natürliche bei Luther: Vorträge des Dritten Internationalen Kongresses für Lutherforschung*, edited by Ivar Asheim, 20–59. Göttingen: Vandenhoeck & Ruprecht, 1967.
Ökenfädernas tänkespråk. Skellefteå: Artos & Norma, 2019.
Ottosson, Åsa, and Mats Ottosson. "Gudomlig guidning. Låt tankarna vandra." In *Svenska leder: På äventyr i andras spår*, 119–31. Stockholm: Svenska Turistföreningens Årsbok, 2011.
Pasaban, Edurne. *Tilting at Mountains: Love, Tragedy, and Triumph on the World's Highest Peaks*. Seattle: Mountaineers, 2011.
Peterson, Michael, et al. *Reason and Religious Belief*. Oxford: Oxford University Press, 1991.

———, eds. *Philosophy of Religion: Selected Readings*. Oxford: Oxford University Press, 1996.
Peura, Simo. "Christ as Favor and Gift: The Challenge of Luther's Understanding of Justification." In *Union with Christ: The New Finnish Interpretation of Luther*, edited by Carl E. Braaten and Robert W. Jenson, 42–69. Grand Rapids: Eerdmans, 1998.
Pietsch, Stephen. *Of Good Comfort: Martin Luther's Letters to the Depressed and their Significance for Pastoral Care Today*. Adelaide: ATF, 2016.
Pulkkanen, Johannes. *The Dark Night: St. John of the Cross and Eastern Orthodox Theology*. Uppsala: Uppsala universitet, 2009.
Rose, David, and Ed Douglas. *Regions of the Heart: The Triumph and Tragedy of Alison Hargreaves*. London: Penguin, 1999.
Stein, Edith. *The Science of the Cross*. Washington, DC: ICS, 2002.
Steinmann, Anne-Elisabeth. *Karmelitorden: Historia–helgon–anda*. Tågarp and Glumslöv: Karmeliterna, 1981.
Stinissen, Wilfrid. *Den enkla vägen till helighet: En bok om Thérèse av Lisieux*. Örebro: Libris, 1999.
———. "Företal." In *Själens dunkla natt*, 9–20. Tågarp and Glumslöv: Karmeliterna, 1990.
———. *Inre vandring*. Örebro: Libris, 1999.
———. *Natten är mitt ljus*. Tågarp and Glumslöv: Karmeliterna, 1990.
———. "Om Thérèses andliga utveckling." In *De svagas styrka: Om Thérèse av Jesusbarnet*, 41–77. Tågarp and Glumslöv: Karmeliterna, 1998.
Stjerna, Kirsi. "Introduction." In *Spirituality. Toward a 21st Century Lutheran Understanding*, edited by Kirsi Stjerna and Brooks Schramm, 5–12. Minneapolis: Lutheran University Press, 2004.
———. "Luther, Lutherans, and Spirituality." In *Spirituality. Toward a 21st Century Lutheran Understanding*, edited by Kirsi Stjerna and Brooks Schramm, 32–49. Minneapolis: Lutheran University Press, 2004.
———. *Women and the Reformation*. Malden, MA: Blackwell, 2009.
Stolt, Birgit. *'Laßt uns fröhlich springen!' Gefühlswelt und Gefühlsnavigierung in Luthers Reformationsarbeit. Eine kognitive Emotionalitätsanalyse auf philologischer Basis*. Berlin: Weidler, 2012.
———. "Luther's Faith of 'the Heart': Experience, Emotion, and Reason." In *The Global Luther: A Theologian for Modern Times*, edited by Christine Helmer, 131–50. Minneapolis: Fortress, 2009.
———. *Martin Luther: Människohjärtat och Bibeln*. Skellefteå: Artos & Norma, 2016.
Svenska Kyrkans bekännelseskrifter. Stockholm: Verbum, 1985.
Svenskt bibliskt uppslagsverk. Gävle: Skolförlaget, 1948.
Swan, Laura. *The Forgotten Desert Mothers: Sayings, Lives, and Stories of Early Christian Women*. Mahwah, NJ: Paulist, 2001.
Taylor, Charles. *A Secular Age*. Cambridge, MA: Belknap, 2007.
Teresa of Avila. *The Book of Her Foundations*. In *The Collected Works of Saint Teresa of Avila*, 3:95–309. Translated by Kieran Kavanaugh OCD and Otilio Rodriguez OCD. Washington, DC: ICS, 1985.
———. *The Book of Her Life*. In *The Collected Works of Saint Teresa of Avila*, 1:15–365. Translated by Kieran Kavanaugh OCD and Otilio Rodriguez OCD. Washington, DC: ICS, 2019.

———. *The Collected Letters of St. Teresa of Avila, Volume 1*. Translated by Kieran Kavanaugh, OCD. Washington, DC: ICS Publications, 2001.

———. *Her Life in Letters*. Translated by Kavanaugh, Kieran OCD. Notre Dame, IN: Christian Classics, 2018.

———. *The Interior Castle*. In *The Collected Works of Saint Teresa of Avila*, 2:263–452. Translated by Kieran Kavanaugh OCD and Otilio Rodriguez OCD. Washington, DC: ICS, 2017.

———. *Spiritual Testimonies*. In *The Collected Works of Saint Teresa of Avila*, 1:369–438. Translated by Kieran Kavanaugh OCD and Otilio Rodriguez OCD. Washington, DC: ICS, 2019.

———. *The Way of Perfection*. In *The Collected Works of Saint Teresa of Avila*, 2:15–204. Translated by Kieran Kavanaugh OCD and Otilio Rodriguez OCD. Washington, DC: ICS, 2017.

Thérèse of Lisieux. *Her Last Conversations*. Translated by John Clarke OCD. Washington, DC: ICS, 1977.

———. *Letters of St. Thérèse of Lisieux. Volume I, 1877–1890*. Translated by John Clarke OCD. Washington, DC: ICS, 1982.

———. *Letters of St. Thérèse of Lisieux. Volume II, 1890–1897*. Translated by John Clarke OCD. Washington, DC: ICS, 1988.

———. *Story of a Soul: The Autobiography of St. Thérèse of Lisieux*. Translated by John Clarke OCD. Washington, DC: ICS, 2017.

Tournier, Veronica. "Egeria." In *Kyrkomödrar*, edited by Ann-Ida Fehn and Hedvig Larsson, 107–23. Skellefteå: Artos & Norma, 2017.

Wiberg Pedersen, Else Marie. "This Is not About Sex? A Discussion of the Understanding of Love and Grace in Bernard of Clairvaux's and Martin Luther's Theologies." *Dialog* 50 (2011) 15–25.

Wolterstorff, Nicholas. *Lament for a Son*. Grand Rapids: Eerdmans, 1987.

Wrede, Gösta. *Unio Mystica: Probleme der Erfahrung bei Johannes Tauler*. Stockholm: Almquist & Wiksell, 1974.

Yeago, David S. "The Promise of God and the Desires of Our Hearts. Prolegomena to a Lutheran Retrieval of Classical Spiritual Theology." *Lutheran Forum* 30 (1996) 21–30.